The Palgrave Review of British Politics 2006

KV-086-391

The Palgrave Review of British Politics

Titles include

Michael Rush and Philip Giddings (*editors*)
THE PALGRAVE REVIEW OF BRITISH POLITICS 2005
THE PALGRAVE REVIEW OF BRITISH POLITICS 2006

The Palgrave Review of British Politics Series
Series Standing Order ISBN 0–230–00190–4

You can receive future titles in this series as they are published by placing a standing order. Please contact your bookseller or, in case of difficulty, write to us at the address below with your name and address, the title of the series and one of the ISBNs quoted above.

Customer Services Department, Macmillan Distribution Ltd. Houndmills, Basingstoke, Hampshire RG21 6XS, England

 **Blackburn**
College

Library
01254 292120

Please return this book on or before the last date below

~~2 9 OCT 2007~~

2 9 OCT 2007

The Palgrave Review of
British Politics 2006

Edited by

Michael Rush
Emeritus Professor of Politics
University of Exeter, UK

and

Philip Giddings
Senior Lecturer in Politics
University of Reading, UK

HANSARD
SOCIETY

© Editorial matter and selection © Michael Rush and Philip Giddings 2007
All remaining chapters © respective authors 2007

All rights reserved. No reproduction, copy or transmission of this publication
may be made without written permission.

No paragraph of this publication may be reproduced, copied or transmitted
save with written permission or in accordance with the provisions of the
Copyright, Designs and Patents Act 1988, or under the terms of any licence
permitting limited copying issued by the Copyright Licensing Agency,
90 Tottenham Court Road, London W1T 4LP.

Any person who does any unauthorised act in relation to this publication
may be liable to criminal prosecution and civil claims for damages.

The authors have asserted their rights to be identified as the authors of this
work in accordance with the Copyright, Designs and Patents Act 1988.

First published 2007 by
PALGRAVE MACMILLAN
Houndmills, Basingstoke, Hampshire RG21 6XS and
175 Fifth Avenue, New York, N.Y. 10010
Companies and representatives throughout the world

PALGRAVE MACMILLAN is the global academic imprint of the
Palgrave Macmillan division of St Martin's Press LLC and of
Palgrave Macmillan Ltd.
Macmillan® is a registered trademark in the United States,
United Kingdom and other countries. Palgrave is a registered
trademark in the European Union and other countries.

ISBN-13: 978–0–230–00259–3 hardback
ISBN-10: 0–230–00259–5 hardback

This book is printed on paper suitable for recycling and made from
fully managed and sustained forest sources. Logging, pulping and
manufacturing processes are expected to conform to the environmental
regulations of the country of origin.

A catalogue record for this book is available from the British Library.

A catalogue record for this book is available from the Library of Congress.

Hansard Society   www.hansardsociety.org.uk

BLACKBURN COLLEGE
LIBRARY

Acc. No. BB46357
HSC 320.941
Date July 07 Ru

10   9   8   7   6   5   4   3   2   1
16   15   14   13   12   11   10   09   08   07

Printed and bound in Great Britain by
Antony Rowe Ltd, Chippenham and Eastbourne

Contents

List of Tables and Figures

Tables

Figures

Notes on Contributors

Tim Bale is Senior Lecturer in Politics at the University of Sussex. He has published in the fields of comparative, European, and British politics. His latest book is *European Politics: A Comparative Introduction* (Palgrave Macmillan, 2005).

Jonathan Bradbury is Senior Lecturer in Politics, University of Wales, Swansea. He is the author of numerous essays and articles on territorial politics and devolution in the UK.

Michael Cole is Hon. Research Fellow at the LGC Elections Centre (University of Plymouth). He has published widely in the fields of local government, quangos, elections, devolution, the UK Parliament and the NHS.

Philip Cowley is Professor of Parliamentary Government at the University of Nottingham, and his most recent books are *The Rebels: How Blair Mislaid His Majority* (Politico's, 2005) and (co-editor with P. Dunleavy, R. Heffernan and C. Hay) *Developments in British Politics 8* (Palgrave Macmillan, 2006).

Oonagh Gay is Head of the Parliament and Constitution Centre, the House of Commons Library and co-editor (with Patricia Leopold) of *Conduct Unbecoming: The Regulation of Parliamentary Behaviour* (London: Politico's, 2004).

Philip Giddings is Senior Lecturer in Politics at the University of Reading. He is editor of and contributor to *The Future of Parliament: Issues for a New Century* (Palgrave Macmillan, 2005).

Wyn Grant is Professor of Politics, University of Warwick. His most recent books are (co-editor with David Coen) *Business and Government: Methods and Practice* (Barbara Budrich, 2005) and (with Philippa Sherrington) *Managing Your Academic Career* (Palgrave Macmillan, 2006).

Andrew Gray is Emeritus Professor of Public Management, University of Durham, and a freelance academic. His recent publications include (with W. I. Jenkins) 'Checking Out? Accountability and Evaluation in the British Regulatory State', in M-L. Bemelmans-Videc, J. Lonsdale and B. Perrin (eds), *Accountability and the Role of Evaluation* (Transaction Publishers, 2007), and (with S. J. Pearce and L. Marks) 'The Training Needs of Doctors Working in English and Welsh Prisons: A Survey of Doctors', *International Journal of Prisoner Health*, 2006.

Andrew Hindmoor is Senior Lecturer in Politics, University of Queensland. His most recent books are *New Labour at the Centre: Constructing Political Space* (Oxford University Press, 2004) and *Rational Choice* (Palgrave Macmillan, 2006).

Stephen Ingle is Emeritus Professor of Politics, University of Stirling. He is author of a number of books, including *The British Party System* (Continuum, 3rd edn 1999) and *Narratives of British Socialism* (Palgrave Macmillan, 2001). His most recent book is *The Social and Political Thought of George Orwell* (Taylor and Francis, 2005).

Bill Jenkins is Professor of Public Policy and Management, University of Kent at Canterbury. He is Deputy Editor of *Public Administration* and his most recent book (with E. C. Page) is *Policy Bureaucracy: Government with a Cast of Thousands* (Oxford University Press, 2005).

Tim Jones is a postgraduate researcher at the LGC Elections Centre (University of Plymouth) and the Leader of Restormel Borough Council.

Richard Kelly is a Senior Researcher in the Parliament and Constitution Centre, the House of Commons Library.

Steve Leach is Professor of Local Government in the Local Governance Research Unit, Leicester Business School, De Montfort University, Leicester. He is the author of *Local Political Leadership* (Policy Press, 2000) and *The Changing Politics of Local Government* (Policy Press, 2006).

Philip Norton (Lord Norton of Louth) is Professor of Politics, University of Hull. He chaired the Constitution Committee of the House of Lords from 2001 to 2004 and is the author/editor of 25 books, the latest being *Parliament in British Politics* (Palgrave Macmillan, 2005).

Lawrence Pratchett is Professor of Local Democracy and Director of the Local Governance Research Unit, Leicester Business School, De Montfort University, Leicester. He is the author (with Vivien Lowndes) of *Developing Democracy in Europe* (Council of Europe, 2004), as well as a number of edited collections and articles on British local government.

Sue Prince is Lecturer in Law at the University of Exeter. She is currently researching access to justice in the civil courts, examining the role of court-based mediation.

Michael Rush is Emeritus Professor of Politics, University of Exeter. He has authored numerous articles and books on British politics, particularly Parliament. His most recent book is *Parliament Today* (Manchester University Press, 2005).

Andrew Russell is Senior Lecturer in Politics at the University of Manchester. He is co-author (with E. Fieldhouse) of *Neither Left Nor Right? The Liberal Democrats and the Electorate* (Manchester University Press, 2005). He has published widely in the fields of party politics and party systems, electoral turnout and engagement, and young people and politics.

Meg Russell is Senior Research Fellow at the Constitution Unit, University College London. Her publications include *Reforming the House of Lords: Lessons from Overseas* (Oxford University Press, 2000) and *Building New Labour: The Politics of Party Organisation* (Palgrave Macmillan, 2005).

Maria Sciara is a Research Assistant at the Constitution Unit, University College London.

Christopher White is Lecturer in International Relations at the University of Reading. He is currently researching globalisation and New Labour foreign policy, with a particular focus on security.

Dominic Wring is Senior Lecturer in Communication and Media Studies, Loughborough University. He is author of *The Politics of Marketing the Labour Party* (Palgrave Macmillan, 2005) and co-editor (with Jane Green, Roger Mortimore and Simon Atkinson) of *Political Communications: The British General Election of 2005* (Palgrave Macmillan, 2007).

Ross Young is Senior Researcher in the Social and General Statistics Section, House of Commons Library.

Preface

In this, our second annual review of British politics, we have continued our policy of providing systematic and up-to-date coverage of the main developments written by acknowledged experts in their fields. This year we are joined by Dr Christopher White of the University of Reading, who has taken on the task of reviewing the United Kingdom's foreign policy. We are again grateful to Ross Young for providing the statistical appendix which we believe will become an increasingly useful source of reference for detecting trends (or confuting those who claim to have done so!) as the years go by. Without our contributors the Review would not exist, but we are particularly grateful to them for meeting a more demanding production schedule, which should see the Review available in the shops before too much of the current year's events have clouded our recollections and analysis.

When asked what he found his biggest problem as Prime Minister, Harold Macmillan reputedly and famously replied, 'Events, dear boy, events!' In spite of annual fixtures like the party conferences, the Queen's Speech, the Pre-Budget Report and the budget itself, and EU and G8 summits, it is other events that make each year politically distinctive: some rapidly and visibly, as with natural disasters, wars and other acts of violence; others slowly, almost imperceptibly, as with movements of population, economic change and fundamental values. In the Review we seek to offer a systematic way of mapping those changes, whatever their speed.

Thanks are also due to Jenny Cook of the Department of Politics, University of Exeter, for her help in preparing the manuscript for publication, and we are once again indebted to our publishers for support and encouragement, particularly Alison Howson, Amy Lankester-Owen, and Gemma D'Arcy-Hughes, and to Ray Addicott and Tracey Day for their swift and efficient preparation of the typescript for publication.

Michael Rush
University of Exeter

Philip Giddings
University of Reading

February 2007

1
Labour's Love Lost
Stephen Ingle

It is the task of the first contribution to this Review to try to capture the flavour of the year in question so as to provide a context for the more detailed analyses to follow, but the truth is that few years are punctuated by an event or events so dramatic as to characterise that year. From the end-of-year perspective, 2006 produced no single event, issue or personality to seize the public imagination to the extent that in future it will be remembered primarily for that person, issue or event. Perhaps some revisionist historian of the future will tell us that it was in 2006 that for the first time the problems of climate change made a serious impact on the public consciousness (the Stern Report on global warming was presented in October), if not on the government's policies; in 2006 that the dismembering of the United Kingdom was discussed as a serious possibility in the English as well as the Scottish press; perhaps when, in a few years, David Cameron is enthusiastically welcomed to Downing Street as the latest agent of national reform and regeneration, he will be able to see that his sun first rose unmistakably above the horizon in 2006. From today's perspective, however, neither these issues nor Cameron's potential can be said to have shaped the year. Rather, it has been characterised by the continuation of service as usual: which is to say the steady erosion of the public's trust in its government and political leader and in the efficiency and 'fitness for purpose' of the main institutions of the state.

Trials and tribulations: the Liberal Democrats

The main events at the beginning of the political year did not have to do with the Labour government, however; seamlessly they followed on from 2005 and the problems confronting the Liberal Democrats. The year had ended with Charles Kennedy's senior colleagues seeking to engineer his resignation as party leader because of his admitted problems with alcohol; admitted, it seems, only because a former press secretary and now chief political correspondent

1

for ITV News was known to be working on a news report on the problem. Kennedy had toyed with the idea of resigning and then contesting the ensuing election in the plausible belief that party members would be likely to stand by him. After all, these members, and indeed the public at large, had been brought up on the rumour that Churchill had successfully fought a world war while consuming considerable quantities of wines and spirits. What his colleagues maintained was that, unlike the great man, Kennedy was not doing his job effectively. When he had sought their support at a party meeting only two MPs stood with him, Mark Oaten and Lembit Opik, and both men were known to be chiefly concerned to secure the former's eventual succession as leader. This episode was embarrassing and damaging to the party but, if they thought that successfully securing their leader's resignation would put an end to this embarrassment, they were deluded. In the ensuing election, two of the frontrunners were forced by media disclosures to admit to homosexual affairs: the up-and-coming (and apparently happily married) Mark Oaten – who withdrew – and party chairman Simon Hughes – who finished a poor third in the first ballot. The problem was not their sexual orientation but their apparent duplicity. *Faute de mieux*, and with little enthusiasm, the party chose their elder statesman, Sir Menzies Campbell, over the young but little-known Chris Huhne in the second ballot. Notably, only 72 per cent of members bothered to vote, and 'Ming', whose considerable reputation was based chiefly upon his foreign affairs expertise, proved as ineffectual in Prime Minister's Questions as his detractors had feared. In this early part of the year, support for the Liberal Democrats fell to 15 per cent, the lowest for five years.

But this is not the whole story. Campbell's electoral victory was on 2 March. Three weeks earlier, in the middle of this whole sorry episode, the Liberal Democrats won a simply stunning by-election victory at Dunfermline and West Fife, stunning for several reasons. First, the constituency was next to Gordon Brown's patrimony of Kirkcaldy and Cowdenbeath; second, the 'Cameron factor' was expected to improve Conservative performance; and third, the Scottish National Party (SNP) was enjoying a surge in support. Nothing prepared the political media for the 16.4 per cent swing to the Liberal Democrats, giving Labour its first by-election defeat in Scotland since the SNP took Govan in 1988 and the Liberal Democrats (and the Liberals before them) their first ever victory over Labour in a Scottish by-election. What an extraordinary discontinuity between events in and around the Palace of Westminster and perceptions of those events amongst the voting public! If this result showed that voters still held the party in some esteem despite its best efforts to discredit itself, it also showed a worrying collapse in support for second-placed Labour and a lack of any observable improvement in Conservative fortunes (the party came fourth). It was, as the *Daily Telegraph* reported, a staggering blow in a Scottish working-class constituency.

Since we have begun the story of 2006 with the Liberal Democrats, it will make sense to continue to follow the party's fortunes. Campbell's position as leader has not been challenged, nor is it likely to be in the near future. He has faced a number of problems, chief amongst which are the challenge posed by a resurgent Conservative Party (two-thirds of party members accept that the Conservatives now pose a 'real threat' to their party) and a disenchantment with their party's perceived closeness to Labour, though polls showed that 40 per cent of party members wished the party to remain left-of-centre. At the Scottish Labour annual conference, Alistair Darling called the Liberal Democrats 'inconsistent and opportunistic' and questioned the viability of the coalition between the two parties at Holyrood. This was a theme that First Minister Jack McConnell pursued later in the year, declaring that the stability that coalition brought constrained his party's natural radicalism. One of his colleagues was dispatched to New Zealand to see how Labour managed a minority government there. For their part the Liberal Democrats claimed to be focused not on coalition but on becoming, themselves, the largest party in Scotland. Possibilities of coalition were also discussed at Westminster where, for the first time since 1997, the Liberal Democrats were being asked to declare which major party they would support in a hung Parliament. Ken Clarke declared that the Conservatives should be willing to form a coalition with the Liberal Democrats following an inconclusive election, describing Campbell as an 'Old Tory'. As for a Lib-Lab coalition, such is Blair's current unpopularity that no Liberal Democrat leader could contemplate such an alliance, but a Brown-led Labour Party could be a different proposition. Given that the Liberal Democrats have always been more or less equally divided between those prepared to 'do a deal' with Labour, those prepared to 'do a deal' with the Conservatives, and those prepared to 'do a deal' with no one, Campbell would surely be best advised to restate Ashdown's position in a similar predicament: express no preference before an election but simply reiterate Liberal Democrat policy priorities. Campbell's problem is compounded by the possibility that, Dunfermline notwithstanding, his party might represent a diminishing asset. In the May local elections in England, the Liberal Democrats, until recently the second party of local government, gained three councils but lost two, making a net gain of only 11 councillors. The Conservatives, by contrast, made a net gain of 320 councillors and now control nearly six times as many councils as the Liberal Democrats.

The party conference at Brighton was a mild success. Campbell's speech, in which he spent more time attacking Labour over growing economic inequality, threats to civil liberties and Iraq than he spent attacking the Conservatives, whom he called superficial, received a six-minute standing ovation. More significant, perhaps, was the leadership's change in taxation policy. The party had been unique in the 2005 election for promising to increase the rate of taxation for high earners, but had decided to withdraw this commitment in favour of taxing carbon emissions and other environmental taxes. A rough ride for the leadership had been anticipated but, in the event, a 'good' debate ended with support for the leadership's proposals. Indicative of Campbell's perceived 'image problem', however, was the fact that prior to his speech the conference was privileged to see film footage of the young Ming, for example as a successful Olympic athlete: 'Ming the Movie', as the *Guardian's* Simon Hoggart called it. One last problem for the party: a sword of Damocles hangs suspended over party finances: their largest backer at the 2005 election, Michael Brown, the Scots millionaire who donated £2.4 million, is currently in jail in Spain for fraud. The party might be called upon to repay this sum.

Rebuild or make-over: Cameron's Conservative Party

David Cameron is now a recognisable feature of the political landscape, though uncertainty continues as to exactly what he represents. In one of their early confrontations at the dispatch box, Cameron mocked Blair, saying that he could remember when Blair used to represent the future. It is not easy, however, to remember that in Blair's early days as leader, much speculation focused on what he represented: was he Old Labour in bright new regalia or was he serious in claiming that he wanted to remake Labour? Most commentators thought either that he was not serious about remaking Labour or that if he were, he would be as unable to do it as Kinnock and Gaitskell had been. In fact, Blair was brilliantly successful. If Cameron is indeed – as he is often said to be – 'just' another Blair, then perhaps the Conservative hierarchy, or at least the Thatcherite elements within the hierarchy, do have cause to be apprehensive.

Like his predecessors, Cameron has had to deal with the Thatcher legacy, less divisive as time passes but still potent. At least he is not a part of that legacy and does not feel the need to define his Conservatism in direct response to Thatcherism. Cameron has abstemiously avoided identifying specific policy commitments; instead, he has sought to articulate his view of Conservatism's fundamental and working principles. 'There is a we as well as a me in politics', he claims, stressing traditional Tory organicism and its values. He goes on to identify the all-powerful state and, interestingly, the large corporation as the enemies of this organicism. Traditional Conservative organicism was to be encouraged in political life through the rebuilding of local communities. Cameron sees New Labour as the enemy of community because it has espoused 'the steady encroachment of the state into the private sphere of voluntarism'. Hybrid organisations, nominally independent but in reality parasitic appendages of the state, such as public–private partnership ventures, Network Rail and foundation hospitals have mushroomed since 1997. Cameron wishes to reinvigorate the sense of community via what is being called localism. In giving control back to local communities Cameron is stressing that, contrary to Thatcher's dictum, there is such a thing as society, and society, not the individual or the state, is the motor of well-being. We should take note that, again in contrast to Thatcherism, the goal is not wealth and the primacy of the individual but well-being and the primacy of local communities. It is too early to make any judgement on how seriously we are to take what appears to be a genuine reappraisal of modern Conservatism, but at least Cameron and his advisers appear to have cast aside the post-Thatcher laager mentality of xenophobia. Disraeli told electors at Buckingham once that collectivism, if unchecked, posed a threat to the national character, and concluded with an aphorism that, suitably amended, Cameron could take to heart: 'England should be governed by England, not by London.'

Financing the Conservative machine is not getting easier and controlling this 'arms race' proved problematical in the 2005 election, when both major parties augmented their funds by soliciting loans as well as donations. Although the Conservatives have been successful fundraisers since the election, with a number of loans being converted into donations, the party is still over-dependent on major donors. Loans taken on commercial terms do not have to be declared, but in 2006 it was reported that the Conservative Party would have to repay £20 million of a total debt of £53 million. However, they had spent £16 million on buying back the freehold of their former headquarters, and this could be sold at a profit or used as security against debt. Nevertheless, reliance on such large loans or donations must mean that campaigns (and hence perhaps policies) are likely to be influenced by a small number of rich individuals and major interests. (In 2006 the party received a donation of £300,000 from the Midlands Industrial Council and £200,000 from the Scottish Business Group.) It would be astonishing if Cameron, having identified large corporations as enemies of his one-nation organicism, were actually to construct policies harmful to the interests of such supportive groups.

Cameron's leadership has had its critics both within and without the party. The basis of the criticism is similar to that which Blair attracted in his early years as leader: that there was no substance to his politics, only image. Cameron has countered this by making it clear that the time is not right for creating a platform of specific policies. Rather, the task is to establish a general approach to current problems; in respect, for example, of environmental issues, it has been necessary to establish the party's 'green credentials' in the most general terms and to float the general topic of 'carbon taxes' for discussion. More specifically, Cameron has set up a number of commissions and taskforces to examine policy areas. Blair did much the same thing, but not until he became Prime Minister in 1997. In addition, the party's symbol, the torch, has been replaced by, of all things, a tree, exciting among his opponents, perhaps, the possibility that Cameron might turn out to be King Log. Voters' cynicism has been aroused by Cameron's photo-rich expedition, husky dogs and all, to see the diminishing ice fields around Svarlbad and his much-publicised cycling to the House of Commons (with an English flag attached to his handlebars during the World Cup!), especially when it was revealed that his official car, complete with papers, was bringing up the rear. At the end of 2006, Cameron announced that the Conservative Party, and not Labour, was the party for the poor and for ordinary working people. He promised that 2007 would witness the flowering of party policy to back up these claims. Certainly the policy groups that the party commissioned to advise on specific areas of policy are beginning to make their reports. But the question will not go away: is this a genuine attempt to remake the party or is it another attempt to out-Blair Blair, by appearing to prise out of Labour's grasp those areas of the policy agenda they believed to be their own by right? A subsidiary question demands our attention. If the attempt is genuine, how will the party stalwarts react? Finally, showing an astute awareness of the possibilities of technology, in late 2006 Cameron introduced another innovation, WebCameron, his own web page, which anybody can access, with a video in which we can all see the leader at home doing his chores and passing on his thoughts, and we can communicate with him directly if we wish. Is this an imaginative attempt to bring the leadership closer to the people? We could see it, perhaps, as an appropriate symbol for Cameron's leadership to date: innovative, democratic and with a popular touch – or as a vacuous gimmick. If election results offer any guide on public perceptions, local government elections in England were good, but the Dunfermline result was disappointing and a by-election in the seventeenth-safest Conservative seat of Bromley and Chislehurst was positively alarming. The party held the seat against a strong Liberal Democrat challenge, but its majority was slashed from 13,342 to 633. If we were to add to the balance the postal ballot of members that was held to endorse *Built to Last*, the statement of Cameronian aims and values, in which the leader's attempted annexation of traditional Labour territory was demarcated, then we might feel that the 92.7 per cent support received tells us what we wish to know about the leader's hold over the party membership. A less publicised statistic, however, is that only 26.7 per cent bothered to vote at all. No ringing endorsements yet then.

The wagon that lost its wheels: the Labour government

2006 has not been a good year for the Labour Party. It seems hard to believe, given the party's inability to be sure of putting major legislation on the statute book, that it secured a massive majority in a general election some 18 months ago. It is frequently suggested that the Prime Minister's lack of control over the parliamentary party is self-inflicted: his declaration, prior to the 2005 election, that he would not lead the party through the whole of the new Parliament, undermined him fatally. This suggestion seems to be based upon faulty memory and faulty logic. The decision was announced to counter Blair's deep personal unpopularity with the party and the public, and to win Labour a third term. Moreover, if his many critics today did not know that he will probably be retiring from the leadership sometime within the next 12 months, he would almost certainly have been forced out before now. The reason for Blair's lack of control over the parliamentary party is precisely that unpopularity that caused him to announce his retirement, and the reason for that unpopularity was and is that Blair has consistently taken the party where many did not want to go. This underlying malaise has been greatly exacerbated during 2006, as several contributors show, by a series of headline-making improprieties or alleged improprieties that stand comparison with the Major years (as a consequence of which, as the world well remembers, Blair declared that an incoming Labour administration would need to be purer-than-pure, whiter-than-white). First came the case of Culture Secretary Tessa Jowell and her husband David Mills. The public was informed that Ms Jowell was simply unaware that the family finances had been boosted by a gift of some £350,000, allegedly for legal services to the former Italian Prime Minister, Silvio Berlusconi. The propriety of such a gift to the husband of a Cabinet minister ceased to be an issue when the public was further informed of the couple's separation. The general media and public reaction (not always the same thing!) was that this was a sordid political ploy. The Deputy Prime Minister, John Prescott, whose long-standing affair with his diary secretary was revealed by the press, provided the next set of headlines. The charge against Prescott was that he was a womaniser who had used his position to obtain sexual favours. Prescott was not forced to resign, presumably because the process of replacing him would have been divisive, but his reputation as a plain-speaking, honest man of the people was in tatters and he was no longer of use to the Prime Minister. Worse for Prescott's image was the *Daily Mail*'s front-page photograph of the hapless Deputy Prime Minister playing croquet on the lawns of his official residence. What would his rugby league-following Hull constituents make of their representative? In July, it was disclosed that Prescott had spent two nights at the Colorado ranch of the owner of the Millennium Dome, who is anxious to see his property house a casino. The Deputy Prime Minister denied that his acceptance of a stetson and a pair of cowboy boots breached the Ministerial Code. Fortunately for the nation, Prescott was not photographed playing croquet in his new gear. Finally, Prescott was a special target in the Blunkett memoirs, a widely publicised exercise in self-justification by another tarnished Labour leading figure.

To these charges of financial impropriety and moral turpitude was later added that of gross inefficiency, when Home Secretary Charles Clarke was forced to admit that his department had no idea of the whereabouts of over 1,000 immigrants released from prison, some of whom were dangerous and many of whom should promptly have been deported. Clarke was dismissed and his place taken by the abrasive John Reid, who promptly declared that the Home Office was 'not fit for purpose' and stood in need of major reform. A sign of the level of incompetence of the Home Office was its estimate of how many would come to Britain seeking employment after 2004 from the new member states of the European Union: 13,000. In the event some 600,000 came. But Reid's performance in office has, to date, been no more effective and he has been obliged to admit to more departmental shortcomings.

One of the charges made against Reid was that his responses to problems have been prompted by the Murdoch media and Dominic Wring, in his chapter in this volume, alerts us to the importance of the Murdoch press generally. Piers Morgan, former editor of the *Daily Mirror*, published his private diaries in 2005 under the title *The Insider*. He tells us that, when President Clinton visited Belfast some time after the Good Friday Accord, he had discussed the possibility of Clinton writing a piece for his paper. He was told by Number 10 that Clinton could be asked to sign a prepared piece, and so Morgan asked his Northern Irish specialist to prepare such a piece for Clinton's signature and forwarded it to Number 10. Next day, said Morgan, the scoop appeared sure enough – but in the paper's arch-rival, the *Sun*. Like Morgan, we can only assume that Alastair Campbell considered that a scoop for Murdoch was worth the *Mirror*'s displeasure. And what displeasure! Such, it seems, is the influence of the Murdoch press on the present Labour government. In January's 'Who Runs Britain?' poll for the BBC's *Today* programme, Murdoch came second, behind the EEC President, but ahead of both Parliament and Blair. Playing to the tabloid gallery was a charge laid at the door of former Foreign Secretary Jack Straw when, writing in the *Lancashire Evening Telegraph*, he suggested to his Muslim constituents that 'wearing the full veil was bound to make better, positive relations between the two communities more difficult'. A week later, Constitutional Affairs Minister Harriet Harman joined the bandwagon: 'If you want equality, you have to be in society, not hidden away from it', she told the *New Statesman*. Indeed, Straw's comments received the support of a number of his colleagues in the Labour Party, including the Prime Minister himself, Gordon Brown, Hilary Armstrong and Phil Woolas. The controversy was further extended when Aishah Azmi, a teaching assistant, was sacked from her post in the West Riding after refusing to remove her veil in front of adult men. The *Daily Express* took the opportunity to launch a campaign to ban the wearing of veils.

Straw would not be the first politician to have sought to gain support through exploiting such issues, but it seems odd that so many government figures should have voiced similar misgivings around the same time. In the face of evidence of the alienation of many young British Muslims and of a corresponding backlash amongst non-Muslim voters, Labour politicians have clearly retreated from the policy of multiculturalism that they had hitherto pursued enthusiastically in favour of an agenda of an incorporative Britishness. Straw has since argued that his comments have at least put an important issue into the public domain. His opponents would argue that he was playing to the tabloid agenda.

Of all the controversies to embroil the Labour government though, the most important and enduring was that of the financing of the 2005 election. With the passage of the Political Parties, Elections and Referendums Act of 2000, for the first time a regulatory framework for party finances at the national level was established. A new agency, the Electoral Commission, was set up to oversee the operation of the Act. In the 2001 election, the major parties stayed well within the limits established, though they had secured large donations before the Act came into force. In 2005, both parties augmented their funds by securing loans as well as donations, and loans were not required to be declared so long as they were made at a commercial rate of interest. The Electoral Commission, looking at Labour's 2005 returns, following a complaint by the SNP MP Angus MacNeil, discovered that some loans were made at an allegedly uncommercial rate by wealthy individuals who were subsequently offered life peerages. Moreover, the party treasurer, Jack Dromey, publicly declared the he knew nothing of such loans. A Scotland Yard inquiry was established and as the year wore on its net grew tighter around Number 10. After interviewing those who had sought to attract funding to the government's flagship specialist academies, attention shifted in July to Lord Levy, the party fundraiser and close friend of the Prime Minister. Lord Levy was formally arrested and released on bail after being interviewed. In the autumn, a number of ministers were contacted, including the Chancellor and the Deputy Prime Minister. Patricia Hewitt was interviewed as a witness. We shall know the outcome of these events when Assistant Commissioner Yates makes his report to the Crown Prosecution Service early in 2007, and included in that report will doubtless be the gist of the proceeding that occurred on 12 December when, for the first time, a serving Prime Minister was questioned by the police in the course of a criminal investigation. It might excite some interest and perhaps not a little cynical conjecture, that by an odd coincidence, this interview was held on the very day that the Stephens Inquiry into the death of Diana, Princess of Wales, reported, and that widespread closure of post offices was announced. What luck, a good day for bad news! Equally interesting is the fact that neither the Conservatives nor indeed the Liberal Democrats were very forceful in their criticism. Michael Howard had already himself been interviewed on behalf of his own party, and the Liberal Democrats, as we have seen, had their own funding difficulties.

Apart from these problems it was 'business as usual' for the government. Blair loyalists, such as Stephen Byers and Alan Milburn, had been openly critical of Brown's handling of the tax credit system; later in the year Byers returned to the attack, this time over inheritance tax. Charles Clarke went further, calling the Chancellor a control freak. In September, Brown supporters turned on the Prime Minister when, coming back to London reinvigorated by his summer holiday, he indicated that he had no immediate plans to step down. Talk of a strong letter to the Prime Minister by previously loyal MPs and rumours of a coup were in the air; a junior minister felt obliged to resign but it was then reliably reported that Blair would indeed be gone within the year. At the party conference, however, each extolled the virtues of the other. Blair yet again refused formally to endorse Brown as his preferred successor, and indeed, in an off-the-cuff remark, later unconvincingly denied, his wife Cherie was acutely dismissive of the veracity of some of the statements that Brown was making in his speech.

It was said that Labour had only to wait before its substantially increased investment in the National Health Service (NHS) and state education paid dividends. It now seems that their wait is likely to be as fruitless as that of Vladimir and Estragon in Samuel Beckett's *Waiting for Godot*. Labour's rationalisation of NHS hospital provision drove the party chairman Hazel Blears to demonstrate against a hospital closure in her own part of Manchester. She was in favour of the policy as policy, she explained, but it was her job as a constituency MP to oppose its application in her own area. We may recall that this was one of Vladimir and Estragon's problems: they were never certain they were in the right place! Labour's planned expansion of its specialist academies is likely to go ahead with the approval only of the Conservative Party. Andrew Hindmoor, in his chapter in this volume, traces the developments of the debate on city academies, especially the issue of selection, through the year. He concludes that Blair was obliged to compromise on selection and on the role of local education authorities. Perhaps this was an exercise in *reculer pour mieux sauter*, because towards the end of the year the Prime Minister and his Education and Skills Secretary, Alan Johnson, announced the launch of the first three National Skills Academies. The first, in central London, is Philip Green's Fashion Retail Academy, and bids have been received from the nuclear, chemical and creative and cultural industries, along with the hospital sector.

By the end of 2008, the government aims to have 12 operational National Skills Academies, one per major sector of the economy, investing £90 million in the programme, which will be delivered through the Learning and Skills Council. Two bidding rounds have taken place so far, a third is planned for early 2007. In his final New Year message in 2007, Blair promised the establishment of 400 city academies and more trust schools. It would be quite wrong to say that these developments are not welcomed by any Labour backbenchers, but they are opposed by most on ideological grounds. In general, backbenchers and party supporters are unenthused by the policy aspirations of their own government in respect of the key areas of health and education. The government's likely endorsement of nuclear fuel as a main source of energy supply has angered backbenchers and supporters perhaps even more. But of all Labour's stated policy preferences, that which has infuriated its traditional supporters most is the likely replacement of Trident, Britain's nuclear deterrent. Research into the values of traditional Labour supporters over the past 40 years has consistently shown that opposition to the independent nuclear deterrent is a bedrock of their faith. It is coincidental that that earlier moderniser, Hugh Gaitskell, was preoccupied with the twin issues of reform of Clause IV and nuclear deterrence. They undermined his leadership. Having successfully challenged the traditionalists over Clause IV,

Blair may well be confident of victory over nuclear defence. But once again, his strongest support would come naturally from the Conservatives and not from his own party.

The life of a modernising Labour Prime Minister was never going to be easy, but Iraq and its consequences hang around the neck of this incumbent like an albatross. Labour's claims to pursue an ethical policy seem to belong to bygone age, a fact brought home by the extraordinary decision to terminate a criminal investigation by the Serious Fraud Office into alleged corruption surrounding a huge arms deal between British Aerospace (BAE) and Saudi Arabia. Extraordinary, not because of the nature of the decision – not only was the continuation of the inquiry likely to damage relations between Britain and Saudi Arabia, but no convictions would have resulted as a consequence of the law's lack of clarity – but because the decision appears to have been taken not by the Attorney General, who has responsibility for such matters, but by the Prime Minister himself, who personally assumed 'full responsibility'. But the public was assured that the decision had not been taken because of Saudi threats or defence industry lobbying, for that would have been unethical, but for security reasons. Not only was the government's ethical policy called into serious question, but 2006 saw the special relationship with the US also exposed, following comments made by State Department analyst Kendall Myers that it is a thing of no substance – a myth. Only government ministers resist the claim that the invasion of Iraq was unjustified and illegal, and its consequences utterly disastrous.

While assuring the public that, contrary to all evidence, the invasion of Iraq has not made Britain less safe from terrorist attack, the government has been consumed by the need to protect society, and this preoccupation, as Sue Prince shows in her chapter in this volume, has frequently put it at loggerheads with the judiciary. Hastily enacted legislation restricting individual liberties, such as the Prevention of Terrorism Act 2005, falls foul of the Human Rights Act of 1998, which, in turn, is defended by the judiciary. Senior government figures, especially the Home Secretary, John Reid, but including the Prime Minister himself, are openly critical of senior judges – using them, says Prince, as scapegoats for shortcomings in their own legislation – and thus weakening public confidence in the rule of law. In his chapter, Philip Norton highlights other constitutional issues that the government has attempted to address during the year. He is right to point out that no serious attempts have been made to address the notorious West Lothian question, though serious suggestions of reform have emanated from Conservative ranks, and we might be inclined to conclude that, while Labour continues to benefit from the loyalty of Scottish backbenchers, nothing much is likely to happen. It is true that the completion of House of Lords reform is back on the agenda, though no urgency has been shown by ministers. In their chapter, Meg Russell and Maria Sciara suggest that the Lords, even as presently constituted, is strengthening the legislature against the executive in a way that the government did not foresee. This is not altogether surprising, and Norton rightly bemoans the lack of an 'intellectually coherent' government approach to constitutional issues. All the same, it is fair to point up the Prime Minister's continuing efforts to move forward on the impasse concerning the reintroduction of devolved government to Northern Ireland, where some progress has been made.

We are approaching the end of the Blair era: it is hardly conceivable that he will be in office a year from now. He has transformed the Labour Party and, in government, has pursued policies that neither friend nor foe would have thought possible in 1997. In the short term, Labour has benefited in securing three consecutive electoral victories. Scotland and Wales have measures of self-government, and Northern Ireland is nearer to securing a stable devolved system of power-sharing than seemed feasible when Labour came to office. Labour's stewardship of the economy has, on the whole, been exemplary. Its attempts at reform in health and education have not so far been successful and certainly not popular. When we contemplate the Blair legacy in the round, despite the fact that it, together with Afghanistan, merited only one reference in his valedictory 2007 report to the nation, Iraq outweighs all other considerations. Unless Gordon Brown is in office before the May elections in Scotland and has a programme to extricate British forces, or something equally dramatic takes place, Labour's hegemony north of the border could be broken and the importance of this both for the Union and for the Labour Party in the United Kingdom context cannot be exaggerated. The response of the British public, including some within the Labour Party, prompted especially by the Iraq invasion and its legacy, might be to summon up Oliver Cromwell's famous response to the Rump Parliament made 353 years ago, and repeated by L. S. Amery to Neville Chamberlain in 1940: 'You have sat here too long for any good you may have been doing. Depart, I say, and let us have done with you ...'

2
The Constitution: Fragmentation or Adaptation?

Philip Norton

The constitution continued to witness formal changes and, more fundamentally, unintended pressures resulting from earlier reforms of the nation's constitutional arrangements. The most significant pressures occurred in the relationship between the executive and the courts and between the different parts of the United Kingdom.

The executive and the courts

The tense relationship between ministers and the courts apparent in 2005[1] continued into 2006. At the heart of the tension was judicial interpretation of the Human Rights Act 1998, empowering the courts to issue declarations of incompatibility where measures or actions by public authorities did not comply with the provisions of the European Convention on Human Rights (ECHR).

The Prevention of Terrorism Act was enacted in 2005 after the courts had declared provisions of the Anti-Terrorism, Crime and Security Act 2001 to be incompatible with the provisions of the ECHR. During the bill's passage in 2005, the Joint Committee on Human Rights expressed concern that its provisions for control orders – enabling the Home Secretary to restrict the movement of particular individuals – may also fall foul of the ECHR.[2] Its concerns were vindicated in 2006 when on 12 April Mr Justice Sullivan held that a control order imposed on a particular individual, 'MB', breached Article 6 of the Convention and then again on 28 June when he held that control orders on six men breached their rights under Article 5. 'I am left in no doubt whatsoever', he said in June, 'that the cumulative effect of the order has been to deprive the respondents of their liberty, in breach of Article 5. I do not consider that this is a borderline case.' He made clear that he had taken into

13

account the importance of protecting the public from acts of terrorism, but 'human rights or international law must not be infringed or compromised'.[3] In delivering his judgment, he criticised the Home Secretary for having claimed that the courts could quash control orders but then later telling the courts that it would be 'inappropriate' to quash them. This change, he said, was more than unfortunate and had 'the potential to undermine the government, to undermine confidence in public administration and its integrity'.

The decision elicited an immediate response from ministers as well as from the Chairman of the Home Affairs Committee in the Commons. Home Secretary John Reid argued that the legislation was necessary to combat terrorism. In appealing against the judgment, counsel for the Home Secretary accused the judge of a string of legal errors and misunderstandings. Ian Burnett QC also argued that the decision to impose control orders 'was a policy judgement primarily for the executive – not the courts'. 'The taking of measures to combat terrorism', he declared, 'involves a heavy political responsibility, and it is critical that there be proper accountability if errors are made.'[4] John Denham, Chairman of the Home Affairs Committee, said it was not over the top to talk of an emerging constitutional crisis. 'This is not a battle between government and the judiciary', he declared. 'This is between the elected parliament and the judiciary.'[5] Former Home Secretary Charles Clarke also weighed in to criticise judges for failing to meet him to discuss human rights legislation in the light of the terrorist threat. 'One of my most depressing experiences as Home Secretary', he said, 'was the outright refusal of any of the Law Lords to discuss the principles behind these matters in any forum, private or public, formal or informal.'[6]

The dispute then entered a second phase. On 10 May, the High Court, again in the form of Mr Justice Sullivan, held that nine Afghans, who had hijacked a plane in 2000 and forced it to fly to Britain, could remain in the UK. (The men had been jailed in 2001 but the Appeal Court had quashed their convictions in 2003 because of a mistake in the judge's direction to the jury.) Mr Justice Sullivan criticised ministers for failing to follow correct procedures and for delaying implementing an immigration appeal panel's decision of 2004 while they sought ways to deport the men. To show his 'disquiet and concern', he made an order that the Home Office should pay costs on an indemnity basis – the highest level possible. His decision again attracted intense criticism from ministers and other politicians. 'It's not an abuse of justice for us to order their deportation,' declared the Prime Minister, 'it's an abuse of common sense frankly to be in a position where we can't do this.'[7] 'When decisions are taken which appear inexplicable or bizarre to the general public,' said the Home Secretary, 'it only reinforces the perception that the system is not working to protect or in favour of the vast majority of ordinary decent, hard-working citizens in this country.'[8] Former Home Secretary David Blunkett announced: 'Any judge who fails to understand the signals which are sent in difficult circumstances such as this has missed the point.'[9]

The government suffered a further blow on 1 August when the Appeal Court upheld Mr Justice Sullivan's ruling on the six control orders. They found that his reasons for quashing the orders had been compelling and that the orders had amounted to a deprivation of liberty in breach of Article 5. The court, headed by the Lord Chief Justice, Lord Phillips of Worth Matravers, said there was no merit in the Home Secretary's attack on the principles involved, refused leave to appeal and invited the government to come up with an alternative to the illegal orders. 'Within minutes of the ruling ... John Reid attacked the judges' decision.'[10] The Home Secretary did, though, agree 'reluctantly' to implement the ruling, while noting that amended orders would not be 'as stringent as the security services believe are necessary'.[11]

The government took some comfort from the fact that the Appeal Court quashed Mr Justice Sullivan's ruling in the 'MB' case on the grounds that the review powers were not incompatible with the right to a fair trial under Article 6. There was some more good news for the government later in the month when, on 24 August, the Special Immigration Appeals Tribunal, under Mr Justice Ouseley, held that changed conditions in Algeria made it possible to deport foreign terror suspects back to Algeria.[12] It was one judgment that received a positive response from the Home Secretary. In another case (*Gillan*), the Law Lords held that the stop and search provisions of the Terrorism Act 2000 were not incompatible with the ECHR.

Such welcome outcomes for the government were rare. The relationship between ministers and the courts was such that the Lord Chief Justice felt the need to defend the judges. In evidence to the House of Lords Constitution Committee, he said 'The judge is just doing his job of applying the law and enforcing the rule of law. It is the law that has changed.'[13] It was a point he reiterated, in defending judges against criticism of sentencing policy, at the Lord Mayor of London's annual judges' dinner. The Lord Chancellor, Lord Falconer – under a statutory duty to uphold the principle of the rule of law – also felt compelled to warn ministers not to interfere in judicial cases. 'Whilst it is perfectly legitimate for ministers to address policy issues raised by individual judgements, ministers should not criticise judges.'[14] However, in a speech on the role of judges in a modern democracy, delivered in Australia on 13 September, he conceded that human rights were a 'pressure point' – 'where the position and role of the judges takes on a new dimension, and become the subject of political debate'.[15] Though stressing the case for judicial independence, he nonetheless stressed throughout his speech the need to recognise the respective roles of executive and judiciary. In respect of combating terrorism, he said, it was for the executive or legislature to decide how the fight should be conducted.

The role of the courts is not to determine what individual measures to take. It is to decide whether the measures others have decided on are lawful.

The courts must always be clear that they are not making either political or intelligence decisions.

The courts, he argued, must be sensitive to the needs of the state and the values of society. 'They must therefore command the respect of the public. If the public lose confidence in where the balance is struck, then the system is undermined.'

The judgments of the courts led the government to contemplate changing the law. The picture was further complicated when the Leader of the Opposition, David Cameron, on 26 June promised to replace the Human Rights Act with a 'British bill of rights'. The Human Rights Act, he declared, had hampered the task of fighting crime and terrorism.

A modern British Bill of Rights needs to define the core values which give us our identity as a free nation. It should spell out the fundamental duties and responsibilities of people living in this country both as citizens and foreign nationals. And it should guide the judiciary and the government in applying human rights law when the lack of responsibility of some individuals threatens the rights of others.[16]

He planned to set up a panel of experts to advise on the contents.

Cameron's proposal was immediately attacked by ministers and by some of his own supporters, including Kenneth Clarke, who was chairing the party's taskforce on democracy. Another leading Tory, Lord Tebbit, attacked the proposal since it did not involve repudiating the ECHR. 'European law', he said, 'would override it and we would be back where we are now, but in a bigger muddle perhaps.'[17]

Human rights thus remained a 'pressure point', but with little prospect of relief. There remained the prospect of continuing tension between the executive and the courts, with little sign of any concrete steps to resolve the pressure. The Prime Minister in June ruled out repealing the Human Rights Act and, following a review of the Act by the Department for Constitutional Affairs,[18] conceded that it may not be possible to make major amendments. The review concluded that the effects of the Act had largely been beneficial. David Cameron's proposal got a bad press, with few commentators seeing it as a realistic option.

Devolution

The principal legislative changes affecting the devolution settlement were the passage of the Government of Wales Act 2006 and the Northern Ireland (St Andrews Agreement) Act 2006. However, the year was significant also for tensions in the settlement affecting Scotland.

The Government of Wales Act provided for the transfer, on a case by case basis, of legislative competence in areas where the Assembly already exercised powers. This was to form the second stage of a three-stage process by which legislative devolution would take place. The final stage, involving the transfer of legislative powers in 20 policy areas where the Assembly already exercised some functions, would take place after a referendum was called by the Secretary of State. Though there was some pressure to implement the recommendation of the Richard Commission,[19] under which the transfer of legislative powers would occur in one stage, the bill completed its passage relatively unscathed. Its provisions included a ban on dual candidacy, that is, a candidate standing for both a constituency and a party list. The House of Lords initially opposed the ban, not least since dual candidacy was common in other countries, but eventually gave way. (An attempt by a Labour peer to achieve a similar ban in Scotland, through the medium of a Private Member's Bill, was unsuccessful.)[20] Less controversially, the Act also separated the executive from the National Assembly for Wales.[21]

There were various attempts to make progress in re-establishing devolved government in Northern Ireland. After a reconvened meeting of the Northern Ireland Assembly in June failed to make any progress, the Prime Minister and the Irish Taoiseach, Bertie Ahern, set a deadline of 24 November for agreement to be reached on the restoration of the institutions agreed in the 1998 Belfast Agreement. In October, the governments brought together the various Northern Ireland political parties for a three-day meeting in St Andrews, Scotland, and produced proposals for power-sharing and the devolved institutions as well as a detailed deadline for the restoration of devolved government.[22] Power-sharing would be based on acceptance of the Police Service of Northern Ireland and the rule of law. The goal was for the St Andrews Agreement to be endorsed by the electorate of Northern Ireland in March 2007, with power being devolved by the end of that month. 'Failure to agree to establish the Executive', it declared, 'will lead to immediate dissolution of the Assembly, as will failure to agree at any stage.'[23] In November, both Houses of Parliament rushed through the Northern Ireland (St Andrews Agreement) Bill to give effect to the agreement. On 24 November, three days after the Act was passed, the Northern Ireland Assembly met for the purpose of nominating a First Minister and First Deputy Minister. The leader of the Democratic Unionist Party (DUP), Ian Paisley, declined to be nominated for the post of First Minister and the proceedings were overshadowed by an armed convicted murderer, Michael Stone, attempting to storm into the Assembly.[24] Despite the deadline not being met, Northern Ireland Secretary Peter Hain said there were grounds for optimism, in that both the DUP and Sinn Fein appeared willing to do a deal, but he reiterated that if agreement could not be reached on devolution, the Assembly would be dissolved.[25]

The devolution settlement in Scotland also looked increasingly unsettled. There were tensions on both sides of the border. The 'West Lothian' question was pursued at Westminster. Lord Baker of Dorking introduced a Parliament (Participation of Members of the House of Commons) Bill to deliver on the principle of English votes on English measures in Parliament. The bill, as is the practice in the Lords, passed all its stages. There was no prospect of it going further, but it fulfilled its purpose of keeping the issue on the agenda. Former Conservative Foreign Secretary, Sir Malcolm Rifkind, advocated an English Grand Committee to consider English bills – a proposal echoing that of the Norton Commission Report of 2000[26] – or a convention that no bill should pass unless it had the support of a majority of MPs sitting for English seats.[27] The principle was one that was embraced by the Conservative Party.

There was evidence of growing support for independence on both sides of the border. A YouGov poll in September found that 44 per cent of Scots would be inclined to vote for Scotland to become an independent country.[28] (Only 42 per cent would be inclined to vote against.) This, as the *Sunday Times* noted, represented almost a doubling of the figure since 2000, when only 23 per cent of Scots said they would favour independence. An ICM poll in November found that the figure had increased to 52 per cent.[29] The same poll found that 59 per cent of English voters favoured Scottish independence. It also suggested that there was a surge in support for an English Parliament. An Ipsos MORI opinion poll in June found that more than a quarter of those questioned favoured a law-making English Parliament (up from 16 per cent in 2003).[30] According to the ICM poll, 68 per cent of English voters supported such a Parliament; 48 per cent also wanted a complete break, with Wales and Northern Ireland being separated from England. The 'truly depressing finding, for friends of the Union', editorialised the *Sunday Telegraph*, 'is the surge in English nationalism'.[31]

Other tensions

The clash between the executive and the courts was not the only tension revealed within the British polity. As Philip Giddings discusses in Chapter 7 of this volume, there was a clash between government and the Parliamentary Commissioner for Administration, the Ombudsman. Since the inception of the Ombudsman's office in 1967, only four reports had been made to Parliament by the holder of the office reporting that maladministration had been found and that there had not been, nor would be, a remedy. Two of these were made in the 2005–06 parliamentary session. Both occasions led to the Commons Public Administration Select Committee (PASC) siding with the Ombudsman and issuing reports critical of the government. The Committee declared:

> The government has been far too ready to dismiss the Ombudsman's findings of maladministration. Our investigations have shown that these findings were sound. It would be extremely unfortunate if government became accustomed simply to reject the findings of maladministration,

especially if an investigation on [sic] this Committee proved that there was indeed a case to answer.[32]

PASC's stance was robust, but neither it nor the Ombudsman could force government to act. What gains had been made in the development of the Ombudsman's office would be lost, as Richard Kirkham noted,

> if the government were to adopt a stance towards the finding of the PO [Parliamentary Ombudsman], whereby it claimed to have the final word on interpretations of maladministration. As with other aspects of the British constitution, to ensure that the institution of the ombudsman maintains its required authority, we are reliant on the intervention of a healthy and active Parliament.[33]

There was also an apparent tension between government and the armed forces. In an interview with the *Daily Mail* in October, the Chief of the General Staff, General Sir Richard Dannatt, warned that the continued presence of British troops in Iraq 'exacerbates the security problems' and that 'we should get ourselves out sometime soon' – a stance contrary to that taken by the government – and that it was naive to try to create a liberal democracy in the country.[34] He also offered the opinion that a 'a moral and spiritual vacuum' had opened up in British society. His comments caused a political storm and raised an important constitutional issue: to what extent should the head of the armed services publicly question the position of Her Majesty's Government? There was little obvious precedent. The Prime Minister had the choice of either sacking the General as Chief of the General Staff, thus fuelling the controversy, or backing him. Despite apparent anger in Downing Street, the latter option was pursued. Downing Street offered 'full support', claiming there was no difference between Sir Richard and the government on the issue. Sir Richard himself gave interviews to try to calm the situation – 'We are going to see this through', he said[35] – but did not deny the comments attributed to him.

Proposed changes

The year was notable also for other pressures to make further changes to the nation's constitutional arrangements. Two of the most prominent were in respect of the House of Lords and the royal prerogative.

House of Lords reform

Labour's 2005 manifesto committed the government to a review by a committee of both Houses to seek agreement on codifying the key conventions of the Lords and developing alternative forms of scrutiny that complement rather than replicate those of the Commons.[36] It also committed the party to legislate to place 'reasonable limits on the time bills spend in the second chamber – no longer than 60 sitting days for most bills'. In addition: 'As part of the process of modernisation, we will remove the remaining hereditary peers and allow a free vote on the composition of the House'.

Little progress was made in 2005, but Lords reform came back on the agenda in 2006. In an interview with the *Daily Telegraph* published on 1 April, the Lord Chancellor, Lord Falconer, raised the prospect of reducing the powers of the Lords as part of a wider package of reform.[37] The statement, apparently made without Cabinet clearance, elicited a frosty response. Advocating enhanced legitimacy through election and concomitantly reducing the powers of the House was seen as illogical.[38] The focus then shifted to the proposal for a joint committee. Agreement was eventually reached, and the Joint Committee on Conventions was established in May. The 22-member committee, under Labour peer and former Cabinet minister Lord Cunningham of Felling (who previously chaired the Joint Committee on House of Lords Reform), was asked to consider the practicality of codifying the key conventions on the relationship between the two Houses which affect the consideration of legislation, in particular the Salisbury-Addison convention, the convention on secondary legislation, the convention that government business in the Lords should be considered in reasonable time, and the conventions governing the exchange of amendments between the two Houses. The committee was to report by 21 July, but both Houses later agreed that it should have longer and report by the end of the session.

The new Leader of the House of Commons, Jack Straw, speaking at the Hansard Society annual general meeting on 11 July, expressed support for a second chamber divided 50:50 between elected and appointed members. He indicated that after the Joint Committee had reported, the government would produce a White Paper and there would be a vote on the composition of the second chamber in the New Year. His plans appeared predicated on the Joint Committee coming up with substantive proposals for codifying conventions. In the event, the report of the Joint Committee – published on 3 November – essentially endorsed existing practices.

> We are unanimously agreed that all recommendations for the formulation or codification of conventions are subject to the current understanding that conventions as such are flexible and unenforceable, particularly in the self-regulating environment of the House of Lords. Nothing in these recommendations would alter the present right of the House of Lords, in exceptional circumstances, to vote against the Second Reading or passing of any Bill, or to vote down any Statutory Instruments where the parent Act so provides. The resolutions which we propose are couched in sufficiently general terms to make this self-evident.[39]

On a time limit for the consideration of bills in the Lords, it said that there was no definition of 'reasonable' and it did not recommend that one be invented. Even before the report was published, the government itself, in the light of evidence of the time taken to get bills through, also appeared to abandon its commitment to a 60-day limit.

Straw continued to pursue the issue of composition through a cross-party working group. A paper he prepared for the group was leaked.[40] His quest for a part-elected House was not supported by all his Cabinet colleagues – Deputy Prime Minister John Prescott publicly opposed election – and he had difficult meetings with Labour peers and the Parliamentary Labour Party. Appearing before the Labour peers, the Prime Minister emphasised that he wanted to achieve a consensus and that the Parliament Act would not be used to get a measure through.[41] In the Queen's Speech on 15 November, the government committed itself only to 'work to build a consensus on reform of the House of Lords' and bring forward proposals.[42] By the end of the year, the House of Lords had not debated the Joint Committee report, which was to take place before publication of a White Paper, and there was little evidence of consensus.

Within the Lords itself, there was one change that dispensed with several hundred years of tradition. Following the enactment of the Constitutional Reform Act 2005, which provided that the Lord Chancellor need not be a peer, the House decided to elect its own presiding officer – to be known as the Lord Speaker – in place of the Lord Chancellor. Nine candidates stood for election and, under the Alternative Vote system, the eventual victor (who led in each stage of the ballot) was former Labour minister Baroness Hayman. The result was declared on 4 July and the new Lord Speaker took her place on the Woolsack. The Lord Speaker, like the Lord Chancellor, has no independent powers – the House remains a self-regulating body – and is seen by the House as having an important external role as the public face of the Lords.

The royal prerogative

The royal prerogative comprises those powers traditionally vested in the Crown and which have not been displaced by statute. The extent of prerogative powers has never been clearly defined. PASC identified the principal prerogative powers (which it termed 'ministerial executive powers') but noted that ministers had said that it would be impossible to produce a precise list of the powers.[43] There were, as PASC noted, various demands for restrictions on the prerogative. There were two approaches: a pragmatic approach, making the case for a particular change on its merits, and a comprehensive approach, transferring most or all prerogative powers to statute. Both approaches were apparent in 2006.

The pragmatic approach was reflected in calls for the war-making power to be subject to parliamentary consent. Various Private Members' Bills had previously been introduced to give effect to this. Support for such a move also came in the form of the report of the House of Lords Constitution Committee, published in July, on *Waging War: Parliament's Role and Responsibility*. Though not advocating a statutory requirement for Parliament's approval to be given to the deployment of British forces overseas, it argued that there should be a convention that government should seek approval for such deployment (which on occasion may have to be retrospective).[44] Support also came from two contenders for the office of Prime Minister. Opposition leader David Cameron included support for Parliament having the power to vote on war and treaties in the party's statement of aims and values[45] and reiterated his support in evidence to the Conservative Party's taskforce on democracy. The Chancellor of the Exchequer, Gordon Brown, in his speech to the Labour Party Conference in Manchester, also argued that, apart from emergency action, Parliament should make 'the final decisions on matters as important as war and peace'.[46]

David Cameron also expressed support for a Civil Service Act, a measure on which the government appeared to stall. The government had published a draft Civil Service Bill for consultation in 2004. The case for a bill, embodying the principles underpinning the operation of the civil service, was made by a number of bodies, including PASC, the Lords Constitution Committee, and the Committee on Standards in Public Life. In January, the government published a Civil Service Code for consultation but no commitment was made on a Civil Service Bill. On 3 March, government whip Lord Bassam of Brighton said that the government would make a statement 'in due course'. In an exchange of correspondence with the Chairman of the Lords Constitution Committee, Lord Holme of Cheltenham, the minister refused to say when such a statement would be made. Challenged on why the government had not published the responses to the consultation on a bill (which under the Cabinet Office Code of Practice should have been published within three months of the consultation), Lord Bassam said the responses were being considered alongside those on the Civil Service Code. When the final version of the Code was published in June, the minister said that the responses to the 2004 consultation continued to be studied. 'At this stage, therefore, I am afraid that I am unable to be more specific on the timing of the response.'[47]

The comprehensive approach was embodied in a Private Member's Bill, the Constitutional Reform (Prerogative Powers and Civil Service etc.) Bill introduced by Lord Lester of Herne Hill. Introduced in March, the bill sought to put prerogative powers on a statutory footing. The bill placed under parliamentary authority the prerogative powers exercised by ministers (it excluded those exercised personally by the monarch), embodied the principles underpinning the operation of the civil service, provided for parliamentary approval for some appointments to leading public offices, and provided for direct access to the Ombudsman. Lord Lester declared:

A central question raised by this Bill 'is: who should be sovereign – Parliament or the Executive? ... The principle on which this Bill is based is that in our modern democratic society Parliament rather than the executive should be sovereign, as was envisaged by those who made the constitutional settlement in 1688.[48]

The bill received support from different parts of the House. The leader of the Liberal Democrat peers, Lord McNally, declared: 'I sniff reform in the air.'[49] The smell did not reach the nostrils of ministers. From the government front bench, Lord Bassam declared: 'In the government's view, the prerogative is ... a well established part of our constitutional arrangements.'[50] He contended that it offered flexibility and the capacity to respond quickly in emergencies. Apart from offering the prospect of some change in the Ponsonby rule governing the laying of treaties before Parliament, he failed to embrace any of the bill's provisions. Following the usual practice, the bill was given an unopposed second reading. It completed all its stages but made no further progress. It served, though, to keep the issue of the prerogative – and the case for a Civil Service Act – on the agenda.

A constitution in flux

The year also saw other changes to the nation's constitutional arrangements and to demands for other changes. The Electoral Reform Act was passed in order to encourage greater participation in elections and in order to reduce electoral fraud. Among other provisions, it conferred power to create an online record of electors and extended the powers of electoral registration officers in order to generate a more accurate registration of electors. It also reduced the qualifying age for election to public office to 18 years. (Various attempts to reduce the voting age to 16 were defeated.) As a response to allegations that some peerages may have been awarded in return for loans made, late amendments were made to ensure that loans were disclosed. (Under the Political Parties, Elections and Referendums Act 2000, donations had to be disclosed, but not loans made at commercial rates.) As the awarding of honours for financial gain was prohibited by law, the police investigated whether any breach had occurred: in the course of the investigation, various people were arrested, including Lord Levy, the Prime Minister's principal fundraiser and envoy to the Middle East, and a number of others were questioned.

PASC issued an interim report urging steps to ensure the propriety of the system for awarding peerages and honours. These included greater transparency in the process, the creation of a statutory appointments commission, and a review of anti-corruption legislation.[51] The committee delayed any final report because of the continuing police investigations.

PASC was also active in making proposals for other changes. In September, it issued a report recommending that the Parliamentary Commissioner for

Standards or the Ombudsman should be empowered to investigate alleged breaches of the Ministerial Code.[52] The decision of the Prime Minister in March to appoint the Comptroller and Auditor General, Sir John Bourn, to advise on alleged breaches was described as a 'small step' in the right direction. The committee's recommendation, declared its Chairman, Tony Wright, would not interfere with the political accountability of ministers or the responsibility of the Prime Minister to determine the fate of ministers, 'but would reduce the regular frenzy and provide a more informed basis upon which political judgments can be made'.[53]

Nor was PASC the only committee making recommendations for change. In March, the Merits of Statutory Instruments Committee in the Lords published a report advocating a more co-ordinated management of statutory instruments within government.[54] In September, the Commons Modernisation Committee published a report arguing that bills should normally stand referred to evidence-taking Special Standing Committees, or Public Bill Committees, for consideration.[55] In October, the Law Commission published proposals for post-legislative scrutiny; it advocated the creation of a Joint Committee of the two Houses.[56] Of the three, the Modernisation Committee achieved remarkable success. At the beginning of November, MPs agreed a motion welcoming the committee's proposals and approving 'in particular the proposals for the committal of bills to committees with powers to take evidence to become the normal practice for programmed government bills which start in this House'.[57] Bills began to be so committed in the new session.

The prospect of wider constitutional reform was raised by Chancellor Gordon Brown in his speech to the Labour Party Conference. In addition to proposing that Parliament should have power over matters of peace and war, he advocated 'a radical shift of power from the centre' and separating politicians from administrative decision-making. He also raised the prospect of a written constitution. Without committing himself to the proposal, he noted 'We do not today have a written constitution.' Conservative leader David Cameron also held out the prospect of various reforms to the constitution, including – as we have noted – a British Bill of Rights, parliamentary approval for war, a Civil Service Act, and 'a constructive Unionist response to the West Lothian question'.[58]

What the various changes and the proposals for reform demonstrated was the unsettled nature of the British constitution. They also revealed a lack of direction. They reflected a lack of coherence in constitutional debate by politicians and political parties – there was no clear articulation of an intellectually coherent approach to constitutional change, no clear delineation of what type of constitution advocates wanted for the United Kingdom.[59] There were, as Patrick Dunleavy has noted, different approaches,[60] but these were not necessarily embraced by politicians, were essentially prescriptive, and failed to take account of the fact that reforms could have unintended consequences. The Human Rights Act and devolution may have had the beneficial consequences intended, but they have also had unintended consequences. Lord Falconer, as we have seen, identified human rights legislation as a 'pressure point'. A number of such pressure points have created tensions within the UK's constitutional arrangements.

These tensions could lead in certain circumstances to undermining the core feature of the British constitution, the doctrine of parliamentary supremacy. The point was touched upon in 2005 by the Law Lords in deciding the challenge to the Hunting Act 2004. Lord Steyn touched upon the basic point. The doctrine of parliamentary sovereignty was, he said, still the '*general principle*' of the constitution. It was a construct of common law. 'The judges created the principle. If that is so, it is not unthinkable that circumstances could arise where the courts may have to qualify a principle established on a different hypothesis of constitutionalism.'[61] The constitution continued sailing into largely uncharted waters.

Notes

1. P. Norton, 'The Constitution: Selective Incrementalism', in P. Giddings and M. Rush (eds), *The Palgrave Review of British Politics 2005* (Basingstoke: Palgrave Macmillan, 2006), pp. 14–29.
2. Joint Committee on Human Rights, *Tenth Report: Prevention of Terrorism Bill*, HL 68/HC 334, 2004–05.
3. *Guardian*, 29 June 2006.
4. *Guardian*, 4 July 2006.
5. *Guardian Unlimited*, 29 June 2006.
6. *Guardian*, 4 July 2006.
7. BBC News Online, 11 May 2006 <www.bbc.co.uk/hi/uk_politics>.
8. Ibid.
9. *Sun*, 11 May 2006.
10. *The Times*, 2 August 2006.
11. *Guardian*, 2 August 2006.
12. *Guardian*, 25 August 2006.
13. Select Committee on the Constitution, *Fourteenth Report: Meeting with the Lord Chief Justice*, HL Paper 213, 2005–06, Q59.
14. BBC News Online, 18 July 2006. See also BBC News Online, 4 July 2006 <www.bbc.co.uk/hi/uk_politics>.
15. Lord Falconer of Thoroton, 'The Role of Judges in a Modern Democracy', Magna Carta Lecture, Sydney, Australia, 13 September 2006 <www.dca.gov.uk/speches/2006/sp060913.htm>.
16. David Cameron, speech to the Centre for Policy Studies, 26 June 2006.
17. *Guardian*, 26 June 2006.
18. Department for Constitutional Affairs, *Review of the Implementation of the Human Rights Act* (London: Department for Constitutional Affairs, 2006) <www.dca.gov.uk/peoples-rights/human-rights/pdf/full_review.pdf>.
19. Commission on the Powers and Electoral Arrangements of the National Assembly for Wales, *Report of the Richard Commission* (Cardiff: National Assembly for Wales, 2004).

20. The Scottish Parliament (Candidates) Bill introduced by Lord Foulkes of Cumnock. The bill had its second reading on 3 March. HL Debs, 679, 3 March 2006, cc. 487–505.
21. For a more detailed discussion see Chapter 12, this volume.
22. St Andrews Agreement <www.nio.gov.uk/st_andrews_agreement.pdf>.
23. St Andrews Agreement, Annex D.
24. *The Times*, 25 November 2006.
25. Speaking to Andrew Marr on BBC TV, 26 November 2006.
26. The Commission to Strengthen Parliament, *Strengthening Parliament* (London: Conservative Party, 2000).
27. M. Rifkind, 'The East Lothian answer', *Prospect*, 125 (August 2006).
28. *Sunday Times*, 17 September 2006.
29. *Sunday Telegraph*, 26 November 2006.
30. <www.ipsos-mori.com/polls/2006/ecc.shtml>.
31. *Sunday Telegraph*, 26 November 2006.
32. PASC, *Sixth Report – The Ombudsman in Question: The Ombudsman's Report on Pensions and its Constitutional Implications*, HC 1081, 2005–06, p. 3.
33. R. Kirkham, 'Challenging the Authority of the Ombudsman: The Parliamentary Ombudsman's Special Report on Wartime Detainees', *Modern Law Review*, 69 (2006), 818.
34. *Daily Mail*, 10 and 12 October 2006.
35. BBC News, 13 October 2006 <www.bbc.co.uk/hi/uk_politics>.
36. *Britain Forward Not Back*, Labour Party Manifesto 2005 (London: Labour Party, 2005), p. 110.
37. *Daily Telegraph*, 1 April 2006.
38. See, for example, the editorial in the *Sunday Times*, 2 April 2006.
39. Joint Committee on Conventions, *Conventions of the UK Parliament*, HL Paper 265-I, HC 1212-I, 2005–06, para. 281.
40. *Sunday Times*, 22 October 2006. The document is reproduced at <www.www.times-archive.co.uk/onlinespecials/lordsreform.pdf>.
41. BBC News Online, 25 October 2006 <http://news.bbc.co.uk/go/pr/fr/-/hi/ik_politics/6085746.stm>.
42. HL Debs, 687, 15 November 2006, c. 3.
43. PASC, *Fourth Report – Taming the Prerogative: Strengthening Ministerial Accountability to Parliament*, HC 422, 2003–04, para. 12.
44. Select Committee on the Constitution, *Fifteenth Report – Waging War: Parliament's Role and Responsibility*, Vol. 1: Report, HL Paper 236-I, 2005–06.
45. *Built to Last: The Aims and Values of the Conservative Party* (London: Conservative Party, 2006), p. 9.
46. See especially P. Riddell, *The Times*, 26 September 2006.
47. Lord Bassam of Brighton to Lord Holme of Cheltenham, 3 July 2006. The exchange of correspondence is published on the Constitution Committee website at <www.parliament.uk/parliamentary_committees/lords_constitution_committee/cwm.cfm>.
48. HL Debs, 679, 3 March 2006, c. 444.
49. Ibid., c. 464.
50. Ibid., c. 479.
51. PASC, *Fourth Report – Propriety and Honours: Interim Report*, HC 1119, 2005–06.
52. PASC, *Seventh Report – The Ministerial Code: The Case for Independent Investigation*, HC 1457, 2005–06.

53. *The Times*, 6 September 2006.
54. Merits of Statutory Instruments Committee, *Twenty-ninth Report – The Management of Secondary Legislation*, HL Paper 149-I, 2005–06.
55. Select Committee on Modernisation of the House of Commons, *First Report: The Legislative Process*, HC 1097, 2005–06.
56. Law Commission, *Post-Legislative Scrutiny* (Law Com No. 302), Cm 6495 (London: The Stationery Office, 2006).
57. HC Debs, 451, 1 November 2006, c. 404.
58. *Built to Last: The Aims and Values of the Conservative Party* (London: Conservative Party, 2006), p. 9.
59. See P. Norton, 'The Unsettled British Constitution', *Politics Review*, 16 (2006), 6–9.
60. P. Dunleavy, 'The Westminster Model and the Distinctiveness of British Politics', in P. Dunleavy, R. Heffernan, P. Cowley and C. Hay (eds), *Developments in British Politics 8* (Basingstoke: Palgrave Macmillan, 2006), pp. 315–41.
61. *R (on the application of Jackson)* v. *Attorney General* [2005] UKHL 56, para.102.

3
Elections and Public Opinion: A Modest Conservative Resurgence

Michael Cole and Tim Jones

It is conceivable that political historians of early twenty-first-century British politics might focus on 2006 as the year in which a 'traditional' pattern of Labour–Conservative competition started to re-emerge. The year might herald the return of the phenomenon of the mid-term slump in support for the government that has been absent from British electoral politics for almost a decade. The Conservatives established a notable and persistent lead in the opinion polls and strengthened their position in local government, while Labour did badly in by-elections and suffered significant erosion in its councillor base. However, in comparison with the progress made by oppositions that defeated the government at the subsequent general election, David Cameron's advance is modest and in private many Conservatives remain sceptical about their chances of winning a majority at the next general election.

For Labour politicians, the most immediate struggle for power concerned the timing of the Prime Minister's departure and the succession. The controversy erupted in September in what some commentators interpreted as a Brownite plot intended, at a minimum, to destabilise the Blair premiership. This process led to a flurry of speculation about a Blairite challenger to Brown, a debate fuelled by concern that Brown lacked sufficient charisma, dislike of the Chancellor amongst many key colleagues, and concern about whether he would be able to 'connect' with the electorate. However, by the end of 2006 most of the potential Cabinet-level rivals had ruled themselves out of the race, although Home Secretary John Reid remained a possible candidate.

Before analysing the year's elections, we focus on trends identified in the opinion polls, primarily the fluctuations in support for the main political parties. This analysis is supplemented by an evaluation of changes in approval and disapproval ratings for Tony Blair, David Cameron and Sir Menzies Campbell. The focus on the Prime Minister's popularity was timely, given the debate about Blair's departure from Downing Street; while analysis of public perceptions of Cameron's performance as Leader of the Opposition should be placed in the context of his PR offensive to soften the image of the Conservatives and establish a parliamentary party that better reflects the gender and ethnic composition of the country. We also consider support for the parties in Scotland ahead of the 2007 Scottish Parliament elections and data on the popularity of potential contenders for the Labour leadership.

Coverage of the year's local elections is split into sections on the May council elections, the four mayoral contests and the referendum, and local authority by-elections, which occur throughout the year.[1] The three Westminster by-elections held in Blaenau Gwent, Bromley and Chislehurst, and Dunfermline and West Fife; the Scottish Parliamentary by-election in Moray, and the by-election for the Welsh Assembly seat at Blaenau Gwent are also discussed. The incumbent party retained four of the seats, although the Conservatives came close to defeat in south-east London. Labour lost Dunfermline and West Fife to the Liberal Democrats, a result that gave a boost to a party whose morale had been diminished through the trauma of Charles Kennedy's ousting as leader.

Opinion polls

In the first four months of 2006, opinion polls suggested that Labour and the Conservatives enjoyed almost equal levels of support among the electorate. An average of opinion polls in January, February and April identified a tie between the two main parties, while Labour had a 1 per cent lead in March. From May to October, however, the Conservatives established and consolidated a lead over Labour. As can be seen from Table 3.1, which shows the monthly average of polls throughout 2006, from May to October the Conservatives had a 4–8 per cent lead over Labour. This shift reflected primarily a decline in support for Labour, which achieved an average of 34 per cent or less from April onwards. Apart from March, April and November the Conservative average was within a 37–39 per cent range throughout the year. In the final two months of the year the gap between the Conservatives and Labour narrowed to 3 per cent. Support for the Liberal Democrats also shifted little during the year: averaging between 17 per cent and 20 per cent every month. Even the negative publicity following Charles Kennedy's deposition as leader and the personal revelations involving Mark Oaten and Simon Hughes had little impact on the poll ratings. The 2006 polls contrasted substantially with those from a similar stage in the last Parliament. In 2002, Labour led in every month, although the Liberal Democrats' 2002 average of 20 per cent was close to their 19 per cent score in 2006.[2]

Public opinion about the main political parties was also reflected in and influenced by attitudes towards the party leaders. As can be seen from Table 3.2, which records approval and disapproval levels[3] for the three main party leaders, Tony Blair had a negative net rating throughout the year, which ranged from 8 per cent to 44 per cent and averaged 31 per cent. In contrast, David Cameron had a net rating that ranged from –6 per cent in November to +33 per cent in March. Overall, Cameron averaged a net +10 per cent score, although his average approval rating was only 5 per cent above that recorded by the Prime Minister. Furthermore, Cameron's highest scores occurred in the early months of the year; from May onwards his net rating averaged +3 per cent. Ironically, Cameron's approval ratings declined as the Conservative position in relation to Labour strengthened. Sir Menzies Campbell had a net rating high of +18 per cent in March, a low of –14 per cent in September and an overall net rating of –2 per cent. Campbell's best scores were also concentrated in the early part of 2006: from 30 May onwards he averaged a rating of –8 per cent. These results contrasted markedly with the position at a similar stage during the 2001–05 Parliament. For example, in January 2002, Tony Blair had a net satisfaction rating of +12 per cent, while the then Conservative leader, Iain Duncan Smith, had a rating of –8 per cent and Charles Kennedy a score of +37 per cent.[4]

Table 3.1   Monthly average of opinion polls, 2006

Month	Con. %	Lab. %	Lib. Dem. %
January	38	38	17
February	37	37	18
March	36	37	19
April	34	34	20
May	38	32	19
June	38	33	19
July	38	33	17
August	39	31	20
September	37	33	18
October	38	33	18
November	36	33	19
December	37	34	17

Dissatisfaction with the Prime Minister and Labour's modest British opinion poll ratings have been matched by mediocre percentages when Scottish voters where asked about voting intentions in relation to the 2007 elections to the Scottish Parliament (see Table 3.3). Eleven opinion polls about support for the parties in the regional list elections for Holyrood taken from July onwards gave Labour an average of 28 per cent compared with 30 per cent for the Scottish National Party (SNP). These figures raised the possibility that the SNP might become the largest party in the Scottish Parliament in 2007, and the spectre of the Scottish government making serious moves towards separatism.

Table 3.2 Approval and disapproval ratings for the main party leaders, 2006

Polls	Survey end date	Tony Blair % App.	Dis.	David Cameron % App.	Dis.	Menzies Campbell % App.	Dis.
MORI/*Financial Times*	23 January	36	57	31	17	–	–
YouGov/*Telegraph*	26 January	33	57	39	17	–	–
MORI/*Sun*	20 February	–	–	31	16	–	–
YouGov/*Telegraph*	22 February	–	–	46	19	–	–
ICM/*Guardian*	12 March	37	45	37	16	31	13
YouGov/*Sunday Times*	17 March	36	61	55	22	29	24
MORI	21 March	31	62	32	19	22	17
YouGov/*Telegraph*	29 March	30	60	38	24	26	24
YouGov/*Sunday Times*	28 April	–	–	51	31	31	32
YouGov/*Sunday Times*	29 April	33	64	–	–	–	–
MORI/*Financial Times*	2 May	29	64	29	27	26	20
MORI/*Sun*	30 May	26	67	33	27	22	31
MORI	26 June	32	60	32	28	22	28
MORI/*Financial Times*	24 July	23	67	29	31	22	28
YouGov/*Telegraph*	26 July	27	63	35	33	–	–
MORI/*Sunday Times*	6 September	26	66	30	28	22	28
ORB	14 September	34	58	–	–	–	–
YouGov/*Sunday Times*	22 September	31	65	49	33	30	44
MORI/*Financial Times*	16 October	32	60	31	32	22	31
YouGov/*Telegraph*	26 October	–	–	42	28	–	–
MORI/*Observer*	14 November	27	65	25	31	23	26
YouGov/*Daily Telegraph*	30 November	–	–	39	30	–	–
MORI	12 December	30	64	28	33	22	31

Table 3.3 Holyrood voting intentions – regional vote, 2006

Polls	Survey end date	Con. %	Lab. %	Lib. Dem. %	SNP %
TNS System Three	4 July	9	29	17	33
TNS System Three	1 August	10	29	15	32
TNS System Three	29 August	11	28	19	27
YouGov/*Sunday Times*	8 September	14	27	15	29
Progressive Partnership/*Sunday Mail*	20 October	11	25	26	28
ICM/*Scotsman*	30 October	14	28	17	28
TNS System Three	31 October	9	30	17	33
YouGov/*Telegraph*	17 November	17	29	15	28
YouGov/SNP	20 November	15	26	15	30
ICM/*Scotsman*	23 November	12	26	19	31
TNS/*Sunday Herald*	30 November	11	32	15	30

Opinion polling also strengthened Gordon Brown's position as the strong favourite to succeed Tony Blair as Prime Minister. A series of polls taken in September, for example, showed that Brown was the clear favourite of the electorate, although there was also notable support for John Reid (see Table 3.4).

Table 3.4   Preferred leader of the Labour Party – all voters, 2006

Polls	Survey end date	Gordon Brown	Alan Johnson	John Reid	Jack Straw	David Miliband	John McDonnell
YouGov/*Telegraph*	7 September	31	4	14	–	3	2
Populus/*Times*	10 September	30	–	11	11	–	–
YouGov/*Sun*	14 September	28	7	15	–	4	2
ICM/*Sunday Mirror*	14 September	33	5	7	–	2	–
YouGov/*Sunday Times*	22 September	23	3	10	5	1	–
ICM/*Sunday Mirror*	30 September	35	2	14	–	2	–

Local elections

Local council elections were held in 176 English authorities on 4 May 2006. Whole council elections took place in 32 London boroughs, while in 36 metropolitan boroughs, 20 unitary councils and 88 shire district councils there were elections for approximately one-third of the seats. In total, 4,414 seats in 3,123 wards were contested (see Table 3.5). More than 15,000 candidates stood, an average of 3.5 candidates per seat, and only 19 seats, mostly in the shire districts, went uncontested. Almost a third of the candidates were women, 1,371 of whom were elected.

Table 3.5   Summary of local election results, 2006

Party	Votes	%	Seats	%
Conservative	2,731,229	34.6	1,820	41.2
Labour	2,215,619	28.0	1,441	32.6
Liberal Democrat	1,854,838	23.5	912	20.7
Green	364,496	4.6	29	0.7
Independent	190,518	2.4	65	1.5
Other	544,799	6.9	147	3.3
Total	7,901,499	100.0	4,414	100.0

The Conservatives made net gains of 320 seats and 11 councils, the tenth consecutive set of elections where they have made net gains, and reinforced their position as the largest party in local government in England. In contrast, Labour's support continued to dissipate with net losses of 350 seats and 17 councils. In England, the Conservatives now control 168 councils and have over 8,200 councillors compared with Labour's 5,200 councillors and

54 councils. The Liberal Democrats have 32 councils and 4,400 councillors, while the remaining 127 councils are in no overall control.

Conservative forward momentum was most noticeable in London, where the party made a net gain of 130 seats and six councils, winning control of four councils from Labour (Bexley, Croydon, Ealing and Hammersmith & Fulham) and three that were previously in no overall control (Harrow, Havering and Hillingdon). Labour's electoral strength in London declined, with net losses of 177 councillors and loss of control in nine councils, including five (Brent, Camden, Hounslow, Lewisham and Merton), which went to no overall control. For the first time since 1982, Labour has fewer council seats in London than the Conservatives. The sole glimmer of good news for Labour was gaining control in Lambeth. The Liberal Democrats increased their share of the vote in London to a record 17 per cent, although this was a modest advance on the levels recorded in 1994 and 2002. In terms of councils, the Liberal Democrats gained Richmond upon Thames from the Conservatives but lost Islington to no overall control. In both Kingston and Sutton, the ruling Liberal Democrats saw their majorities reduced significantly, while expected advances in Haringey and Southwark failed to materialise.

Outside London, the Conservatives gained control of eight councils including Bassetlaw, Hastings, Mole Valley and Winchester. Coventry became the fifth Conservative-controlled metropolitan borough, four of which are in the West Midlands. The Conservatives lost Gosport, Harrogate and West Lindsey to no overall control. Progress was made in the more affluent areas of some northern towns like Bolton and Wakefield, but there are still no Conservative councillors in Liverpool, Manchester or Newcastle-upon-Tyne, where the party's vote fell by five percentage points. There are also no Conservative councillors in either of the university cities of Oxford and Cambridge. Labour lost Crawley to the Conservatives and eight authorities, including Derby, Plymouth, Stoke-on-Trent and Warrington, to no overall control. The May poll had little impact on the number of councils controlled by the Liberal Democrats. The party gained South Lakeland and St Albans from no overall control but lost Milton Keynes to no overall control.

Almost 8 million votes were cast, with more than one in three going to the Conservatives, whose candidates contested the most seats. Labour was over half a million votes behind, despite the fact that these elections were concentrated in their urban heartlands. The combined vote share for the three major parties was 86 per cent, illustrating the extent to which, in local elections, voters are prepared to support the smaller parties and Independent candidates. The Greens fielded 1,290 candidates and fought one in three wards.[5] They gained five seats on Lewisham council and four in Norwich, bringing their total to nine – the largest Green group in England and Wales. There were also Green gains in several other authorities, including Islington, Sheffield and Southwark. Respect mounted its strongest campaign in Tower Hamlets, where the party leader, George Galloway, holds his parliamentary seat. After winning 11 seats the party is now the main opposition to Labour. In Birmingham's Sparkbrook ward the Respect candidate won with almost 50 per cent of the vote.

The BNP fielded over 350 candidates, won 32 seats and now has approximately 50 councillors. Before the election, the situation in Barking & Dagenham attracted considerable attention, following the comments of the local MP and minister, Margaret Hodge. She speculated that a significant proportion of voters in her constituency were tempted to vote for the BNP because Labour was not listening to their concerns. In the event, the BNP won 12 out of the 13 seats they contested, becoming the second largest party.

Concerns about malpractice in local elections were heightened by the conviction and jailing for 18 months of two Liberal Democrat councillors from Burnley. Manzur Hussain and Mozaquir Ali defrauded dozens of voters in the 2004 local elections. Signed blank forms were collected through door-to-door canvassing and subsequently completed to suggest that those people would be on holiday and unable to vote in person. The two men then used the resulting proxy-voting forms to cast ballots for the Liberal Democrats on behalf of voters who were unaware of their activities. The improbable number of proxies, especially given the deprived nature of the ward and the fact that the election was all-postal, attracted the suspicion of the returning officer, who initiated a police investigation.

Mayoral elections and referendum

Currently, there are 13 directly elected mayors in England,[6] and elections for four of them were held in May 2006. There were contests in the London boroughs of Hackney, Lewisham and Newham, and the shire district of Watford (see Table 3.6). In each case, the incumbent was re-elected. The three major political parties fought each election. However, in the London boroughs a notable percentage of first-preference votes went to candidates from the smaller parties: 25.4 per cent in Hackney, 22.8 per cent in Lewisham and 32.5 per cent in Newham. In Newham, Respect took second place, winning 21.6 per cent of first-preference votes and 31.8 per cent at the second stage. Three of the contests went to a second, 'run-off', count involving the top two candidates, while in Watford, Dorothy Thornhill won on the first round of counting.

One mayoral referendum was held in 2006. On 4 May, the electors of Crewe and Nantwich voted 61.4 per cent to 38.6 per cent to reject a directly elected mayor. The loss of a majority of mayoral referendums and the small number held in the last few years[7] led the government to propose, in the local government White Paper,[8] to remove the requirement to stage a referendum if local authorities wanted to convert to the directly elected mayor model.

Table 3.6   Mayoral election results, 2006

Council	Candidate	Party	Council	Winner's 1st vote (%)	Winner's 2nd Vote (%)
Hackney	Jules Pipe	Lab.	Lab. (held)	46.9	73.4
Lewisham	Steve Bullock	Lab.	NOC[a] (from Lab.)	37.7	57.1
Newham	Sir Robin Wales	Lab.	Lab. (held)	47.9	68.2
Watford	Dorothy Thornhill	Lib. Dem.	Lib. Dem. (held)	51.2	–

[a] NOC = no overall control.

Local by-elections

During 2006, there were 284 local authority by-elections. Overall, the outcomes support the theme that the year witnessed a modest resurgence in the support for the Conservatives (see Table 3.7). The party made a net gain of 18 seats compared with a net loss of nine councillors by Labour. The Liberal Democrats also made modest advances with a net gain of 17 seats. In total, the Conservatives defended 120 seats at local government by-elections, losing one in six. Labour defended 64 seats and lost almost a third of them, while the Liberal Democrats lost a slightly higher percentage of the seats they held at the start of the year. The Independents were again the largest losers, with a net loss of 28 councillors. Almost 85 per cent of the seats previously held by Independents were won by party politicians.

Table 3.7   Local by-election results, 2006

Party	Gains	Held	Lost	Net
Conservative	38	100	20	+18
Labour	12	43	21	–9
Liberal Democrat	35	31	18	+17
Independent	5	6	33	–28
Scottish National Party	4	1	1	+3
Plaid Cymru	1	2	1	0
Mebyon Kernow	0	0	1	–1
British National Party	0	0	1	–1
Green	1	0	0	+1
Other	2	3	2	0
Total	98	186	98	

The Scottish National Party's encouraging opinion poll ratings were matched in local by-elections, which saw the party make a net gain of three seats and win five of the 11 seats contested in Scotland during the year. The other parties made little impact, Plaid Cymru emerged with an unchanged number of councillors, while the British National Party (BNP) lost a seat in

Bradford, Mebyon Kernow lost a councillor in Bude (North Cornwall) and the Greens made a gain in Scarborough. Six seats were won by unopposed candidates. In Market & West Deeping ward (South Kesteven) the Labour Party failed to contest one of their seats and thus handed the Conservatives a gain without holding a ballot.

Parliamentary by-elections

The first by-election of the year was held in Dunfermline and West Fife on 9 February, following the death of the Labour MP, Rachel Squire, after a long illness. At the 2005 general election, she had a majority of 11,562 votes and 27.3 per cent over the Liberal Democrats. However, in the by-election the Liberal Democrats overturned Labour's lead and secured a majority of 1,800 votes over the Labour candidate, Catherine Stihler. The result sent Willie Rennie, a former chief executive of the Scottish Liberal Democrats, to the House of Commons as the 63rd Liberal Democrat MP. The outcome was spun as a personal setback for the neighbouring Labour MP, Gordon Brown, and a triumph for Sir Menzies Campbell, an MP from a local constituency in Fife, who was trying to maintain his position as favourite for the then vacant leadership of his party. A by-election to the Scottish Parliament was staged in Moray on 27 April, after the death of the veteran SNP MSP, Margaret Ewing, whose parliamentary career began over 30 years ago. The Scottish Nationalist candidate, Richard Lochhead, held the seat, increasing the SNP majority; the Conservatives retained second place, while Labour slumped to fourth behind the Liberal Democrats.

The other by-elections were held on 29 June. Two of them occurred in Blaenau Gwent, a constituency steeped in Labour history, which incorporated areas represented in Parliament by Aneurin Bevan and Michael Foot. The contests resulted from the death of Peter Law, an Independent Member of the Welsh Assembly and House of Commons, who won his Westminster seat in 2005 following a split in the local Labour Party about the imposition of a Blair-friendly candidate chosen from an all-woman shortlist. The 2006 election led to Independent heirs to Law retaining both seats. Dai Davies, who had served as his election agent in 2005, won the Westminster constituency, although the Labour Party reduced the Independent majority, from 9,121 (25.9 per cent) to 2,484 (9.1 per cent). In the contest for the Welsh Assembly seat, Trish Law, widow of the late MP and Assembly Member (AM), obtained an Independent majority of 4,464 (16.3 per cent) over the Labour candidate. Her triumph meant that Labour failed to regain the majority in the assembly, which had been lost following Law's defection last year.

The other by-election on 29 June resulted from the death of Eric Forth, the Conservative MP for Bromley and Chislehurst. The Conservatives circumvented the pressure to choose an A-list candidate by selecting Bob Neil, who represented the area in the London Assembly. The Conservatives ran a traditional campaign with few obvious echoes of Cameron's reformist agenda. It was suggested that such an approach suited local conditions and reflected the legacy of Eric Forth, a combative and traditionalist Tory. This strategy failed, however, to yield electoral dividends. The Conservative majority was slashed from 13,342 (28.9 per cent) to 633 (2.2 per cent); the Liberal Democrats replaced Labour as the main challenger, while the government's representative finished fourth behind Nigel Farage of the UK Independence Party (UKIP). The contest ended in controversy, with the victor launching a public attack on the conduct of the Liberal Democrat campaign.

Conclusion

The events of 2006 gave the Conservatives some cause for optimism. A persistent lead over Labour in the opinion polls, positive ratings for David Cameron, negative ratings for Tony Blair and the gains made in the local elections were encouraging for the Conservatives. However, Cameron's disapproval levels have started to climb, while the party's performances in parliamentary by-elections have been weak. In particular, at Bromley and Chislehurst the Conservatives almost lost their 18th safest seat. Even the party's local election results were less impressive when placed in the context of the performance of Conservative oppositions against Labour governments in the 1960s and 1970s. The contrast is at its most apparent in the large cities. For example, in 1968 the Conservatives took control of Sheffield; in 2006 the party had two councillors. Similarly, in 1978 the party had 33 councillors on Newcastle-upon-Tyne city council, compared with none after the 2006 elections.

At the end of 2006, assessments about prospects for the political parties are more difficult than normal because the impact of the expected transition from Blair to Brown is difficult to estimate. Blair's departure might diminish the negative electoral legacy of the Iraq war, which could be presented as the project of the former Prime Minister. However, Brown's ability to 'connect' with the electorate remains unproven, although he can take some comfort from the polls on the Labour Party leadership. Similarly, the impact of a Brown premiership on public perceptions of David Cameron is difficult to estimate. Next to Brown, Cameron might appear voter-friendly and dynamic; alternatively, a case can be made that the contrast will make him seem inexperienced and shallow. Calculations about the medium- to long-term impact of David Cameron are particularly hard to guess given the incomplete state of his modernisation agenda. A Conservative Party with personnel better reflecting the ethnic and social composition of Britain and with policies attuned to swing voters might make substantial gains at the general election, but such changes could alienate traditional Conservatives and provoke them to abstain or shift to parties such as UKIP. It is also possible that the party leadership could match the actions of William Hague and Michael Howard and move to the right as the general election nears in order to persuade core

Conservatives to vote. At December 2006, perhaps the only safe prediction is that British politics is entering a fluid period in which the voting patterns and political assumptions of the last decade are under threat.

Notes

1. We are indebted to Colin Rallings and Michael Thrasher for permission to use analysis in relation to the following sections – local elections, mayoral elections and local by-elections. Much of this information is also available in C. Rallings and M. Thrasher, *Local Elections Handbook 2006* (Plymouth: LGC Elections Centre, 2006).
2. C. Rallings and M. Thrasher, 'Elections and Public Opinion: Conservative Doldrums and Continuing Apathy', *Parliamentary Affairs*, 56 (2003), 271.
3. The polls asked slightly different questions: the ICM and MORI questions related to 'satisfied' and 'dissatisfied'; YouGov used the terms 'well', 'badly' and 'good'; ORB used 'approve' and 'disapprove'. We have used 'approval' and 'disapproval' because those terms were used in UK Polling report summaries: see <www.pollingreport.co.uk>.
4. Rallings and Thrasher, 'Elections and Public Opinion: Conservative Doldrums and Continuing Apathy', 272.
5. The Greens fought 29 per cent of the seats.
6. See C. Copus, *Leading the Localities* (Manchester: Manchester University Press, 2006).
7. Since December 2002 there have been five mayoral referendums in Ceredigion, Isle of Wight, Fenland, Torbay, and Crewe and Nantwich.
8. Department for Communities and Local Government, *Strong and Prosperous Communities*, Cm. 6939-I-II (London: The Stationery Office, 2006).

4
Parties and the Party System: On the Edge of Bankruptcy?

Andrew Russell

Last year's Review suggested two contradictory shifts in the British party system. On the one hand, there is real evidence that the grip of the main political parties is loosening dramatically. However measured, the number of effective parties has risen and independents and minor party candidates appear to have an increased chance of electoral breakthrough and sustained success. On the other hand, the major parties still find it relatively easy to appropriate mainstream issues that might otherwise provide a significant challenge to the party system.[1] However, it is possible that 2006 was the year in which permanent change began to take hold.

Party finance

The perilous state of party finance in Britain was a major theme in 2006. It became apparent that the parties had exploited a loophole in the legislation on the declaration of donations, encouraging potential donors to remain anonymous by making loans rather than donations. Furthermore, it is also clear that Labour were struggling to repay some loans and were attempting to renegotiate their terms. In March, the relationship between donors and political patronage came under scrutiny. It emerged that four Labour supporters who had made undeclared loans to Labour were nominated for peerages, only to have their nominations blocked by the Appointments Commission. A criminal investigation began, resulting in the arrest of Lord Levy, Tony Blair's fundraiser, and Des Smith, a headmaster who had raised funds for specialist schools. In addition, several Cabinet ministers were interviewed by the police, as was the former Leader of the Opposition, Michael Howard, along with a number of Number 10 aides. In December, Blair became the first serving Prime Minister to be questioned by police in a criminal investigation. Whatever the outcome, the matter is unlikely to have a quick resolution in

2007. Indeed, it could haunt the next Labour administration as much as it has the Blair government.

Details of party spending during the 2005 election were published during the year, amounting to £17.9 million by Labour, £17.8 million by the Conservatives, and £4.3 million by the Liberal Democrats. Although these totals were capped under the Political Parties, Elections and Referendums Act 2000, it left all three parties in financial difficulty. Towards the end of the year, the Electoral Commission revealed the extent of debt of the main political parties: Labour owed £23.4 million, the Conservatives £35.3 million and the Liberal Democrats £1.1 million in loans.[2]

Faced with these problems, the government announced a review of party funding headed by Sir Hayden Phillips, former Permanent Secretary of the Lord Chancellor's Department. All the parties agreed that more substantial public funding of parties was the solution, though it was often couched in terms of 'having to pay for democracy'.

The publication of the Phillips Review was deferred until January 2007.[3] It was widely anticipated that the review would have far-reaching consequences for the financing of politics. It was reported that it would recommend a £50,000 cap on donations from both individuals and organisations and the registration, as donors, of everyone paying an annual levy to a party through a trade union. This would fundamentally change the organic relationship between the unions and the Labour Party. It was also reported that there would be limits on spending between as well as during election campaigns (including those in marginal seats) in return for public funding related to electoral performance.

These changes have serious implications for political life in Britain. It is unlikely that Labour would accept a system that undermined its main financial base and would press for different caps on group and individual donations. The Conservatives have also benefited from large donations but appear more comfortable with the proposed £50,000 cap. Limits on spending during and between elections and in individual seats would dramatically transform the conduct of electioneering, which has increasingly concentrated on targeting key voters in marginal seats.

The parties need to react intelligently to the Phillips Review to justify a greater influx of public money. Matters could move swiftly: the Conservatives have long opposed extensive state funding, but by the spring of 2006 the party had come out in favour of public subsidies as a means of regulating financial affairs. The government will also find it difficult to do nothing.

Challenges to the party system

Two of the three major parties began 2006 with new leaders, while Labour faced the prospect of a new leader in 2007, but these were not the only challenges the parties faced.

The Power Inquiry, the Rowntree Trust-funded project into the state of British democracy, strongly criticised the role of the political parties, especially the straitjacket imposed by party discipline.[4] Despite noting the 'good practice' of many MPs of informing constituents about their parliamentary activities, it decries the lack of 'formal, resourced and high profile methods by which all MPs can listen and respond to the concerns of their constituents between elections' ... [to] ... 'help to counter the undue influence of the whips which is a major source of alienation from the public'.[5] Yet the report largely ignored the ample evidence that access to decision-makers is more open than ever and, in particular, that 'stringent whipping' did not prevent the 2001 Parliament being the most rebellious ever (a record the 2005 Parliament is likely to surpass).[6]

Clare Short's resignation of the Labour Whip in October is instructive here. She claimed that

> Our political system is in trouble and the exaggerated majorities in the House of Commons have led to an abject Parliament and a concentration of power in Number 10 that has produced arrogant, error-prone government. Given that the next election might well produce a hung parliament, I want to be free to argue that this creates a valuable opportunity to reform our voting system so that the House of Commons more accurately reflects public opinion, and we have a Parliament more able to hold the government to account and to ensure that policy is well considered.[7]

Short's resignation showed the power of the protestor against the party machine. She had earlier been reprimanded by the Chief Whip rather than having the whip withdrawn, which had seemed likely, given her declaration that she would campaign for a hung Parliament rather than a Labour victory at the next election. The 'undue influence of the whips' also failed to prevent the signing of an open letter by MPs from the 2001 intake and a junior minister calling for the Prime Minister's resignation; nor were they able to prevent the Home Secretary, the Labour Party chairman and other ministers from joining local campaigns against hospital closures in their constituencies, despite having voted for the government's NHS reforms, not least because one of them was the Chief Whip, Jacqui Smith. The hollowing out of British political parties has continued. The Conservative leadership election of November 2005 suggested a party membership of just under 260,000;[8] the Liberal Democrat leadership election revealed a membership of 72,000; and Labour's membership in 2006 was said to be 198,000. According to Jon Cruddas, one of the candidates for the deputy leadership, Blair had turned Labour into 'a virtual party' operating through the media rather than the grassroots.[9]

Local elections

Labour's standing in the polls, the problems it was experiencing with the NHS and at the Home Office, and lurid tabloid headlines about John Prescott's private life, minimised expectations with regard to the May local elections. Indeed, the elections were fairly disastrous for Labour, with a net loss of 350 seats and 17 councils.

The Conservatives fared much better, winning an extra 320 councillors and gaining control of 11 authorities. Nevertheless, the party had gone into the elections hoping to make a comeback in northern cities, such as Manchester and Liverpool, and their failure to make an impact suggests that the Cameron revolution is far from complete. Moreover, the Conservative victory was rather stifled. Given the anti-Conservative bias in the electoral system (much of which is likely to survive the next redistribution exercise and the results of differential turnout), obtaining a 40 per cent share on a 36 per cent turnout is sufficient to produce an overall Conservative majority at the next general election.

The Liberal Democrats made only modest gains, electing only a handful of new councillors and control of one new council. As a first test of Menzies Campbell's leadership, it was disappointing given the party's success in local elections in recent years. The fear for the Liberal Democrats is that the electoral strategy that allowed them to make gains from both the Conservatives and Labour may have run its course.[10] Manchester was an interesting test for the Liberal Democrats in 2006. The party was hopeful of building on local election success since 2000 and its spectacular capture of the Manchester Withington seat from Labour at the 2005 general election instilled even greater confidence. Some commentators speculated that the Liberal Democrats could even take control of the city's council.[11] In the event, Labour's dominance in the city was reasserted and the seemingly inevitable Liberal Democrats advance was not only halted but reversed.

Labour: lame ducks and legacies

Historians are likely to remember 2006 as the beginning of the end of the Blair regime. Having already announced his decision to resign before the next election, the Prime Minister came under immense pressure to name a date. His reluctance to do so was apparently fuelled by his perception that it would increase the pressure on him to resign forthwith, doubtless increased by the Conservatives' standing in the polls and his own ratings. Blair's desire to leave a lasting legacy almost certainly strengthened his resolve, but he came under much pressure. David Cameron mocked him: 'The Prime Minister made a great mistake pre-announcing that he was going to go because his authority started to drain away from that moment.' This sentiment was echoed by Labour MPs like Mark Fisher: 'I think we have paralysis now. The speculation of not knowing when the Prime Minister is going to go is even more damaging.'[12]

On 5 September, an open letter urging Blair to set out a timetable was signed by 17 MPs from the 2001 Labour intake, including one minister and seven Parliamentary Private Secretaries. All resigned. In his letter of resignation, Tom Watson, Parliamentary Under-Secretary at the Ministry of Defence, said:

> Your leadership has been visionary and remarkable. The party and the nation owes you an incalculable debt. So it is with the greatest sadness that I have to say that I no longer believe that your remaining in office is in the interest of either the party or the country.[13]

This was a remarkable blow to Blair and his plan for a 'stable and orderly transition'. However, by the time of the party conference he had managed to regain some ground with a well-received speech, described by *The Times* as a 'masterclass for Brown ... a passionate and perfectly delivered speech which provided a stark contrast with Mr Brown's more pedestrian effort'. Blair sought to make a virtue of both innovative and traditional themes in government policy and ended with an appeal for party unity. However, he refused to name a favoured successor, though a few weeks later in the Commons, he spoke of looking forward to seeing Cameron dealt with by one of Labour's political heavyweights with 'his big clunking fist', taken as a reference to Gordon Brown. Some polls show Brown with a clear lead over Cameron; others the reverse: 2007 will see the reality.

Aside from the rivalry at the top of the Labour Party, the government was also beset by personnel crises in 2006. April proved to be particularly troublesome. Health Secretary Patricia Hewitt misjudged the mood of health workers in declaring that 2006 was the 'best year ever for the NHS' and became an early target, but she was soon overshadowed by John Prescott and Charles Clarke.

The Office of the Deputy Prime Minister, with its cumbersome portfolio scope, has long been seen as a problem, but the difficulties of the Deputy Prime Minister in 2006 were largely self-inflicted. He was personally embarrassed by the publication of revelations about his private life, especially as they involved a member of his staff, and open season was soon declared on Prescott. His visit to the Colorado ranch of entrepreneur Philip Anschutz raised questions about his involvement in the bidding for Britain's new super-casino site, and photographs of him playing croquet at his official country residence led to media calls for his resignation. Immediately after the local elections, the Prime Minister reshuffled his Cabinet to draw some of the sting from criticism of the party's electoral performance. To the surprise of many, John Prescott remained as Deputy Prime Minister, but with much-reduced responsibilities. Although Prescott survived, Charles Clarke did not. The Home Office had been beset with immigration problems for a long time (in 2004, Beverley

Hughes had lost her post as Immigration Minister for misleading the House of Commons), but the admission that over 1,000 foreign prisoners (including sex offenders and murderers) had been released rather than deported was the final straw. Clarke was sacked and replaced by John Reid. The reshuffle may have drawn some attention away from the local elections, but it did not ease the pressure on the Prime Minister. The exit of Clarke, who refused a new portfolio, and the emasculation of the Office of the Deputy Prime Minister made the headlines, but there was the continuing subtext of the Prime Minister's future. Damagingly, some former ministers had harsh words for Blair. Frank Dobson claimed that the reshuffle demonstrated that the government was now rudderless and claimed that 'Quite frankly we need the party under new management.'[14]

Throughout the jockeying to succeed Blair, Gordon Brown was in pole position. Other potential candidates surfaced but Brown remained the favourite. Alan Johnson, elevated to Education Secretary in the May reshuffle, was tipped by some as the man most likely to defeat Brown for Labour's leadership,[15] but ended the year as a candidate for deputy leader only and confirmed his support for Brown. John Reid, one of Labour's most experienced ministers (having been in charge of six portfolios as well as party chairman) was also touted as a candidate, especially after becoming Home Secretary. Well-known for his abrasive approach, he was even more abrasive at the Home Office, famously declaring it 'not fit for purpose'. The airport-terror threat unearthed by British intelligence in the summer raised Reid's profile even higher when he led the government response to the new airport security measures in the absence of the Prime Minister, apparently in preference to the Deputy Prime Minister. At the party conference, Reid made a bullish speech about security, contrasting starkly with the Chancellor's, further fuelling speculation about his candidacy. However, towards the end of the year, more problems at the Home Office appeared to make a Reid candidacy less likely. Meanwhile, support for Brown came from several other possible candidates, despite periodic speculation that Brown would not inherit the crown and the damage done by some of his supporters in trying to force the issue in the autumn. At the end of 2006, there was only one declared leadership candidate – not Gordon Brown but the left-wing MP, John McDonnell.

If the 2007 leadership contest is destined to be a foregone conclusion, the contest for the deputy leadership looks likely to be hotly contested. At the end of 2006, five candidates had declared their intention to run for the post (Hilary Benn, Jon Cruddas, Peter Hain, Harriet Harman and Alan Johnson), while at least two others, Hazel Blears and Jack Straw, were considering running. Of these, only Cruddas is not a minister and, of the rest, only Harman not a member of the Cabinet, but the relationship between the leader and deputy, and the party machine and the membership might be redefined by the contest. The present incumbent, John Prescott, is Deputy Prime Minister, but this post is in the hands of the Prime Minister and there is no guarantee that Prescott's successor will hold that post. What role the deputy leader plays in both the government and the party will be of at least as much interest as who becomes deputy leader, which itself is a crucial factor.

The Conservatives: oak trees from little A-lists?

David Cameron's objective as Conservative Leader has been to transform the way the party is seen by the public. Local associations were encouraged to choose candidates for the next election from a centrally approved A-list. Unlike the long-standing approved list of Conservative candidates, the A-list included more women, more black and minority ethnic, and more openly gay candidates. It was not just a cosmetic exercise intended to improve the image of the party, but an attempt to make the parliamentary party more representative.

Labour's introduction of all-women shortlists when in opposition prior to 1997 was designed to make the Labour Party appear more modern and, of course, to address the gender imbalance in the Parliamentary Labour Party, but it also led to a public discourse about whether the election of a much higher proportion of women MPs would transform political life at Westminster. However, the controversy about the Conservative A-list centred less on the issues of representativeness and more on local party autonomy. There has been much hostility to the A-list, partly because it has been seen as an attempt to control the party from the centre but also because local autonomy in selection has been deeply embedded in Conservative politics. Conservative-Home, an influential website of Conservative members, published a version of the list and identified three problems with it. First, despite the publicity, there continued to be a shortage of women applicants for Conservative-held seats. Second, there was a notable reluctance among those on the A-list to apply for less safe seats, and, third, a marked tendency for local associations to select non A-list candidates.

Cameron also sought to play a significant role in setting the political agenda. In particular, he associated himself closely with environmental policy, and other areas such as the impact of the Human Rights Act. However, for the most part he and his frontbench colleagues refused to commit the party to detailed polices, especially over tax cuts. Instead, Cameron set up a series of commissions in broad policy areas, mostly headed by senior Conservative MPs. One consequence was that Cameron was increasingly accused of having no policies, only vague aspirations. His aim, however, was to shift his party to the crucial centre ground of politics. In February, he claimed that 'The right test for our policies is not how they help the rich, but how they help the least well-off in society.'[16] In November, a leading Cameronite MP, Greg Clark, urged the party to follow the poverty agenda set by *Guardian* columnist Polly Toynbee rather than that of Winston Churchill, and Cameron spoke of the need for a Conservative government to address the plight of the 'relatively disadvantaged'. In December, Cameron signalled a desire to move to 'territory that Labour should never have conceded: social mobility and the role of schools in enabling every child to reach their potential' and claimed that 'a fully-fledged Conservative intellectual revival is under way' as the Conservatives were now 'the party of social mobility'.[17] Under the guidance of his Director of Strategy, Steve Hilton, Cameron demonstrated good communication skills: meeting Nelson Mandela and the US rap star Rhymefest; calling for the understanding rather than condemnation of 'hoodies'; visiting Norway to draw attention to climate change; and setting up 'WebCameron'. Cameron has shown a willingness to reach out to the disengaged, a refreshing change from the 2005 general election, when the parties focused almost exclusively on target voters in marginal seats and core voters elsewhere. The imagery of the party was overhauled both literally and metaphorically. The party's emblem was changed from a muscular torch-bearing arm to a depiction of an oak tree. The design was not warmly received, however, seeming rather simplistic to many.

The Conservatives led the polls for much of 2006.[18] In the spring the party opened up a clear lead over Labour, although the lead narrowed significantly towards the end of the year. Doubtless pleased to have sustained a lead in the polls for the first time since 1992, Conservative support seldom surpassed the 40 per cent mark, the minimum the party would need to have a chance of winning the next election. Furthermore, there was little sign of opening up a decisive gap over the Liberal Democrats. The Conservatives need to recapture 15–20 seats won by the Liberal Democrats in 1997 and since, but are finding it difficult to make significant inroads in these areas. The evidence from the local elections in cities like Manchester and Liverpool is that, once established as the anti-Labour party, the Liberal Democrats are able to resist a Conservative revival. The Bromley and Chislehurst by-election showed that the Liberal Democrats can mount a fearsome challenge to the Conservatives where they are seen as a credible alternative.

Indeed, the by-election, in one of the Conservatives' safest seats, was a near disaster: they held the seat, but there were two sources of discomfort. First, despite Labour being pushed into fourth place, the UK Independence Party (UKIP) came third (almost certainly attracting many disaffected Conservatives). Second, the Liberal Democrats were only 600 votes behind the Conservatives. The Cameron leadership did not quite declare war on the party rank and file, but it did little to discourage discontent within the party. Like the movement towards New Labour in the mid-1990s, the changes in the Conservatives are as important for their symbolism as their actual impact. If the rank and file is unhappy, then it reinforces the fundamental message that the party has changed during Cameron's first year as party leader. Nevertheless, the extent of hostility to the Cameron agenda appears to be deep. Former minister and touchstone of the rank and file, Lord Tebbit first criticised the direction in which the new leadership was taking the party in January; he went on to accuse the new regime of attempting to 'purge the memory of Thatcherism'.[19] During the course of the year the depth of intra-party discomfort became clear, ConservativeHome conducted a poll of party members which concluded that the numbers with reservations about 'Project Cameron' would have been extremely worrying for the leadership. Its panel of 2,000 party members shows that support for Project Cameron fell in 2006. In January, 82 per cent were satisfied with David Cameron's performance, but by November this had fallen to 67 per cent; and 32 per cent were dissatisfied with Cameron's leadership, a sharp rise from 24 per cent in October. Furthermore, the November poll revealed that 43 per cent of Conservative members thought Cameron had gone too far in modernising the party and distancing itself from traditional policies, while 47 per cent thought the pace and extent of change about right and just 11 per cent wanted Cameron to go further.[20]

In setting a radical course, Cameron not only was aware that it might lead him into conflict with the rank and file, but seemed to wear the criticism as a badge of honour, regarding it as necessary in order to avoid a fourth electoral defeat. However, this intra-party conflict has been remarkably quick to set in. Parallels with Blair might be double-edged: like Blair, he may find that despite ideological misgivings, the party supports the reforms as long as he seems likely to deliver electoral advance; but like Blair, he may find that rank and file support is conditional.

The Liberal Democrats: tantrums and tiaras

The Liberal Democrats began 2006 in turmoil as the party leader, Charles Kennedy, finally succumbed to enormous pressure and admitted to a serious drinking problem. He resigned the party leadership in January, but hopes of a quick succession were dashed and the party embarked on a leadership election not resolved until March.

The Liberal Democrats are a federal party with a constitution that devolves power through its constituent parts. It was designed for a small parliamentary party, with power focused in local government and regional offices, and the Westminster successes of the party in 1997 and since have rather overtaken its design. When the parliamentary party was small, it was relatively easy to accommodate all MPs within the formal structure of the party by the allocation of multiple portfolio responsibility at Westminster. Now, the parliamentary party is three times the size of its 1992 counterpart and is able to exert a 'de facto power of veto' that constitutionally does not exist.[21] One of the most remarkable features of the 2005–06 leadership crisis is that it was driven by the new intake of Liberal Democrat MPs, rather than by the old stagers or the party at large.[22] The ousting of Kennedy has caused considerable disquiet in the party at large. The then leader of the Association of Liberal Democrat Councillors described the affair as 'a game going on in the Westminster bubble somewhere and the rest of us who live in the real world are slightly surprised to find out what's going on'.[23]

Sir Menzies Campbell, Kennedy's deputy, was the clear favourite but, with the Conservatives skipping a generation, there was some pressure on the Liberal Democrats to follow suit. In the event, there were three candidates: Campbell, the party's president; Simon Hughes; and former MEP (and newly elected MP), Chris Huhne. One of the assumed frontrunners, Mark Oaten, failed to attract sufficient support from the parliamentary party and withdrew his nomination shortly before a national newspaper printed damaging revelations about his private life. Hughes also encountered difficulty with the media when he was forced to admit (contrary to earlier denials) that he had had homosexual relationships. Hughes continued to run, but it is hard to escape the conclusion that his chances were fatally comprised.

The contest did not really reflect the schism in the party between social and economic liberals, but Huhne was the dark horse, and promising to make much of the party's innovative zeal and to make environmental concerns a key issue. Comfortably beating Hughes into second place, and with 42 per cent of the vote in the second round, Huhne could claim to be a moral victor of the contest (see Table 4.1). He was rewarded with the Environment portfolio in Campbell's first Shadow Cabinet.

Table 4.1   The Liberal Democrat leadership election, March 2006

	First round votes	Second round votes
Menzies Campbell	23,264	29,697
Simon Hughes	12,081	Eliminated
Chris Huhne	16,691	21,628
Turnout	52,036	72%

Source: <www.libdems.org.uk>.

Campbell's victory was hardly met with dancing in the streets. Questions about his health and age were never far from the surface, and his early performances in the Commons (first as acting leader, then as leader) did little to inspire confidence. The *Sun's* editorial hyperbole made uncomfortable reading for the Liberal Democrats: 'Having dumped an alcoholic, shunned a rent-boy botherer and rejected a liar, they settle for a man who looks ready to retire.'[24]

Despite a poor media showing during the leadership crisis and election, the Liberal Democrats were able to win Dunfermline and West Fife from Labour in the February by-election. However much this may have been due to Labour's unpopularity in its Scottish heartland, it was still a remarkable victory. Furthermore, second place at Bromley and Chislehurst demonstrated that, whatever the prevailing national mood, the Liberal Democrats remain a formidable local campaigning force.

Shortly after the leadership election, Vince Cable was elected deputy leader and the first Campbell Shadow Cabinet (and a subsequent reshuffle in December) resulted in many of the new stars of the party (mostly associated, often erroneously, with the economic liberal wing of the party) being rewarded. There has also been a concentration of power around the office of the leader, which may be a further indication that the party's powerbase is shifting away from its local government roots.

Campbell's personal ratings have been fairly poor since he became leader, leading to media speculation that he is only a 'caretaker'. However, the standing of the party in the polls has barely changed, although a drift away from the Liberal Democrats was discernible at the end of the year. Furthermore, their fortunes in the first nine months of Campbell's leadership were better than for the early periods of both his predecessors. Campbell's first nine months in charge saw the party average 19 per cent, despite Campbell's apparent shortcomings. In contrast, in Charles Kennedy's first nine months the Liberal Democrats averaged only 15 per cent, and only 9 per cent in the first nine months of Paddy Ashdown's leadership.

The devolved elections in Scotland and Wales in 2007 will be real tests for the Liberal Democrats since, in conjunction with the local elections, they will provide clues as to the future direction of the party. A poor Labour performance in Wales could reopen the potential for another partnership agreement with the Liberal Democrats in the National Assembly, but a poor performance by Labour in Scotland might benefit the Scottish National Party rather than the Liberal Democrats. The prospect of closer relations with both Conservative and Labour parties might be tested in the field of local government in 2007.

Minor parties

The Scottish National Party (SNP) had a good year in 2006: in the 2006 Scottish local elections, the SNP emerged as the winner of the popular vote (35.2 per cent) and the most gains of councils (four); it was at the heart of unveiling the 'cash for peerages' controversy; and it edged ahead of Labour in the polls for the 2007 Scottish Parliament election. Indeed, the SNP could well emerge as the largest party, although it would probably need one or more coalition partners, which could be difficult given its pledge to hold a referendum on independence, a proposal opposed by most other parties.

Plaid Cymru sought to consolidate its position: it changed its name to Plaid (although 'Plaid Cymru – The Party of Wales' would remain the official title) and its logo to a yellow Welsh poppy. Ieuan Wyn Jones was re-elected as leader; and Dafydd Iwan was reaffirmed as president. Plaid hopes to benefit from dissatisfaction with Labour in the 2007 National Assembly elections in the same way that it did in 1999.

Peter Law, the former Labour politician, who had successfully stood in Blaenau Gwent as an Independent against the party in the 2005 general election in protest at the imposition of an all-woman shortlist, died in 2006. His death necessitated two by-elections, since he was both MP and Assembly Member for Blaenau Gwent. His former agent, Dai Davies, contested the Westminster seat while his widow, Trish, stood for the National Assembly. Both stood as Independents but referred to themselves as 'People's Voice' candidates, and both retained the seats held by Law. Labour narrowed the gap in Blaenau Gwent – and Labour chair Hazel Blears referred to the electoral context there as something of a 'family feud' – but the extent of support for disaffected Labour voices in Blaenau Gwent should not be dismissed so readily. Davies held the parliamentary seat by 2,500 votes and Labour has now lost three times in two years in a seat which, because of its association with Nye Bevan, forms part of Labour's traditional electoral heritage. The evidence of Blaenau Gwent suggests that Labour may be in trouble in its Welsh heartland.

The British National Party (BNP) doubled its number of councillors in the May local elections to 52.[25] Winning seats in Epping Forest, Stoke on Trent and in Sandwell, it made limited breakthroughs but made its biggest impact in Barking and Dagenham, winning 11 of the 13 wards it contested and becoming the second largest party. Much of this was anticipated: a Democratic Audit academic report had claimed that the BNP was poised to make an impact in traditional Labour strongholds,[26] and Margaret Hodge, the Labour MP for Barking, said that 80 per cent of her constituents were 'tempted' by the BNP.[27] Some Labour commentators felt that such claims legitimised the BNP, but 52 councillors from a national total of 22,000 does not suggest that the BNP constitutes a major part of the UK party system. Even so, the BNP, which won its first council seat in 1993 and has been represented on Burnley council since 2002, has now shown a resilience that marks it out from a typical 'flash party'.

The Greens, like the BNP, made a sizeable advance in the 2006 local elections, gaining an extra 21 council seats and taking their national total to 92.[28] However, in spite of more widely spread gains, they received less media attention that their extreme-right rival.

UKIP faltered in the local elections, seeing its small councillor base all but wiped out. David Cameron set the tone for the disappointment of May for UKIP by claiming that Conservatives should not be tempted by a party he described as 'fruitcakes, loonies and closet racists mostly'. Under the new leadership of Nigel Farage, UKIP has attempted to broaden its electoral appeal, and the party wrote to 17,000 councillors in late 2006 urging them to defect to the party. However, it is hard to see a better electoral strategy for UKIP than to appeal to that section of the electorate who think of themselves as natural Conservatives but are distrustful of the Cameron-led project taking the Conservatives back to the centre ground. Whether this is a significant gap in the electoral market for UKIP remains to be seen.

Respect will probably be best remembered in 2006 for the television appearance of George Galloway, its leader and sole MP, on *Celebrity Big Brother* and his stated aim of connecting young people to the world of politics through reality television, but the performance of the party in inner London in the May local elections was also significant. In particular, Respect gained a series of credible results in Tower Hamlets, increasing their number of councillors from one to 11; a third seat was won in Newham and the party also won a seat in Birmingham. In particular, Respect seems to have benefited from the collapse of the Liberal Democrat vote in Tower Hamlets, suggesting that the party can be a viable alternative to Labour in certain areas, and bridging the credibility gap must remain Respect's long-term aim.

One potential area for Prime Minister Blair to leave a lasting legacy is Northern Ireland. Indeed, the prospect of power-sharing between the Democratic Unionist Party and Sinn Fein moved from a pipedream to a probable outcome. With new Assembly elections due in 2007, there is a real chance that the two parties could yet come to an agreement over the policing of Northern Ireland and form a joint administration after all.

Conclusion: edging towards bankruptcy?

Historians might come to view 2006 as a pivotal year in the history of party politics in Britain. It was the year when party finance rose to the top of the political agenda and all of the established political parties came out in favour of some form of state funding. The extent of debt owed by the parties was revealed and the nebulous relationship with gifts, loans and political patronage put under scrutiny.

All three major political parties experienced intra-party strife. The Conservatives appear to have the least to worry about since the new leadership is marching the party away from its comfort zone, apparently in order to demonstrate the party's new electability, but there may be a limit to the goodwill of existing members and there is some evidence to suggest that that threshold is not far away. The Liberal Democrat MPs flexed their muscles to dispose of a leader and elected another who has not really impressed in the Westminster circle. Moreover, the physical condition of the Liberal Democrats has again relied on the party's campaigning quality in local and by-elections rather than on the vim and vigour of its leadership. It could well be that 2006 marked the beginning of the end for the dual-identity party as the economic liberals seemed to be in a stronger position than the social liberals. Labour will hope that the party's health in the polls will be restored with the election of a new leader, but history might suggest that coronations and real contests can both be troublesome. Furthermore, there is some evidence to suggest that

Tony Blair's problems are more marked with his own party than with that slice of the electorate that New Labour recruited for the first time in 1997. A new leader will have to ensure that Labour's electoral reach goes further than its ideological heartland and reaches Middle England.

Notes

1. A. Russell, 'Parties and Party Systems: Movement in the System?', in M. Rush and P. Giddings (eds), *The Palgrave Review of British Politics 2005* (Basingstoke: Palgrave Macmillan, 2006), pp. 58–9.
2. See <www.electoralcommission.gov.uk>.
3. An interim report was published in October, see <www.partyfunding review.gov. uk>.
4. *Power to the People: The Report on Power – An Independent Inquiry into Britain's Democracy* (London: Joseph Rowntree Trust Inquiry, 2006), p. 186 – available at <www.powerinquiry.org>.
5. Ibid., p. 250.
6. See P. Cowley, *The Rebels: How Blair Mislaid his Majority* (London: Politico's, 2005).
7. <http://bbc.co.uk/1/hi/uk_politics/6069710.htm>.
8. David Cameron received 134,446 votes and David Davis 64,398 in the run-off ballot. The official turnout was 77 per cent, giving notional membership figures of 258,239.
9. *The Times*, 27 December 2006.
10. E. Fieldhouse, D. Cutts and A. Russell, 'Neither North Nor South: The Liberal Democrat Performance in the 2005 General Election', *Journal of Elections, Public Opinion and Parties*, 16 (2006), 77–92.
11. Professor Jon Tonge predicted the Liberal Democrats would take control of the Council. 'I think we're in for a very dramatic change in Manchester; I'm expecting to see 35 years of Labour dominance in this city ended.' BBC *Politics Show* (North West), Sunday 23 April 2006.
12. <http://news.bbc.co.uk/1/hi/uk_politics/4751197.stm>.
13. <http://news.bbc.co.uk/1/hi/uk_politics/5320760.stm>.
14. <http://news.bbc.co.uk/1/hi/uk_politics/4975938.stm>.
15. See, for instance, *The Economist*, 14 September 2006.
16. 'Cameron urges Tories to back him against right', *Guardian*, 28 February 2006.
17. *Observer*, 3 December 2006.
18. See Chapter 3, this volume, Table 3.1.
19. T. Helm and D. Rennie 'Don't be fooled by Cameron, Tebbit to warn Right', 30 January 2006. <www.bowgroup.org/harriercollectionitems/Tebbit%20article. doc>.
20. See <http://conservativehome.blogs.com/torydiary/2006/12/onethird_of_tor. html>.
21. A. Russell and E. Fieldhouse, *Neither Left nor Right? The Liberal Democrats and the Electorate* (Manchester: Manchester University Press, 2005).
22. G. Hurst, *Charles Kennedy: A Tragic Flaw* (London: Politico's, 2006).
23. A. Russell, E. Fieldhouse and D. Cutts, 'De-facto Veto? The Parliamentary Liberal Democrats', *Political Quarterly*, 78:1 (March 2007).
24. *Sun*, 3 March 2006.

25. Stuart Wilks-Hegg, 'A Slow and Painful Death? Political Parties and Local Democracy in two Northern Towns', ESRC seminar series 'The Future of Political Parties in Local Government', De Montfort University, Leicester, 18 January 2007.
26. P. John, H. Margetts, D. Rowland and S. Weir, 'The BNP: The Roots of its Appeal', Democratic Audit, 2006.
27. <http://news.bbc.co.uk/1/hi/uk_politics/4913164.stm>.
28. Wilks-Hegg, 'A Slow and Painful Death?'

5
Pressure Politics: A Challenge to Democracy?

Wyn Grant and Michael Rush

A widening gap

In a major contribution to the literature on failing democratic politics and the need for more effective and purposive citizen engagement in the political process, Gerry Stoker sees pressure groups and social movements as part of the problem rather than part of the solution. He identifies three major problems that arise from the activities of the new generation of citizen group advocates. The first of these is labelled here as *participatory failure*: 'it is not engaging directly many citizens – its way of operating is through staff-heavy organizations and media-based campaigns'.[1] The second problem can be labelled as *the reinforcement of bias*: 'the new-style groups may have opened up opportunities for representing neglected interests, but many of these interests reflect the concerns of the already privileged, educated and professional classes'.[2] The third problem can be described as *undermining effective governance*: 'the style of advocacy of citizen groups tends to magnify polarized voices'.[3] Stoker thus summarises the key problems posed for a modern democratic polity by group activity, a rather different set of problems from those of pluralist stagnation or corporate bias identified by earlier analysts. He provides a focus for the intellectual agenda that should underpin a much-needed public debate on this subject, although sometimes he seems a little too negative and pessimistic about the role of groups.

Participatory failure

The general trend in group membership is upwards at a time when electoral turnout and political party membership have been declining, but what does this represent in terms of opportunities for participation and engagement? Stoker notes:

When individuals do fight for wider causes, it is also clear that the terms of their engagement are changing, and moving towards an attenuated form of involvement. ... Supporting causes can just become part of a wider identity statement expressed through the sending of an occasional cheque and attendance at a pop concert-based rally.[4]

Studies by Grant Jordan and his colleagues have shown that advocacy groups often have supporters rather than members.[5] 'What is emerging is a pattern of campaigning groups run by professional staffers – effectively advocates without active members.'[6] One aspect of this is the use of celebrity endorsements by advocacy groups, presumably thought to carry more weight than the views of the ordinary citizen, even if the person concerned has no expertise in the area.

The reinforcement of social bias

The reinforcement of social biases by pressure group activity has long been a theme of the pressure group literature. As Schattschneider observed: 'The flaw in the pluralist heaven is that the heavenly chorus sings with a strong upper-class accent.'[7] Social class formations are less important than they were and higher education and the skills it provides is often the best predictor of involvement. However, for socially excluded groups, such as the long-term unemployed and lone parents, the outcome is much the same. They are increasingly the target of government policy, yet if they have spokespersons at all they are professionals speaking on behalf of their 'clients'. What is the case is that class has declined in importance as a social formation: 'The evidence suggests that more *collectivistic* forms of participation have declined and that more *individualist* forms have come to the fore.'[8] This matters because individualistic politics leads to a relative neglect of the impact on the polity or society as a whole as a result of the emphasis on demands for gratification of immediate personal needs.

Undermining effective governance

This links with the third key problem identified by Stoker, that of undermining effective governance. Stoker argues that citizen groups 'may be in part to blame for a negative culture aimed at getting "the government" to do more'.[9] He thinks that this is a particular risk when groups switch into 'outsider' mode and start heaping blame on the government or the bureaucracy. 'Demands to keep sponsors "on side" lead to citizen groups too often taking a populist line in which they blame the government or politicians for their failures and difficulties.'[10] The consequence can be further to undermine citizens' confidence and trust in government, making it more difficult for government to implement policies effectively and creating a vicious circle of underperformance and reinforced disappointment. This may be exacerbated by the tendency of 'Different factions inside government [to] wage a "policy war" through competing interest groups.'[11] Stoker acknowledges that 'The contribution of these citizen groups to the democratic process is substantial.' And that they have, in particular, 'had some successes in challenging and checking the privileged power of business'.[12] But he is overstating the case when he argues that 'the professionalisation of protest activism and the role of the media have created a world of spin-doctoring and manipulation to rival that of the formal electoral and representative politics that protest activists so often purport to despise'.[13] Admittedly, the media, like many of the general public, often treat the positions taken by protest groups too uncritically, too readily accepting their version of events. In a highly competitive media market, protest groups provide dramatic, emotional and highly visual stories, not just for the broadcast media but also compelling photographs for the print media. The media is often simply reacting to market imperatives.

It is tempting to believe in a 'golden age' when there was more effective democratic engagement by citizens. 'People are engaged but in a relatively thin and sporadic way with the political system.'[14] However, it was ever thus. Political participation was always a minority taste. The big change is the decline in party membership. As a consequence, 'Parties are struggling to deliver the political functions of aggregating and cohering interests.'[15] Politicians are faced not only with more demands, but demands that appear in a rawer and unprocessed form, with little regard to their opportunity cost. As Whiteley puts it: 'Unlike parties, interest groups aim to obtain benefits for the people they represent while transferring the costs to the rest of society.'[16]

The example of health

Patient health offers a good example with 'Patients' groups ... growing sharply in strength and influence.'[17] The National Institute of Clinical Excellence (NICE) was supposed to provide a rational and informed mechanism for balancing the cost-effectiveness of alternative treatments within a finite National Health Service (NHS) budget. However, it is relatively easy to attract media attention for an emotional campaign demanding that patients suffering from a potentially terminal illness, such as breast cancer, should be given an unproven treatment. Funds then have to be found from elsewhere in the NHS budget, possibly from conditions that attract less sympathy, such as mental health. Moreover, it would appear that campaigns by patient groups can be used by pharmaceutical companies who wish to promote sales of a particular drug. A study by Patient View found only 11 per cent of the UK's 530 largest patients' groups state publicly that they receive support from the pharmaceutical industry. However, 'In recent years companies including Eli Lilly, Merck and GlaxoSmithKline have been criticised for giving support to patient and professional medical groups that have been associated with publications designed to encourage the sales of their own drugs.'[18]

Seeking a solution

The contours of the problem are evident, but what can be done to tackle it? Any prescriptions must follow a thorough public debate. This has yet to occur, as commentators concentrate on more fashionable topics such as proportional representation, compulsory voting and deliberative democracy. Occasionally, a public figure does make a critical speech about pressure groups, as did Sir John Krebs on retiring after five years as chairman of the Food Standards Agency. He said 'that groups such as Greenpeace and the Soil Association are unaccountable, partisan bodies with agendas as slanted as those of industry lobbyists ... I see pressure groups as businesses – they have a constituency of people who pay their subscriptions to buy their magazines.' He warned: 'Some of these groups that have single issues to pursue tend to be selective in using the scientific evidence.'[19] Such interventions attract instant publicity, but they do not lead to any continuing debate.

There are three groups of actors who need to reflect self-critically on their conduct in relation to single-issue pressure groups. First, citizens themselves need to consider their role in relation to such organisations, although that is unlikely to happen without some outside assistance. Second, non-governmental organisations (NGOs) need to think more systematically about how they conduct their business in a democratic polity. Third, the government needs to think about its stance towards such groups.

Because the emphasis is on feasibility, this approach leaves out three other actors (the media, the parties, the Opposition) who might be considered to be relevant. A number of charges can be made against the media, including confusing fact, speculation and opinion, and an overly adversarial stance towards politicians that encourages 'a culture of contempt'.[20] However, given the market imperatives that drive the media, it is unlikely to put its own house in order anytime soon, although Oxfam has claimed that NGOs are increasingly getting hostile media reporting.[21] As for the political parties, although they could be reinvigorated, the decline in their traditional social bases and the rise of individualised politics makes such an effort unlikely to succeed. The much-canvassed suggestion of state funding is actually likely to make parties more of a creature of the political class and less mindful of their activist base. Turning to the Opposition, the fact that the Conservative Party is rethinking its stance on a wide range of issues might seem to offer an opportunity for reviewing the role of single-issue pressure groups, about which some Conservatives have expressed disquiet from time to time. However, the party is unlikely to want to do anything to alienate potential support. Indeed, the 'Vote blue, go green' slogan presupposes a reluctance to offend the biggest subdivision of advocacy groups, environmental and animal protection organisations.

The heart of Stoker's argument is that citizens should become more competent amateurs: 'Politics is a place for amateurs, but we need to design institutions, structure processes and develop support systems so that amateurs can engage and improve their skills.'[22] This is no easy task when they are relatively unengaged in the first place, distrustful of the political process and hence not inclined to improve their political understanding or skills. Stoker has a whole raft of suggestions which go well beyond the scope of this chapter. However, his suggestion of consultative innovations would provide a range of settings in which citizens could express their views other than through single-interest groups, and thereby become aware of the alternatives to, and possible costs of, apparently straightforward solutions.[23] Information and communications technology also offers new opportunities for interactivity in an ongoing political conversation.[24]

NGOs also need to take more responsibility for their role as intermediaries, promoting transparency and accountability. Codes of conduct have an important role to play here. In June 2006, 11 non-governmental organisations, including Amnesty International, Greenpeace and Oxfam, signed a voluntary 'accountability charter'. Signatories 'recognise that transparency and accountability are essential to good governance, whether by governments, business or non-profit organisations'.[25] They must provide transparent bookkeeping and regular assessments of the organisation's environmental impact and its ethical fundraising standards. Mechanisms are required enabling 'whistleblowers' to report malpractice within organisations. The six-page charter is largely silent on the questions of relations with government. However, Oxfam states: 'In our advocacy work, we may challenge others – for example governments, institutions and companies. If concerns are raised that our claims are inaccurate or unfounded, we will investigate and respond appropriately.'[26]

The Association of British Pharmaceutical Industries has also launched a new code of practice, which will require members for the first time to disclose their support to patients' groups. It also forbids companies from supporting groups with the aim of promoting their drugs. 'However, the new code stops short of requiring companies to disclose publicly either the amount of funding they give to patients' groups or to define the nature of any support in contracts.'[27]

The difficulty with such codes of conduct is that only some groups sign up to them and, even for those that do, there seem to be no mechanisms for monitoring and enforcement. This is why codes need at least to be endorsed by government and perhaps made a condition of consultative access. As Stoker has pointed out: 'The central insight of much rational choice work is that politics requires good *institutions* to frame the process of strategic interaction between different interests.'[28] Although a further extension of the regulatory state through an agency to regulate pressure group activity would be a step too far, there might be a case for extending the remit of the Electoral Commission, given that many organisations registered with it as 'political parties' are, in fact, pressure groups. However, what is needed as a first step is government support for codes of conduct and insistence on the importance of adhering to them.

More generally, government needs to be prepared to stand up to pressure groups, even if it brings media criticism. The signs are not altogether discouraging. A very effective campaign on the issue of bystander exposure to pesticides led the Royal Commission on Environmental Pollution to investigate the issue. Its report was not unsympathetic and proposed a five-metre buffer strip where spraying took place near to dwellings, schools, and so on.[29] This could have been a politically attractive solution, but the government stood firm, saying that it was determined to diminish regulation, not to increase it, and that there was no firm scientific evidence of a health problem. As a result, it received considerable criticism in the media and from pressure groups.

One example does not establish a trend, but it does suggest that government can pay the political price of facing down single-issue pressure groups if it wants to. Instead of such groups obtaining a spurious legitimacy on the basis of apparent popular support and media sympathy, it would be preferable if they earned legitimacy by demonstrating they meet appropriate standards of internal governance. Government, for its part, needs to act on its professed belief in evidence-based policy-making and not be swayed by vociferous campaigns.

Business and government

Tony Blair's aspiration to make Labour the natural party of business looked increasingly under threat as the government entered its third term of office, but business received cold comfort from the new Conservative leadership. Some in business argued that the government's decision in the autumn of 2005 to allow existing public sector workers to continue to retire at 60 was a tipping point in relations between business and government. This was seen as giving way to union pressure in order to avert a strike and a breach in the implicit bargain between business and government that the private sector would sort out its pension funding deficits and the government would resolve the same problems in the public sector.

Another dispute erupted with a warning by Sir Digby Jones, the then Director General of the Confederation of British Industry (CBI), of power cuts in the winter of 2005/06 that could force companies to shut down production. The Energy Minister, Malcolm Wicks, accused Sir Digby of talking 'nonsense' and 'scaremongering' with his claims that Britain risked a return to the three-day working weeks of the 1970s. He took the unusual step of summoning Sir Digby to a meeting at the Department of Trade and Industry (DTI) for what he said would be a 'cool' discussion.[30]

In July 2006, Sir Digby was succeeded as CBI Director General by Richard Lambert, former editor of the *Financial Times* and subsequently a member of the Bank of England's Monetary Policy Committee. His selection represented a return to the rather cooler, more intellectual style of CBI leadership represented by Sir Digby's predecessors. Sir Digby's outspoken style went down well with the CBI's grassroots membership, but was less welcome in the corridors of power. Nevertheless, this did not prevent the CBI enjoying strong channels of communication with government, and Lambert made it clear that he wanted the CBI to be more robust in its dealings with government. He also wanted the CBI to be more proactive and forward-looking in the way that it handled issues.

For all their complaints about what they see as the growing burden of taxation and regulation, business has enjoyed a close and constructive relationship with New Labour. Business leaders are grateful to Gordon Brown for providing a climate of macroeconomic stability. The uncertainty surrounding the succession to Tony Blair was unsettling and concerns have been expressed about a return to a more 'Old Labour' style of leadership should Gordon Brown become Prime Minister. Nevertheless, business relations with Labour governments have often been more comfortable than those with Conservative governments because Labour thinks that it needs business support while the Conservatives often not only take it for granted but see a need to differentiate themselves from big business.

The new Conservative leader, David Cameron, created concern in his first few weeks in office when he criticised big business. Newspaper advertisements quoted him as saying that he would 'not just stand up for big business, but stand up to big business when it's in the interests of Britain and the world'.[31] Business was urged to shoulder more social responsibility with reviews of party policy to consider industry's duties in such areas as the environment, transport and waste disposal, in line with the 'Vote blue, go green' slogan. This stance appears in part to have been driven by research showing that the Conservatives are seen by voters as too close to large corporations and therefore out of touch on issues such as the environment, global warming and poverty that are important to women and younger voters. Some business commentators saw this stance as public relations with very little substance attached to it, but there was a concern that the increased emphasis on issues such as climate change could create public expectations that would make it more difficult to implement business-friendly policy.

In the context of the 2006 Conservative Party Conference, Oliver Letwin, the party's head of policy, tried to address some of these concerns by unveiling what he described as 'the deal we're putting to business'.[32] He pledged that a Conservative government would seek to address factors seen to damage UK competitiveness, such as excessive and intrusive regulation, lack of skills and poor infrastructure. In return, business would be expected to show greater corporate responsibility in areas such as family-friendly employment policies and environmental impacts in the broadest sense of the term. This would be achieved by a mixture of persuasion and coercion, a difficult balance to maintain. Business remained concerned about exactly how the Conservatives would promote greater competitiveness.

There was also concern in business organisations about the support from the Conservatives and Liberal Democrats for dismantling the Department of Trade and Industry. The Liberal Democrats have a policy of scrapping the DTI, while David Cameron has said that it is 'possible' that the Conservatives could axe the department. Nevertheless, a survey of 550 employers commissioned by the British Chambers of Commerce found that 89 per cent thought there was a future need for the DTI, principally to act as the voice of business within government.[33] The fact that business considers that it needs such a voice indicates that not all trade associations representing sectors of business are perceived to be fully effective.

The pledge to stand up to big business won support from a traditional constituency of the Conservatives, small businesses. However, such businesses remain relatively less well-organised and vulnerable to the lobbying power of bigger businesses. This was demonstrated in the summer of 2006, when the government watered down its own policy of requiring sellers of houses to prepare home information packs that were intended to provide additional protection to consumers. The government was put under pressure on the issue from mortgage lenders and estate agents, who were able to use the argument that house prices might be affected and could undermine the government's electoral popularity. The real losers in this decision were the self-employed individuals who had invested considerable sums of money to train as 'home inspectors'. A number of companies had also entered the market and they were represented by the Association of Home Information Pack Providers, but the individual operators were not effectively represented and had to hire legal advice to seek compensation.

Despite complaints about particular policies, business has enjoyed an effective working relationship with the Blair government. Business associations are usually more effective at working with the executive than lobbying Parliament, whichever party is in power.

Government consultation

Government consultation of various interests during policy formulation is not, of course, a new phenomenon, but it has become more widespread, systematic and public in recent years, particularly under the Blair government. In November 2000, the government published a Code of Practice on Consultation which all government departments and agencies are expected to observe.[34] Consultations are normally subject to a minimum period of 12 weeks, with a shorter period being permissible for reasons such as deadlines imposed by EU negotiations or cases of reconsultation following an earlier full consultation. Consultation documents are available on departmental and agency websites, but additional means may also be used to reach particular interests. For example, on the Department for Education and Skills' Youth Green Paper, teachers, other professionals and voluntary workers were used to encourage and facilitate responses from young people aged between 13 and 19, resulting in more than 20,000 responses. Formal consultation is sometimes preceded by seminars, as happened in 2005 and 2006, in considering additional powers for the Greater London Authority.[35]

In 2005, the latest year for which figures are available, government departments and agencies carried out 583 formal consultations, 80 per cent of which lasted 12 or more weeks.[36] Government departments are responsible for most consultations, with the Department for the Environment, Food and Rural Affairs (DEFRA), the Department of Trade and Industry, the Office of the Deputy Prime Minister, the Department of Health, and Department for Transport the most frequent users. Among agencies, the Food Standards Agency and the Health and Safety Executive are the most regular users.

Individual departments and agencies publish details of their consultations and a limited perusal of departmental websites demonstrates the considerable involvement of pressure groups in the consultation process. A DEFRA consultation in 2006 on badger culling and the spread of bovine tuberculosis involved 32 pressure or interest groups, 55 per cent of those responding,[37] while in 2005 another on the environmental impact of agricultural assessment regulations produced a response from 199 groups, 62 per cent of the total.[38] Similarly, 54 per cent of response to a DTI consultation on additional paternity leave and pay and a massive 80 per cent to draft employment regulations on age equality were from groups.[39]

The hunting ban: the saga continues

More than eight months after it came into force, the Hunting Act was successfully used to prosecute a huntsman.[40] However, it took a private prosecution by the League Against Cruel Sports to achieve it: from the moment it came into force, the League claimed that illegal hunting was widespread, but the Crown Prosecution Service (CPS) refused to mount any prosecutions. In August 2006, Tony Wright of the Exmoor Foxhounds was convicted and fined £500.[41] However, in October the CPS prosecuted two members of the Devon and Somerset Staghounds.[42] Earlier, in the year, Kate Hoey, the pro-hunting Labour MP and now chair of the Countryside Alliance, claimed: 'All hunts have far more people going out with them', and an anonymous Cabinet minister was quoted as saying that the Act had been a 'complete waste of [parliamentary] time'.[43] Meanwhile, fears that other field sports and fishing would increasingly become the targets of animal activists, now that hunting with dogs was illegal, were fuelled by an attack on anglers at a fly-fishing centre in Lancashire. It took place on 12 August, the first day of the grouse-shooting season, and it appeared that the initial target of the activists was a shoot which had been cancelled. According to the Lancashire police, attacks on anglers have increased, but it remains to be seen whether, having secured a ban on hunting with dogs, activists are not so much opening another front as extending an existing one.[44] The national umbrella organisation for fishing, the Fisheries and Angling Conservation Trust, demanded a meeting with the Home Office to discuss the safety of anglers. A new organisation, the Lobster Liberation Front, dismantled 60 lobster pots in Scotland and spray-painted slogans on fishermen's sheds, also slashing nets belonging to Dorset fishermen.[45]

Direct action

Media reports of various forms of direct action – some legal, others illegal – were plentiful in 2006, with animal rights activity again figuring prominently and Fathers 4 Justice being replaced by a more militant Real Fathers 4 Justice. However, unusually, the business community also became involved in a form of direct action when protesting against the extradition of three businessmen to the United States.

'The NatWest Three'

US prosecutors sought the extradition of three employees of the National Westminster Bank on fraud charges relating to the financial collapse of the Texas-based Enron Corporation. Business interests objected because, under a new extradition treaty and unlike earlier arrangements, no prima facie evidence need be presented to a UK court, only that charges had been brought. In May 2005, an Early Day Motion in the Commons was signed by 163 MPs from all parties,[46] but protests did not get fully underway until 2006. In conjunction with the *Daily Telegraph*, the CBI and the Institute of Directors (IoD), as well as a number of individual businessmen, organised a campaign to oppose the extradition, involving an open letter to the Home Secretary, John Reid, signed among others by the Directors General of the CBI, the IoD, the British Chambers of Commerce, and the British Retail Consortium and the Chairman of the London Stock Exchange. Other protests were made by the civil liberties group, Liberty, and the legal reform group, Justice. The *Telegraph* invited its readers to add their names to the letter, via its website, and 7,400 did so.[47] Business leaders also joined a protest march on 29 June. Subsequently, the House of Lords sought to suspend the extradition arrangements with the United States, by passing an amendment to the Police and Justice Bill, but it was subsequently rejected by the Commons.[48] Before that, however, the Speaker allowed an emergency debate on 12 July.[49] In the event, these protests were unsuccessful and the 'NatWest Three' were extradited, as were several other businessmen.[50]

Fathers 4 Justice transmutes

Since its formation in 2002, Fathers 4 Justice has achieved considerable publicity through various stunts, but following internal disputes in 2005, between 30 and 40 members were expelled and a more militant group, Real Fathers 4 Justice, was formed. Late in 2005, some members of the latter were reported to be planning to kidnap Tony Blair's son, Leo, leading Matt O'Connor, the founder of Fathers 4 Justice, to disband his organisation.[51] Undeterred, Real Fathers 4 Justice embarked on its own campaign, involving hitting Ruth Kelly, the then Education Secretary, with an egg when she appeared as a witness in a court hearing involving an earlier egg-throwing incident during the 2005 election campaign,[52] interrupting a men's quarter-final at Wimbledon,[53] and a protester dressed as Father Christmas, but carrying a shotgun, climbing onto the roof of a circuit judge's house.[54]

Farmers for Action

Farmers for Action (FFA), one of the more long-standing direct action groups, has faced increasing difficulty in mobilising farmers despite continuing problems in the dairy industry, its main base of support. There were no direct actions organised by the group in the six months to August 2006 because farmers failed to turn out. When the leading dairy company Arla cut its milk prices, Farmers for Action joined forces with the National Farmers Union to protest, but out of 4,000 producers contacted, only 31 turned out. This does not mean that direct action in the farming community has come to an end. However, it has so far done nothing to halt the downward trend in milk prices. When those called on to protest have to work long hours to maintain their livelihood, it becomes increasingly unattractive to devote long hours at night to blockades, and protest fatigue sets in. The calculations about the costs and benefits of direct action are rather different for an economic group compared with the animal rights groups discussed next.

Animal rights

Following the strengthening of legislation against animal rights extremists using violence or intimidation, the British Pharmaceutical Association reported that attacks on its member companies, individual directors and employees had declined from more than 500 in 2004 to 200 in 2005, with the downward trend continuing in the first two quarters of 2006.[55] In May, three activists were sentenced to 12 years' imprisonment and one to four years' for their part in digging up and removing the body of a relative of one of the owners of a guinea pig breeding farm in Staffordshire. Then, in August, Donald Currie, described as the Animal Liberation Front's (ALF's) 'leading bomber', was found guilty of arson and the possession of firebombs, and in December was sentenced to 12 years in prison.[56] Also in August, more than 30 protesters were arrested for disrupting a degree ceremony in Oxford and sent for trial in January 2007.[57]

Nonetheless, attacks against a variety of targets continued, including two of the activists' major quarries – Huntingdon Life Sciences (HLS) and the Oxford University animal experiments laboratory that has been under construction for several years. According to the ALF's website, Bite Back, there were 12 HLS-associated attacks in the UK, 11 in other parts of Europe, and four in the United States. Attacks also took place in the UK and elsewhere against GlaxoSmithKline and Roche;[58] Glaxo shareholders received anonymous letters threatening to reveal their names and addresses unless they sold their shares,[59] and a Glaxo director's home was attacked.[60]

The ALF opened its 2006 campaign against the Oxford laboratory by extending its targets beyond the builders and others directly associated with the project by issuing a statement on the internet: 'We must target professors, heads, students, investors, partners, supporters and ANYONE that dares to deal in any part of the university in ANY way.'[61] In March, for example, Vodafone, which was funding projects at the university, had some of its transmitters damaged, even though the projects were unrelated to animal experimentation.[62] This led to the setting up of a counter-group, Pro-Test, which organised a march in Oxford on 25 February, the first major public response to the Oxford activities of the ALF and other animal rights groups, such as Speak.[63]

But public opinion does not come into the equation for militant activists. A YouGov poll in May showed a substantial majority of respondents in favour of animal testing for medical purposes. Although overwhelming majorities regarded various forms of peaceful protest as 'reasonable', only 10 per cent similarly regarded threatening individuals via the internet, 2 per cent damaging property, and 1 per cent issuing death threats.[64] The same month, the Coalition for Medical Progress organised a petition against animal rights extremists which, by October, had been signed by more than 21,000 people, including the Prime Minister.[65] But in May, Speak revealed where builders working on the Oxford laboratory site were being housed and threatened to demonstrate outside their quarters, although the High Court extended the scope of an injunction to ban such demonstrations.[66]

The attacks by the ALF and other animal rights militants take a number of forms. Persons directly involved are attacked, their vehicles and other property damaged. The suppliers of the main target organisations are also threatened and attacked: for instance, letters are sent to the individuals' neighbours alleging that they are paedophiles. Growing use is also made of electronic means of communication – inundating targets with e-mails, setting up automatic telephone calls, and hacking into websites and credit card records.

The use of the internet

The internet is now a regular and well-established tool in pressure politics, not least as a means of organising direct action. For example, a week-long climate change protest at the Drax Power Station, the UK's largest coal-fired power station, in Yorkshire was largely organised via the internet. Though only small in numbers, the demonstrators succeeded in securing much media attention.[67] Almost all pressure groups now have websites and they are especially useful for umbrella organisations. These bring together an often wide variety of groups focusing on a particular issue or policy area, such as the environment, with some concerned specifically with the issue or policy area and others whose interest are wider but include the same specific concern. Stop Climate Chaos is one such umbrella organisation, comprising a coalition of some 30 groups, including established environmental groups such as Greenpeace, Friends of the Earth, Transport 2000 and the World Wide Fund for Nature, aid groups such as Oxfam and Christian Aid, at least one major trade union – Unison, and long-established groups like the Royal Society for the Protection of Birds and the Women's Institute. In 2006, it organised a wide range of meetings and demonstrations; some local or regional, others national; some on specific climate issues, others broader in scope.[68] Another similar umbrella organisation is Rising Tide.[69]

Conclusion

In this chapter we have looked at the more established groups that represent business and a variety of direct action movements seeking to advance a variety of causes. These two types of group are only part of a much wider array of group activity, ranging from large-scale organisations such as the Royal Society for the Protection of Birds, with more members than all the political parties combined, to spontaneous examples of local action concerned with such issues as the location of mobile telephone masts. This particular form of 'Not in my back yard' (Nimby) group illustrates some of the difficulties that pressure groups pose for modern democracy. On the one hand, it illustrates that a capacity for spontaneous sporadic intervention by citizens still exists and in that sense is indicative of a healthy democracy. However, if the phone mast is not located in one place it may have to go elsewhere, where the citizens are more disadvantaged and less well-organised, so that the objectors to the original location can continue to use their mobile phones. The fragmentation of society leads to highly individualised forms of protest which can flare up and then die away. This makes the task of governance more difficult, but government has not sought to tackle the issues this poses in any systematic way. Extending the regulatory state to regulate pressure groups might be a step too far, but the underlying issues need to be debated more widely.

Notes

1. G. Stoker, *Why Politics Matters* (Basingstoke: Palgrave Macmillan, 2006), p. 111.
2. Ibid., p. 111.
3. Ibid.
4. Ibid.

5. G. Jordan and W. Maloney, *Interest Group Politics: Enhancing Participation* (Basingstoke: Palgrave Macmillan, 2006).
6. Stoker, *Why Politics Matters*, p.107.
7. E. E. Schnattschneider, *The Semi-Sovereign People* (New York: Rinehart and Winston, 1960), p. 35.
8. Stoker, *Why Politics Matters*, p.92.
9. Ibid., p. 112.
10. Ibid.
11. Ibid., p. 108.
12. Ibid., p. 109.
13. Ibid., p. 104.
14. Ibid., p. 92.
15. Ibid., p. 116.
16. P. Whiteley, 'Just the Best of a Bad Bunch?', *Times Higher Education Supplement*, 7 January 2005.
17. P. Jack, 'Few patients' groups admit links to drug companies', *Financial Times*, 1 May 2006.
18. Ibid.
19. M. Henderson, 'Friends of the corporate Earth', *The Times*, 12 April 2005.
20. Stoker, *Why Politics Matters*, p.12.
21. H. Williamson, 'Greenpeace, Amnesty and Oxfam agree to code of conduct', *Financial Times*, 3 June 2006.
22. Stoker, *Why Politics Matters*, p.150.
23. Ibid., pp. 183–5.
24. Ibid., pp. 172–3.
25. Williamson, 'Greenpeace, Amnesty and Oxfam agree to code of conduct'.
26. <www.oxfam.org.uk/about_us/accountability>.
27. Jack, 'Few patients' groups admit links to drug companies'.
28. Stoker, *Why Politics Matters*.
29. See <www.recep.org.uk/pesticides/Crop%Spraying%web.pdf>.
30. *Financial Times*, 26 October 2005.
31. *Financial Times*, 5 January 2006.
32. *Financial Times*, 20 September 2006.
33. *Financial Times*, 18 September 2006.
34. See <www.cabinet-office.gov/uk/regulation/consultation/code/index.asp>. A revised code was published in 2004.
35. <www.cabinet-office.gov.uk/regulation/consultation>.
36. The figures were 621, with 71 per cent compliant with the 12-week minimum, in 2002; 622 and 77 per cent in 2003, and 621 and 76 per cent in 2004.
37. <www.defra.gov.uk/corporate/consult/badgers-tbcontrols/consultlist.htm>.
38. <www.defra/gov.uk/corporate/consult/eia2005/consultlist.htm>.
39. <www.dti.gov.uk.consultations/page25906//.html> (and p. 16395).
40. It had earlier been used to convict a poacher hunting with dogs (see *Daily Telegraph*, 19 October 2005).
41. *Daily Telegraph*, 5 November 2005; 31 July, 1 and 5 August 2006.
42. *Daily Telegraph*, 18 October 2006.
43. *Daily Telegraph*, 17 February 2006.
44. See *Daily Telegraph*, 23 August 2006.
45. *The Times*, 26 August 2006.
46. EDM 241 Extradition Act 2003, 26 May 2006.

47. <www.telegraph.co.uk/news/main.jhtml?xml=news/2006/07/12/natwest12. xml>.
48. HL Debs, 684, 11 July 2006, cc. 625–53.
49. HC Debs, 418, 12 July 2006, cc. 1396–447.
50. The legal aspects of the case are dealt with in Chapter 10, this volume.
51. See <www.guardian.co.uk/uj_news/story/0,36044,1502264,00.html> and <www. bbc.co.uk/1/hi/uk/4626.stm>.
52. <www.bbc.co.uk/1hi/england/manchester/4685496.htm>.
53. *Daily Telegraph*, 6 July 2006.
54. *Daily Telegraph*, 29 November 2006.
55. <www.abpi.org.uk/press_releases>.
56. <www.bbc.co.uk/1/hi/england/525774.stm> and *Dorset Echo*, 14 December 2006.
57. *Daily Telegraph*, 26 August 2006.
58. *Bite Back Magazine* (<www.directaction.info.news.htm>).
59. *Daily Telegraph*, 9 May 2006.
60. *Daily Telegraph*, 30 January 2006.
61. Cited in the *Sunday Times*, 29 January 2006.
62. *Sunday Times*, 19 March 2006.
63. *Daily Telegraph*, 25 February 2006; *Sunday Times*, 26 February 2006. Speak (originally Speac – Stop Primate Experiments at Cambridge) successfully campaigned for the abandonment by the University of Cambridge of its proposed animal experiments laboratory in 2003 (see <www.guardian.co.uk/animalrights/story/0,,1265928,00. html>).
64. *Daily Telegraph*, 29 May 2006.
65. <www.thepeoplespetition.org.uk/sigup/index.cfm?theform> and <www.mdecical-progress.org/news/newsarchive.cfm.news_id=147>.
66. *Daily Telegraph*, 31 May and 13 June 2006.
67. *Daily Telegraph*, 1 September, and the *Sunday Times*, 3 September 2006.
68. See <www.stopclimatechaos/about_us/10.asp>.
69. See <www.risingtide.org.uk/about>.

6
Government and Administration: Fit for Purpose?

Andrew Gray and Bill Jenkins

In the summer of 2006, the new Home Secretary, John Reid, told a startled Home Affairs Committee that his department was 'not fit for purpose'. He had just moved into the job (his sixth Cabinet post in nine years) and reported that the leadership, management systems, processes and information technology of the Home Office were unable to cope with the new age.[1] Whatever its motivations, the admission was unusual. Reid's political critics saw it as an attempt to distance himself from continuing problems, especially the Home Office's inability to keep track of an increasing number of released foreign prisoners. The episode had deeply embarrassed the government and his predecessor, Charles Clarke. In any event, Reid's response was to initiate a fundamental review of his department under its new Permanent Secretary, Sir David Normington.

If the whole episode propelled the term 'fit for purpose' to the top of the lexicon of administrative reform and enthralled journalists in need of summer sustenance, it also raised questions about other parts of the government. Was the demise of the long-criticised Child Support Agency (CSA), for example, a recognition that it had not been fit for purpose? And could the financial sufferings of English farmers as the result of inefficiencies in the Rural Payments Agency be attributed to the same failing?

An early 2006 publication from the Society of Local Government Chief Executives (SOLACE) reminded us that the term was hardly new. It sought to make local government 'fit for purpose in a year of living dangerously'. In his foreword to the essays, Clive Grace confirmed that 'all organisations should be fit for their purpose in being clear about what they should be trying to achieve and organising themselves accordingly'. But in times of changing pressures the task was to rethink what local government was for and to redesign structures and processes strategically to meet these demands.[2]

Later, in the autumn of 2006, the left-wing pressure group Compass published its own contribution on the Labour Party itself, *Fit for Purpose: A Programme for Labour Party Renewal*. One of its authors asked 'why, while society grows ever more devolved and decentralised, are our political parties just about the only institutions being pushed in the opposite direction?'[3] For Compass, 'fit for purpose' involves a programme of organisational and political renewal in a world where politics, governance and administration are inexorably entwined.

The fitness for purpose of its parts will thus be our theme as we chart major developments in British government and administration in 2006. We shall review, first, the centre of government and its leadership; second, the parliamentary monitoring of administration; and third, the machines of service delivery, before returning in our concluding discussion to ask whether the system of government and administration as a whole is fit for its purpose.

The centre and its leadership: imbalances in the internal combustion of government

Funded by the Joseph Rowntree Foundation and Trust, the Power Commission was established in 2004 to investigate how political participation could be increased in the UK. It attributed the decline in voter turnout and political engagement to citizen estrangement from policy-making, disenchantment with parties and the electoral system, and poor information about formal politics. Its solutions included shifting the balance of power from the executive to Parliament and local government, improving the responsiveness of and choice within electoral and party systems, and providing citizens with a more direct say in political decisions by empowering them to initiate legislative processes and inquiries.[4]

If part of the problem identified by the Commission was public alienation from political personnel and institutions, the government leaders in 2006 aggravated the problem. The Secretary of State for Culture, Media and Sport, Tessa Jowell, found herself at the centre of a media circus on how far her husband's remunerated dealings with Italian politicians had financed their mortgage and whether she had breached the Ministerial Code by not declaring this income. Although the Cabinet Secretary, Gus O'Donnell, cleared her of any impropriety, the Prime Minister later appointed the Comptroller and Auditor General, Sir John Bourn, as the first independent adviser on ministerial conflicts of interest.[5]

If Jowell was unlucky, the Deputy Prime Minister, John Prescott, appeared at best accident-prone. First, the press revealed his affair with a civil servant and implied he had abused ministerial privileges; then its photographers caught him playing croquet with staff at his grace and favour residence, Dorneywood, while nominally in charge of the country; and later it questioned his acceptance of hospitality and gifts from an American businessman connected to a casino licence application at the Millennium Dome. His conduct in the casino case was criticised in particular by the Standards and Privileges Committee. Concerns about the Ministerial Code were also raised by the Public Administration Select Committee (PASC), which called for the investigatory machinery into breaches of the code to be independent in order to provide a more informed basis for political judgements.[6]

Meanwhile, the Labour Party and senior officials, including some in Number 10, became embroiled in allegations about party funding and peerages after the party treasurer, Jack Dromey, distanced himself from a series of undeclared loans from wealthy donors. Very soon questions were asked of both main parties whether they offered 'peerages' for donations or loans. To defuse the situation the Prime Minister set up an inquiry into party funding by a former Permanent Secretary, Sir Hayden Phillips. At the same time the Constitutional Affairs and Public Administration Committees launched inquiries into party funding and political honours.[7]

Labour's loss of over 500 seats in the May local elections prompted an extensive Cabinet reshuffle. The machinery of government implications included Ruth Kelly's move from Education to a new Department for Communities and Local Government, and the dismantling of the Office of the Deputy Prime Minister (although Prescott retained his title). David Miliband, having championed the cause of devolved government, found himself out of local government and into Environment, Food and Rural Affairs. His predecessor, Margaret Beckett, was no doubt grateful to escape the problems with farm payments (of which more below), but surprised to become Foreign Secretary. Accompanying these and other changes, the Prime Minister wrote to all senior ministers demanding that they focus on delivery. He also launched a new public consultation on the future of the public services, 'Let's Talk'.

The changes may be explained as an attempt by the Prime Minister to reassert his authority. Yet their administrative logic remains unclear. Why, for example, move the minister (Miliband) most clearly committed to the government's decentralisation plans from the department most able to enact them? For Polly Toynbee the reshuffle indicated 'an indifference to good administration by experienced ministers' and 'a mania for ideological reform without the necessary administrative skills'; for sacked Charles Clarke, Blair had lost his sense of purpose and direction.[8]

The reshuffle also reopened the differences between Blair and Brown over the timing of the Prime Minister's retirement. While the Chancellor pressed for 'a stable and orderly transition' through an agreed timetable, Blair refused to be drawn and wished 'to get on with the business of governing'. It is not only a matter of personal rivalry but also one about policy direction and public spending, especially the next Comprehensive Spending Review (CSR) due in 2007 and many of the government's social policy challenges, including pensions reform.

Ensuring sufficient public and private provision of pensions is a common problem for European governments. The government asked Lord Turner to investigate and make recommendations for the UK. His final report, published on the 63rd anniversary of the Beveridge Report, radically proposed raising the state pensionable age in line with increasing life expectancy and restoring the link between the state pension and average earnings. The latter was vigorously contested in Cabinet, with the Chancellor opposed to its consequence of a decade of higher taxes. Eventually, a deal was struck between Prime Minister and Chancellor, and the Pension Reform Bill was published in May. Turner welcomed it for containing 95 per cent of his recommendations.[9]

In the autumn one junior minister and several Parliamentary Private Secretaries sympathetic to the Chancellor resigned, demanding that Blair state his retirement day. Although unity appeared to have been restored when Brown and Blair 'praised' each other in their respective speeches at the Labour Party Conference, Blair then invaded what the Treasury saw as its territory by announcing a series of Cabinet-level policy reviews of challenges facing Britain over the next decade: economic competitiveness, public services, security, migration and foreign policy. These could be construed, as the Treasury publicly observed, as complementing departmental work on the CSR; they might, however, be another attempt to reassert prime ministerial authority.[10]

In July, the Prime Minister had responded to questions on his 'leadership style' from the House of Commons Liaison Committee. He informed them he did not think it a very good idea to hold votes in Cabinet: 'it would be odd if the Prime Minister did not have a firm view of what he thought was the right thing to do'. He was also unrepentant on the legislative burden on departments; it played an important part in enabling civil servants to do their job. He also believed he had to drive the policy agenda himself to overcome cultural forces in politics and the professions that failed to grapple with change and modernity.[11]

Is the centre 'fit for purpose'? Many have questioned the efficacy of shaping policy through continuous internal trench warfare, unrelated initiatives (often without departmental consultation), and a machinery of government determined by the political wish to constrain personalities. Martin Kettle argued that this exposes the wider limitations of Labour's way of governing and 'even some of the limitations of the modern state itself'.[12] Perhaps, however, it was ever thus.

Parliament, scrutiny and the civil service: monitoring and managing

The evolution of the Schools White Paper into the Education and Inspections Act 2006 was a bruising process for the Labour leadership, secured eventually only with the votes of the Conservative opposition. At issue were choice and contestability in school admissions, the role of local authorities and trust schools, and school expansion. The Education Committee was important in extracting compromises before the publication of the bill. Describing the White Paper as confusing, poorly structured and the victim of the Number 10 publicity machine, the committee sought major changes. Although the government's response appeared lukewarm, the committee claimed it had obtained 80 per cent of what it wanted.[13]

While many of the objections of the Parliamentary Labour Party to the Education Bill were ideological, some resented the hijacking of the bill from the department by the centre and saw a contempt for Parliament in failing to provide information. The Prime Minister admitted to the Liaison Committee that some of the information offered was partial and appeared to contradict evidence given to the Education Select Committee by the then Secretary of State, Ruth Kelly. He agreed to publish more evidence to facilitate the debate and commended the Education Committee for its 'very good and careful piece of work'.[14]

Another contempt of Parliament was highlighted by PASC when it took up the cause of the Parliamentary Ombudsman, who had previously found against the Department of Work and Pensions in its dealings with pensioners suffering from the collapse of final salary pension schemes. The government had rejected the finding of maladministration and the recommendations to recompense those affected. Arguing that the Ombudsman was correct and the government could not simply abandon people it had advised, PASC warned that the Ombudsman was a parliamentary officer and her decisions should be respected. Not to do so raised fundamental issues about the relationship between Parliament and the executive.[15]

In June 2006, the unlikely duo of Michael Howard and David Blunkett gave evidence to PASC's inquiry on 'Ministers and Civil Servants'. Blunkett outlined his frustrations with structures that did not live up to expectation or match the private sector. In contrast, Howard denied that structural reforms were panaceas. Rather, strong political leadership was required: ministers (and prime ministers) who concentrated on initiatives diverted administrative attention from the 'grind of government and the often boring business of making sure that delivery takes place'.[16]

These exchanges were part of a typically wide-ranging and busy year for PASC. In addition to investigations into the Ministerial Code, Propriety and Honours and Ethics and Standards,[17] it began inquiries into strategic thinking in government (even managing eventually to question the reluctant Lord Birt, but gaining nothing from him), the relationship between ministers and civil servants, and the administrative skills required by the service in the modern world.[18]

If PASC and the Public Accounts Committee share a concern with the fitness for purpose of government departments, the latter concentrates on the effective management of public funds. Much of its effort in 2006 sought to learn from its previous inquiries. It saw continued problems with poor policy planning, implementation, and the ability to learn from and share lessons. It exhorted public organisations to understand and consult users more regularly, provide effective redress, and motivate and reward staff. But it also acknowledged progress in some departmental operations, citing 'Job Centre Plus' as an exemplar. Even here, however, it warned that such efficiency improvements should not be at the expense of quality of service.[19]

Evidence for the validity of its concerns emerged from the Work and Pensions Committee's more recent review of activities at Job Centre Plus. While commending staff, the committee noted that substantial organisational changes in IT, staffing and financial programmes had come together with the push for Gershon efficiency savings to overwhelm organisational capacity and result in appalling levels of service in some areas. One of the Gershon tests was that service should not deteriorate as a result of greater efficiency, and, 'as far as Job Centre Plus is concerned, particularly in the summer of 2005, it failed that test and failed its customers and staff'.[20]

Sir Gus O'Donnell, the Cabinet Secretary, told a government conference in June that he aimed to improve matters by creating a 'culture of excellence' in the civil service, combining traditional values with pride, passion, pace and professionalism. A new Civil Service Code was designed to help forge this culture.[21] A month later he published the results of the first departmental capability reviews for Constitutional Affairs, the Home Office, Education and Skills, and Work and Pensions. Conducted by teams convened by the Prime Minister's Delivery Unit and assisted by the National Audit Office (NAO) and Audit Commission, the reviews assessed leadership, strategy and delivery functions. The results were not flattering. The Home Office was judged to be failing seriously in most areas. Other departments, while performing adequately in some respects, had serious weaknesses, particularly in providing effective services, resource management and service prioritisation. Colin Talbot described the results as 'truly appalling. Not one of the departments can really be described as fit for purpose on these scores.' Some weeks later the government announced that various senior officials in the departments concerned had left or been moved.[22]

The Institute of Public Policy Research (IPPR) also published its own study of Whitehall to open 'a long overdue debate of what kind of civil service is needed to be fit for purpose in the 21st century'. The report argued that the key problem lay in the service's traditional culture that made it insular and poor at strategic thinking and performance management. It was also hampered by an outdated convention of ministerial responsibility that could be remedied by either greater politicisation or a clearer distinction between 'policy' (ministerial) and 'operational' (administrative) responsibilities. The authors preferred the latter, as it would give ministers a professional, better-managed and strategic service and more support for making policy. The whole should also be reinforced by a civil service executive (led by a head of the civil service), a governing body appointed by Parliament, and a Civil Service Act.[23]

The delivery machine: creaking under pressure

The Child Support Agency has long been a beacon of administrative inadequacy. Its laudable mission has been to oblige absent parents (mainly fathers) to support their children financially. Despite repeated attempts by successive governments and chief executives, a stream of criticism from Ombudsmen, select committees, MPs, angry lone parents and their advocates, the CSA has palpably failed to realise its mission. In the summer of 2006, the National Audit Office reported that the CSA 'was never structured in a way that would enable policy to be delivered cost-effectively', while Sir David Henshaw, commissioned by the Department for Work and Pensions (DWP) to investigate the totality of child support, found that the CSA was not capable of the radical shift in culture and efficiency needed in any new child support system and consequently a new organisation was required. The DWP duly promised a more streamlined and robust replacement; the aim was to make the child support service simpler to use and administer while maximising the reduction in child poverty.[24]

Meanwhile, a new system of farm payments initiated by the European Union (EU) was causing anger and financial pain for farmers in England. The responsibility of making the new Single Farm Payments fell to the Rural Payments Agency (RPA). By the end of March 2006, by when 96 per cent should have been paid, only 27 per cent of farmers had been paid and only 15 per cent of the money had been distributed causing substantial financial distress. The Environment, Food and Rural Affairs Committee had already argued that, not only was the Department for the Environment, Food and Rural Affairs' implementation model flawed and aggravated by a bungled contract for a new computer system, but that the minister had shown 'unacceptable complacency' of the financial impact of any delay. After the payment failure and the sacking of the RPA's chief executive, the NAO severely criticised the inability to take corrective action and the mothballing of contingency plans.[25] In addition, the delay in payments has resulted in Britain incurring an EU 'disallowance' or fine of some £131 million.

Executive agencies are founded on the differentiation of policy from its administration. As the committee and NAO reports imply, such a division is often hard to sustain; indeed, may not be fit for purpose. Yet, as Simon Jenkins observed, 'it cannot be coincidence that a simple executive reform such as the new single farm payments has been achieved without trouble in Scotland and Wales but is a shambles in London'. For Jenkins, an avowed localist, the causes were the centralising tendencies of the government in general and the Prime Minister in particular: 'he has made almost all public services his responsibility and will indeed be judged on them'.[26] Certainly, an enduring problem for New Labour has been an ambiguity over governance structures and devolved power, particularly in relations with local government.

As discussed elsewhere in this volume, local government's remit, structure and finance were themselves subject to review by an inquiry, headed by Sir Michael Lyons, and a local government White Paper in the autumn. Local government began 2006 under the remit of the Office of the Deputy Prime Minister, with David Miliband as minister, and ended up under the new Department for Communities and Local Government and the stewardship of Ruth Kelly. Miliband had spent a great deal of time on his 'double devolution' agenda – a model extending devolved responsibility to local authorities and within them to neighbourhoods. Geoff Mulgan, one of its principal advocates, argues that double devolution requires local authorities to redefine themselves as centres of local leadership while engaging with neighbourhoods and communities, and therefore real devolution from central government. But before Miliband could put these ideas into practice he was moved. In her first White Paper, Kelly lightened the performance and inspections system, but was ambiguous on the devolution of powers, city-regions, finance and powers to neighbourhoods.[27]

Kelly also acknowledged the difficult task of getting other Whitehall departments to accept the benefits of greater local autonomy. She may well have had the Home Office in mind, particularly in its relations with police forces. Their historical position as an important local responsibility came under further threat following the Inspector of Constabulary's 2005 critical report on the fitness for purpose of policing structures. The then Home Secretary, Charles Clarke, responded with a programme of restructuring in England and Wales, reducing 43 police forces to as few as 17, a change justified by the requirements for fighting organised crime and terrorism in a global context. However, the proposals met with vigorous opposition from the police service, MPs, local authorities and the Treasury. With Clarke's departure the plans were shelved and later the Home Office repaid a proportion of what the forces had spent on the aborted amalgamations.[28]

By the summer, policing was the least of the Home Office's worries. Alarm bells began to ring with a series of announcements that it had lost track of increasing numbers of foreign nationals who should have been deported following release from British prisons. As the Home Affairs Committee later revealed, the problem stemmed principally from the Home Office's Immigration and Nationality Directorate (IND). Under-resourced and struggling with other targets, the lower echelons had identified the problem but not thought it serious. Ministers were therefore not alerted until March 2006.

Once ministers were alerted, the problem appeared to magnify, almost weekly. The IND later admitted to the Home Affairs Committee that it 'had not the slightest idea' how many illegal immigrants there were in the country. And for several weeks no one appeared to know either how many foreign prisoners were on the run, let alone where they were. The committee saw this as a structural and cultural weakness: 'fragmentation and lack of communication is a systemic problem not just within the IND but within the entire immigration system which ought, ideally, to work as a whole'.[29]

John Reid, unnerved by changing statistical reports and discoveries that illegal immigrants had been employed as contract cleaners in the Immigration Service's headquarters at Croydon, castigated his own department in his evidence to the Home Affairs Committee and announced two reviews into the IND and the wider operation of the Home Office. On the basis of their recommendations, he re-established the IND as an executive agency with clearer lines of accountability and responsibility, reorganised the Home Office top management, cut headquarters staff to reinvest in frontline services, subjected 250 senior Home Office officials to an assessment of their operational and delivery skills, and announced new 'contracts' between ministers and civil servants clarifying responsibilities for policy, delivery and management.[30]

Such administrative change may improve matters. But the Home Office remains a highly political department and, as Philip Johnson notes, administrative rearrangements have to be assessed in terms of their ability to handle complex and often cross-departmental problems (including foreign national prisoners). He also advised that one way of relieving pressure on staff would be 'to call a halt to the almost permanent revolution it has undergone ... with reform after reform and pressure from No. 10 to meet targets that often conflict with other priorities'.[31]

Similar observations may be made of the National Health Service. In the flack that the NHS receives in the media, it is easy to lose sight of the improvements to patient outcomes over the past few years. Waiting times for out- and in-patient procedures have shortened dramatically, mortality rates for a range of conditions have fallen, the numbers of clinical professionals have increased to improve capacity, and patients have now more (if uninformed) choice of where to subject their bodies to licensed assault. All this has been funded by very substantial real increases from the Exchequer. And yet, the dominant picture of the NHS in 2006 was financial deficit, endemic hospital-acquired infections (especially MRSA) and inequalities of access to certified therapies.

Although the press likes to regard NHS managers as responsible for all its woes, the main contributor to the financial deficit appears to be the unplanned success in treating patients more quickly. Several systemic factors seemed to aggravate matters: the new financial arrangements of payment by results (by which hospitals are incentivised by fees for the procedures they carry out), a lack of commissioning capability in the primary care trusts who hold the budgets, and a desire in strategic health authorities to secure financial balance for their acute and mental health candidates as foundation trusts. Despite (or perhaps because of) the integration of health policy functions and their delivery through the NHS within the Department of Health, under its Permanent Secretary, Nigel Crisp, health initiatives have been notably volcanic in output and contradictory in effect. It was almost inevitable that, with an unaudited deficit of about £750 million in 2005–06, Crisp should have felt compelled to take early retirement in the summer (straight into the House of Lords), while his Secretary of State, Patricia Hewitt, awash in a sea of confusion, was booed at health conferences for causing further turmoil to frontline staff through ill-thought-out and, in the end, irresolute, reforms, especially to primary care trusts.

At the end of the year, the Healthcare Commission published its annual assessments of the performance of the healthcare organisations under its jurisdiction. Replacing the star system of previous years, it awarded grades (excellent; good; fair; poor) for both quality of services and financial management. Nationally, the assessments portrayed improving quality of service but weak financial management (most organisations judged poor or fair).[32] As a consequence, most government and administrative effort was, at the end of 2006, devoted to improving financial management and restoring financial balance to the NHS as a whole. Mirroring the process that assesses candidate foundation trusts, the new generation of larger primary care trusts was subject to a regime of 'fitness for purpose' reviews of organisational, commissioning and board capacities.[33]

There is no question that the potential of such reviews to improve management system capability in the NHS is considerable. But, as with the other cases reviewed above, the interventions appear to be founded on at best an unclear evidence base (often little more than polemics from interested lobbyists) and their benefits have to be allowed to settle in before that next wave of change. Ministers in 2006 gave every impression of being policy shoppers, attracted by whim to the latest gizmo and fashion accessory, rather than using evidence to secure a lasting functional acquisition.

Conclusion

The 1979 Sale of Goods Act states that goods purchased should be of a satisfactory quality and 'fit for purpose'; this is generally interpreted to mean they should be able to perform the function for which they were designed.[34] Such guarantees empower consumers against rogue traders and shoddy goods and grant rights to seek redress in law. Much of our review thus far has chronicled the equivalent of shoddy goods of government administration. It could thus be read as a testimony of unfitness for purpose. But, are we clear what the purpose is?

In the summer of 2006, the Prime Minister gave a series of lectures on issues he believed would dominate future public and political debate. One of these set out his vision of the modern state: not 'how much government' but government for what purpose? New Labour, he argued, had 'developed the concept of the enabling state, whose job was to empower the individual.

This should support public service risk takers and open up provision to the independent and voluntary sectors.'[35] The Number 10 Strategy Unit followed with an attempt to flesh out Blair's ideas. It pointed to the desire for citizen-centred public services that were responsive, effective and of high quality, but then resorted to the usual emphasis on mechanics: pressure from above to enhance performance management and from citizens below, combined with competition and measures to increase the capacity of public servants.[36] The problem with such well-meant elaboration is that, in common with many earlier initiatives, it has failed not only to allow for the very considerable variety of different services and contexts (including political significance) but also the underlying common purpose in providing them. In its desire to press on with mechanics, it has lost touch with a sense of its fundamentals.

To its credit, the Public Management and Policy Association has sought to act restoratively. It asked a collection of practitioners and academics what they thought public management was for. The answers were, as expected, almost as varied as the contributors.[37] However, there were at least two common features. First, public management exists to serve the proactive growth of distinctly societal values that are in their essence determined through the political process. Second, these values relate to the qualities and properties of outcomes, certainly, but also, and perhaps principally, to those of processes. Thus public management organisations and practitioners exist to serve, first, the political process and its determinations and, second, its processual values such as equity, fairness, and due process. Assessments of the fitness for purpose of the organisations and personnel of government and administration need to be clear on how they are meant to contribute to these purposes.

Notes

1. Home Affairs Committee, *Fifth Report: Immigration Control*, HC 775-III, 2005–06 (evidence taken on 23 May 2006).
2. Clive Grace (ed.), *The Rethinking of Local Government: Fitness for purpose in a Year of Living Dangerously* (London: SOLACE Foundation Imprint, 2006); Audit Commission/Improvement and Development Agency (IDeA), *Fitness for Purpose in the 21st Century: Strategic Choice at the Local Level in the New Millennium*, July 2005.
3. John Cruddas and John Harris, *Fit for Purpose: A Programme for Labour Party Renewal* (London: Compass 2006); John Harris, *Guardian*, 12 October 2006.
4. The Power Commission, *Power to the People: The Report of the Power Commission: an Independent Inquiry into Britain's Democracy* (York: York Publishing, 2006).
5. See Downing Street press briefing, 2 March 2006, <www.number-10.gov.uk)>.
6. Standards and Privileges Committee, *Thirteenth Report: The Conduct of Mr John Prescott*, HC 1553, 2005–06; PASC, *Seventh Report: The Ministerial Code – The Case for Independent Investigation*, HC 1457, 2005–06.
7. Sir Hayden Phillips, *The Review of Funding of Political Parties*, Interim Assessment 19 October 2006, <www.partyfudingreview.gov.uk>; Constitutional Affairs Committee,

Investigation into Party Funding, HC 1060-i-iii, 2005–06; PASC, *Fourth Report: Propriety and Honours*, HC 1119, 2005–06.

8. *Guardian*, 9 May 2006.

9. Second Report of the Pensions Commission (Lord Turner, chair), *A New Pensions Settlement for the 21st Century* (London: The Stationery Office, November 2005); *Security in Retirement: Towards a New Pensions System*, Cm. 6841, May 2006.

10. Colin Talbot, 'Open the Books?', *Public Finance*, 29 September 2006.

11. Liaison Committee, HC 709-ii, 2005–06. Prime Minister's Speeches: 'Our Nation's Future: Criminal Justice', Bristol, 23 June; 'Public Health', Nottingham, 26 July; 'Social Exclusion', York, 5 September <www.number-10.gov.uk>.

12. *Guardian*, 29 April 2006.

13. *Higher Standards, Better Schools for All: More Choice for Parents and Pupils*, Cm. 6677, October 2005; Education and Skills Committee, *First Report: the Schools White Paper – Higher Standards, Better Schools for All*, HC 633, 2005–06; *The Government's Response to the House of Commons Education and Skills Committee First Report: The Schools White Paper*, Cm. 6747, February 2006.

14. Liaison Committee, HC 709-i, 2005–06.

15. PASC, *Sixth Report: The Ombudsman in Question – The Ombudsman's Report on Pensions and its Constitutional Implications*, HC 1081, 2005–06.

16. PASC, *Politics and Administration: Ministers and Civil Servants*, HC 660-vi, 2005–06.

17. See HC 1457, 1119 and 884-i-viii, 2005–06.

18. PASC, *Governing the Future* (evidence of Lord Birt, 16 March 2006), HC 756-iii, 2005–06; *Politics and Administration: Ministers and Civil Servants*, HC 660, 2005–06; *Skills for Government*, HC 1647, 2005–06.

19. Public Accounts Committee, *Seventeenth Report: Achieving Value for Money in the Delivery of Public Services*, HC 742, 2005–06; *Sixty-third Report: Delivering High Quality Public Services for All*, HC 1530, 2005–06; *Fifty-fifth Report: Progress in Improving Government Efficiency*, HC 978, 2005–06.

20. Work and Pensions Committee, *Second Report: The Efficiency Savings Programme at Job Centre Plus*, HC 834, 2005–06.

21. Sir Gus O'Donnell, 'Our 21st Century Civil Service – Creating a Culture of Excellence', speech to Public Service Reform conference, 6 June 2006; *Civil Service Code* published 6 June 2006 (both available on <www.civilservice.gov.uk>).

22. Cabinet Office, *Capability Reviews: The Findings of the First Four Reviews*, July 2006; Colin Talbot, 'Who's the Weakest Link Now?', *Public Finance*, 4 August 2006.

23. Guy Lodge and Ben Rogers, *Whitehall's Black Box: Accountability and Performance in the Senior Civil Service* (London: IPPR, August 2006); and 'Need to Get Out More', *Public Finance*, 18 August 2006; PASC, *Politics and Administration: Ministers and Civil Servants*, HC 660-vi, 2005–06.

24. National Audit Office, *The Child Support Agency – Implementation of Child Support Reforms*, HC 1174, 2005–06; Sir David Henshaw, *Recovering Child Support: Routes to Responsibility* (report to the Secretary of State for Work and Pensions), Cm. 6894, July 2006; *A Fresh Start: Child Support Redesign – The Government's Response to Sir David Henshaw*, Cm. 6895, July 2006.

25. Environment, Food and Rural Affairs Committee, *Fifth Report: The Rural Payments Agency – Interim Report*, HC 840, 2005–06; Environment, Food and Rural Affairs Committee, *The Rural Payments Agency*, HC 1071-i-iv, 2005–06; National Audit Office, *Department for Environment, Food and Rural Affairs and the Rural Payments*

Agency: The Delays in Administering the 2005 Single Payment Scheme in England, HC 1631, 2005–06.

26. Guardian, 3 May 2006.

27. The Lyons Inquiry into Local Government: Consultation Paper and Interim Report, December 2006; National Prosperity, Local Choice and Civic Engagement: A New Partnership Between Central and Local Government for the 21st Century, May 2006 (available on <www.lyonsinquiry.org.uk>); Geoff Mulgan and Fran Bury (eds), Double Devolution: The Renewal of Local Government (London: Smith Institute (in association with the Young Foundation), 2006); Ruth Kelly, 'Check against delivery', speech to the Local Government Association Conference, 5 July 2006 <www.communities.gov.uk>; Strong and Prosperous Communities: The Local Government White Paper, Cm. 6939-I, October 2006.

28. Dennis O'Connor, HM Inspector of Constabulary, Closing the Gap: A Review of 'Fitness for Purpose' of the Current Structure of Policing in England and Wales, Home Office, September 2005.

29. Home Affairs Committee, Fifth Report: Immigration Control, HC 775, 2005–06, para. 548.

30. From Improvement to Transformation: An Action Plan to Reform the Home Office so it Meets Public Expectations and Delivers its Core Purpose of Protecting the Public, Home Office, July 2006.

31. Philip Johnson, 'A Game of Two Halves', Public Finance, 23 June 2006.

32. Healthcare Commission, Results of Annual Healthcheck, 2005–06, October 2006.

33. Department of Health, PCT Fitness for Purpose Programme, October 2006.

34. Department of Trade and Industry, Sale of Goods Factsheet (URN No. 05/1730).

35. Prime Minister's speech on 'Healthy Living', Nottingham, 26 July 2006 <www.number-10.gov.uk>.

36. Prime Minister's Strategy Office, The UK Government's Approach to Public Service Reform: A Discussion Paper, Cabinet Office, June 2006.

37. Public Management and Policy Association, What is Public Management For?, August 2006.

7
Ombudsmen and Tribunals: A Year of Change, Challenge and Opportunity

Philip Giddings

For public service complaint-handling in the UK, 2006 was a significant year: a new tribunals service launched and major legislation for a new statutory framework; the introduction of the public sector Ombudsman in Wales; statutory provision for a military complaints commissioner; and some controversial cases for the Parliamentary Ombudsman, leading to the suggestion that the constitutional position of that office might be under threat. In this chapter we shall look first at those cases and then at the evolving work of other UK public sector Ombudsman offices before addressing the new set-up for the military and the developments in the tribunals world.

The Parliamentary and Health Service Ombudsman: a year of challenge

In 2006, the four difficult cases from 2005 (and before) rumbled on and contributed to the debate on the government's attitude to the work of the Parliamentary and Health Service Ombudsman (PHSO) work. We will look first at the case in which the Ombudsman was clearly vindicated.

A debt of honour

In July 2005, the Parliamentary Ombudsman, Ann Abraham, published a special report, *A Debt of Honour*, highly critical of the Ministry of Defence's (MOD's) handling of the development of an ex gratia scheme for British civilians interned by the Japanese during the Second World War. As the government resisted the Ombudsman's recommendations, the Commons Public Administration Select Committee (PASC) held an inquiry. Its report in January 2006 fully endorsed the Ombudsman's criticisms and recommendations[1] and recommended that the government conduct a full and proper review and reconsider the case of those denied payments because they had no blood link to the UK. In a statement to the House on 28 March, Veterans Minister Don Touhig admitted that the government review had revealed confusion and inconsistency in the administration of the compensation scheme, and announced that the scheme would be widened by changing the criteria for eligibility and that the 'shortcomings' in the administration of the scheme would be the subject of a separate independent review.[2] In June, he announced a new 20-year residence criterion for the Far East prisoner of war scheme, thus substantially meeting the Ombudsman's original recommendation.[3] The following month, David Watkins, a retired civil servant from the Northern Ireland Office who conducted the independent review, produced a devastating critique of the way the scheme had been developed and administered. He listed a catalogue of shortcomings and failings due largely to haste and 'insufficient administrative thoroughness and research'.[4] In a Written Statement on 19 July, the new Veterans Minister, Tom Watson, announced the government's acceptance of the overall thrust of the Watkins Report's recommendations, describing the 'errors in administering the scheme' as 'deeply regrettable'.[5]

The whole saga illustrated both the strengths and the weakness of the Parliamentary Ombudsman system in the UK. In the end, with the support of the select committee, the serious failures in the MoD had been exposed and the victims of maladministration and injustice achieved a remedy. But that 'success' was a long time coming because, even with the aid of the Ombudsman investigation and two judicial reviews, the ministry's defensiveness and intransigence blocked the remedial action so obviously required. It is not clear why the MoD was so unwilling to hold its hand up straight away to the shortcomings revealed by the Ombudsman, but the suspicion must be that senior management in government departments no longer give to the Ombudsman's investigations the attention they once did. Evidently, Watkins found that senior management's attention was elsewhere. His findings clearly vindicated the Ombudsman as well as the complainants.

Tax credits

The outcome in the tax credits was not so clear. Following exchanges with the government and HM Revenue & Customs over her special report on the new tax credits system, Ann Abraham criticised the government for 'picking and choosing' which of her recommendations it wanted to accept.[6] PASC gave Ann Abraham its full support in its January 2006 report, expressing deep concern about the government's handling of the scheme and particularly that a government department was 'presuming to define what constitutes maladministration'. The committee welcomed the Revenue's willingness to look again at the Ombudsman's recommendation to introduce a pause before starting recovery of overpayments and undertook to monitor the Revenue's progress in implementation – noting that the Treasury Sub-Committee was intending to inquire into the administration of tax credits.[7]

In May, PASC published the government's formal response to its January report, and correspondence with the chairman of HM Revenue & Customs.[8] Again the 'picking and choosing' aspect of the response was apparent and reinforced the Ombudsman's anxieties at the government's attitude to her office, which surfaced again in her Annual Report. The outcome of the case might be characterised as a score draw, with the possibility of a replay not ruled out.

Equitable Life

With Equitable Life we have had both replays[9] and repeatedly extended extra time. In October 2005, Ann Abraham had told PASC that she hoped to publish her already delayed second report before the Easter adjournment in 2006 – but she had to write to MPs twice more, in February and October 2006, further deferring the date. At the time of writing, it is expected that she will send her draft report to government in January 2007, so the earliest the final report could be published is May of that year. These repeated postponements indicate how complex assessing prudential regulation in the financial services sector is.

Occupational pensions

Complexity and delay were also features of another high-profile case during 2006 – occupational pensions. In March, the Ombudsman published a rare section 10(3) report, highly critical of the Department for Work and Pensions (DWP), which had rejected both her findings and her recommendations.[10] Her investigation had uncovered evidence of real suffering, distress and uncertainty about the future amongst pension scheme members and their families who had relied on government information when making choices about future pension provision. The official information provided was 'sometimes inaccurate, often incomplete, largely inconsistent and therefore potentially misleading'.[11] The Ombudsman had recommended that the government should consider making arrangements for the restoration of core pension and non-core benefits to the categories of scheme members covered by her report, but the government had responded that it was not minded either to accept her findings of maladministration or to implement her recommendations, except one relating to the process of winding-up schemes. PASC chairman Tony Wright noted with great concern that this was the second time in a year that the Ombudsman had used her powers to report to Parliament that the government had caused maladministration but did not intend to remedy it.[12]

The Ombudsman report was raised at Prime Minister's Questions on the day of publication,[13] and the following day, in a Commons statement, Secretary of State John Hutton sought to set out the reasons why, 'after very careful consideration, the government cannot accept any of her findings of maladministration' and were rejecting all but one of her recommendations.[14] The vigorous questioning which followed indicated that MPs on both sides were deeply uneasy about the government's response, and this was reflected in some Early Day Motions put down the following week.

When PASC began its hearings on the issue on 2 May 2006, Ann Abraham robustly defended her position and took issue with the government's presumption in rejecting her findings of maladministration.[15] In June, the government's full response to her report[16] reiterated that it could not agree with her findings and refused to accept her recommendations because it was not right to use taxpayers' money – 'some £15 billion in cash terms over 60 years' – to compensate people for losses arising from risks inherent in most, if not all, financial and investment decisions.[17]

The issues continued to be explored by PASC, which took evidence from the Pensions Action Group and the Secretary of State.[18] In a further memorandum to the Committee, Ann Abraham argued that, by appearing to draw no distinction between rejecting her findings and rejecting her recommendations for redress, the government's response represented 'a new and significant departure from historical precedent and constitutional practice' which had serious implications for the position of the Ombudsman's office.[19] The issues were aired again in a speech by the Ombudsman to a Constitution Unit seminar on 4 December 2006 and in a Commons debate on PASC's report a few days later.[20]

PASC's report at the end of July set the issue in the wider context of the government's responses to other reports, including *A Debt of Honour*. PASC was highly critical of the government's position, concluding that the Ombudsman was correct and the government far too ready to question the Ombudsman's findings, with the result that there was now a threat to the Ombudsman's constitutional position. As Tony Wright put it in his press statement, 'This was clearly maladministration and the Ombudsman was right to say so ... If government became accustomed simply to reject the Ombudsman's findings ... it would raise fundamental constitutional issues.'[21]

In response, the government sought to find ways of beefing up the financial assistance scheme[22] but in October the position became more complicated when the High Court agreed to allow to proceed a case brought by the Pensions Action Group seeking judicial review of the government's refusal to implement the Ombudsman's recommendations. In early November, the DWP published its formal response to PASC's further report, again rejecting the Ombudsman's findings and recommendations, but proposing further changes to the assistance scheme to mitigate the severity of some people's losses. On 6 November, there was a mass rally at Westminster to protest at the government's refusal to compensate victims of pension schemes that collapsed when employers went out of business. This has all the appearance of an issue on which it will be very difficult to obtain closure.

Ombudsman under threat?

Is there a threat to the constitutional position of the Parliamentary Ombudsman? It is understandable that Ann Abraham should express concern about the government's attitude to her office with two high-profile rejections of her findings and recommendations within so short a period. However, while rare, these are not unprecedented. What matters is the extent to which MPs generally, and specifically members of PASC, are willing to back the Ombudsman against the government. As long as the issues are essentially matters of administrative rather than policy or political judgement, then the Ombudsman has a good chance of success. (See Table 7.1.)

In most cases it is officials, not ministers, who deal with the Ombudsman and it may be here that attention is needed to the PHSO's relationship with 'government'. Cabinet Secretary Gus O'Donnell told PASC in May that he had discussed with Ann Abraham 'how we could improve relations between the Civil Service and the Ombudsman'. From that conversation emerged the designation of 'a permanent secretary champion who could help departments when they are liaising with the Ombudsman'. [23] The chosen champion, Paul Gray, is from HM Revenue & Customs, PHSO's principal Whitehall customer (see Table 7.1(b)), so he should have plenty of experience to draw on.

A crucial feature of any Ombudsman system is the underpinning of the impartiality of the office by the arrangements for appointment and funding. Until 2004–05, the PHSO's budget was sanctioned by the Treasury and approved by Parliament on an annual basis. The Ombudsman and the Treasury have agreed that from 2005–06 there will be a three-year funding cycle aligned with the PHSO's newly introduced strategic plan. [24] This arrangement, endorsed by Parliament, should enable more effective planning of the use of resources in what is a multi-million pound operation with several hundred staff (see Table 7.1(d)). The PHSO's budget for 2006–07 is £22.9 million, and that will rise to £24 million in 2007–08. [25]

Budgets need to be related to workload. The workload of the PHSO office can be viewed in a number of ways. New cases accepted for investigation, at 3,162, were 25 per cent down on 2004–05 but the number of cases reported on (3,606) were up 25 per cent (see Table 7.1(a)). In 2005–06 (previous years are not comparable because of changed reporting procedures), the office received over 21,000 enquiries and requests for information. The service standards for time taken to complete investigations were not met in 2005–06 because of a casework backlog at the beginning of the year and delays caused by the implementation of a 'new business approach'. [26]

An important initiative launched by Ann Abraham in October 2006 was a consultation document on 'Principles of Good Administration'. [27] These 'are not intended to be used as a checklist nor will they be the only means by which the Ombudsman will assess and determine individual cases ... Failure to observe a single principle will not automatically constitute maladministration. We will apply a test of reasonableness, not a test of perfection.'

Table 7.1 The work of the Parliamentary and Health Service Ombudsman, 2004–06

(a) PHSO cases accepted and concluded, 2004–06

Category	No. accepted for investigation		No. reported on in the year	
	2005–06	2004–05	2005–06	2004–05
Parliamentary	1,853	1,715	1,715	–
Health	1,309	1,891	1,891	–
Total	3,162	4,189	3,606	2,886

(b) Most Parliamentary Ombudsman complaints by body, 2005–06

Body	No. accepted for investigation	No. reported on in the year	Upheld in full or part (%)
HM Revenue & Customs – tax credits	404	299	90
HM Revenue & Customs – other	144	114	30
Job Centre Plus	263	221	52
Child Support Agency	209	180	83
Pension Service	97	111	45
Immigration & Nationality Directorate	95	75	88

(c) PHSO outcome of complaints investigated, 2005–06

	% Upheld in full	% Upheld in part	% Not upheld
Parliamentary	31	23	46
Health – continuing care	51	41	8
Health – other	27	29	44
Health – total	41	36	23
PHSO – total	37	30	33

(d) PHSO finance and staffing,[a] 2004–06

	Numbers	
	2005–06	2004–05
Financial resources used	£22.6m	£19.5m
Parliamentary Ombudsman staff	88	81
Health Ombudsman staff	115	111
Corporate management group staff	77	66
Total PHSO staff	280	258

[a] Average no. of full-time equivalent (FTE) persons employed.

Sources: PHSO Annual Reports and Resource Accounts, 2005–06 (HC 163 & 1433, 2005–06) and 2004–05 (HC 348 & 347, 2004–05).

Apart from the changes set out above, the Ombudsman continues to wait for the government to act on the proposals for bringing the English public sector Ombudsman schemes into a more integrated system. A consultation in 2005 on a proposed Regulatory Reform Order to facilitate joint working has, at the time of writing, still to bear legislative fruit. As we shall see below, in both Scotland and Wales, integrated public sector Ombudsman schemes have been established. For the time being, England and the UK (not the same!) must wait.

The Local Government Ombudsman

Now that the devolved assemblies have set up unified public sector Ombudsman offices, only England has a specific Local Government Ombudsman (LGO) office – and that is working ever more closely with the Parliamentary Ombudsman. The offices, now co-located in Millbank Tower in London, are seeking to develop a single point of reference for complainants. Legislation is required to enable them to carry out joint investigations (though parallel ones are possible, as with the *Balchin* case)[28] and the offices are also planning to issue joint guidance and some joint reports.

The bulk of the LGO's work remains dealing with complaints. (See Table 7.2.) As Table 7.2(a) shows, the volume of complaints remains around 18,600 but the subject matter is changing, with the recent increase in complaints about education, particularly school admissions, balanced by a declining proportion of housing benefit cases (see Table 7.2(b)). In common with most Ombudsman offices worldwide, many of the complaints made to the LGO cannot be taken up – in 2005–06, nearly 40 per cent were either outside jurisdiction or premature (see Table 7.2(c) and (d)). Of the 60 per cent which were taken up, the outcome of about a quarter of them was a 'local settlement'. But in a further 1 per cent of cases where that was not possible, the Ombudsman investigated, found 'injustice in consequence of malad-ministration'[29] and recommended a remedy which the local authority then accepted. So, in 27 per cent of the complaints determined in 2005–06 the Ombudsman achieved a remedy for citizens from their local authority: either an apology, a review of policy procedures or some specific action (see Table 7.2(d)). Sometimes, especially where it is too late to reverse the consequences of a decision, the remedy takes the form of a financial payment: in 2005–06, the LGO recommended payments totalling £1.67 million[30] arising from just under 3,000 cases.

The LGO continues to seek the necessary legislative changes to implement the Collcutt Review's proposals made six years ago for more integrated public service Ombudsman provision in England.[31] As mentioned above, reforms along those lines have already been introduced in Scotland and Wales, but to date the UK government has not been willing to find time in its legislative programme to carry through the required changes in the governing

Table 7.2 The work of the English Local Government Ombudsman, 2003–06

(a) Volume of complaints

	2005–06	2004–05	2003–04
No. complaints received	18,626	18,698	18,982
No. complaints decided	18,321	18,487	18,658

(b) Complaints received by category

Category	2005–06	% 2004–05	2003–04
Housing benefit	6	8	10
Housing – other	24	24	25
Planning	24	23	21
Highways	10	10	9
Education	9	7	8
Social services	8	8	7
Local taxation	5	6	6
Environmental health	4	4	4
Other	10	10	10

(c) Outcome of complaints

Outcome	2005–06	% 2004–05	2003–04
Local settlements[a]	25.9	25.3	27.5
Maladministration causing injustice[a]	1.1	0.15	1.5
Maladministration, no injustice found[a]	0.1	0.002	0.1
No maladministration*	0.0	0.0	0.2
No evidence of maladministration[a]	48.6	47.5	46.5
Discretion exercised not to pursue[a]	24.3	25.4	24.2
Outside jurisdiction[b]	12.9	13.0	12.5
Premature complaints[b]	27.0	25.5	24.7

[a] Percentage of total decided, excluding premature complaints and those outside jurisdiction.
[b] Percentage of all complaints decided.

(d) Type of remedy of settlement obtained

Remedy/settlement	2005–06	No. 2004–05	2003–04
Apology	744	809	n.a.
Action taken	1,636	1,618	n.a.
Review of policy or procedures	282	244	n.a.
Payment made	1,660	1,948	1,842

(e) Finance and staffing

	2005–06	2004–05	2003–04
Annual expenditure	£11.85m	£11.06m	£11.08m
Number of staff (average FTE)	197.0	201.7	202.6
Average output per investigator	131.2	140.5	151.3
Average cost per complaint	£640	£592	£583

Sources: LGO Annual Reports.

statutes. However, in the October 2006 White Paper on local government, the government did commit to 'modernise and clarify the role and working practices of the [local government] Ombudsman'.[32] The question is when? Meanwhile, but one suspects with increasing frustration, the LGO is seeking other ways of enhancing co-operation with the PHSO in order to provide a more accessible service for users of public services. The LGO's Corporate Plan[33] outlined its plans for a new Access and Advice Centre based in Coventry which will contribute to this. The LGO currently employs about 200 staff and spends just under £12 million a year (see Table 7.2(e)).

The Prisons and Probation Ombudsman

Another Ombudsman service awaiting government legislative action is the Prisons and Probation Ombudsman (PPO). Currently this is a non-statutory scheme, established under the administrative authority of the Home Secretary, dealing with a small but growing caseload (see Table 7.3). Expressing his disappointment that once again the legislation to place the PPO on a statutory basis with appropriate powers had been postponed, the Ombudsman, Stephen Shaw, commented: 'I am beginning to feel like Billy Bunter and his postal order: continually promising that the my legislation will turn up when somehow it never does.'[34] Although for most of the time its practical effect is negligible, 'just occasionally the absence of statutory powers really does make a difference: there have regrettably been a number of occasions during fatal incident investigations when doctors have declined to submit for interview'. Moreover, a statutory basis gives greater weight to the claim that the PPO is genuinely independent of the Home Office and the Prisons and Probation Services – a feature which is necessary to meet the requirements of Article 2 of the European Convention on Human Rights.

The Public Service Ombudsman for Wales

On 1 April 2006, a unified public service Ombudsman service came into being in Wales. The Public Service Ombudsman for Wales (PSOW) brought together the previously separate local government, health, Welsh administration and social housing complaints functions. Adam Peat's first Annual Report as the new 'unified Ombudsman', in June 2006, necessarily dealt mostly with the work of the separate schemes, the total caseload of which was 1,915 (see Table 7.4(a)). In that period, there had been a marked increase in caseload – over 40 per cent. Although 70 per cent of cases were dealt with within six months, there were in his view too many cases – around 10 per cent – which took more than a year.

In his work as Local Government Ombudsman for Wales, Peat noted that there had been widespread problems with implementation of the

Table 7.3 The Prisons and Probation Ombudsman, 2003–06

(a) Complaints received

Service	2005–06	2004–05	2003–04
Prisons Service	4,159	4,076	3,527
Eligible complaints	40%	41%	46%
Probation Service	307	309	282
Eligible complaints	11%	13%	10%
Total	4,466	4,385	3,809

(b) Complaints investigated

| Service | | No. | |
	2005–06	2004–05	2003–04
Prisons Service	1,469	1,582	1,501
Probation Service	38	19	28
Total	1,507	1,601	1,529

(c) Deaths reported

| | | No. | |
	2005–06	2004–05	2003–04
Total	197	227	n.a.
Eligible for investigation	193	224	n.a.
Cause found natural	94	107	88
Cause found self-inflicted	83	94	93

(d) Finance and staffing

	2005–06	2004–05	2003–04
Overall cost	£5.73m	£3.90m	£2.59m
– of which staffing	£3.21m	£2.27m	£1.49m
Staff numbers	86	71	53

Source: PPO Annual Reports.

Homelessness Act 2002 which, in February 2006, led him to issue the first ever Special Report by the Welsh Local Ombudsman. Addressed to all 22 county councils, the report provided guidance on how to operate the Act. Later in the year, he issued a second Special Report jointly with the English Local Government Ombudsman on the troublesome topic of memorial safety in local authority cemeteries.[35]

Another first recorded by Peat in 2006 was a Further Report on a complaint to a council which had refused to implement the recommendations contained in the Ombudsman's first report. In December 2005, Conwy County Council

Table 7.4   The Public Service Ombudsman for Wales, 2004–06

(a)   Caseload, 2004–06

Category	No. 2005–06	No. 2004–05
Brought forward	477	308
Local government complaints	904	676
Local government allegations	281	175
Health	180	159
Welsh Administration	45	42
Social housing	28	–
Total	1,915	1,360

(b)   Outcomes, 2005–06

Outcome	%	No.
Outside jurisdiction	23	287
Premature	17	213
Insufficiently serious	3	41
Discontinued	39	494
Early settlement at PSOW's suggestion	3	36
Voluntary settlement (after PSOW investigation)	9	110
Report issued – complaint not upheld	1	18
Report issued – complaint upheld	4	55

(c)   Local government complaints
(i)   Complaints against county council by category, 2005–06

Category	%
Planning and budget control	31
Housing	23
Social services	10
Highways	7
Education	6
Environmental health	6
Finance	6
Other	5
Land and property	4
Legal and administration	2

(ii)   Complaints by type of local authority, 2005–06

Type of council	No.
County/county borough councils	136 (of which 66 = decision not to investigate)
Community and town councils	155 (of which 84 = decision not to investigate)
National parks and police authorities	8 (of which 4 = decision not to investigate)
Total	299 (of which 154 = decision not to investigate)

(d) Health service complaints
(i) Complaints by category, 2005–06

Category	%
Family health services	30
Hospitals	30
Continuing care	20
Ambulance	1
Other health services	19

(ii) Outcomes, 2005–06

Outcome	Local health boards (no.)	NHS trusts (no.)	GP and other (no.)	Total no.	%
Out of jurisdiction	2	8	3	13	5
Premature	10	36	10	56	21
Discontinued	15	23	7	45	17
Early settlement	1	1	1	3	1
Settlement after investigation	16	8	0	24	9
Report – complaint not upheld	10	3	0	13	5
Report – complaint upheld	11	16	5	32	12
Carried forward	23	44	12	79	30
Total	88	139	38	265	100

(e) PSOW finance and staffing

Year	Expenditure	Staff no.
2003–04	£1.73m	27
2004–05	£1.79m	29
2005–06	£2.29m	34

Sources: PSOW Annual Reports.

refused to accept his recommendations in a homelessness case, leading him to set out his recommendations again in a Further, Special Report issued in February 2006. On this second occasion, the council resolved to agree with the Ombudsman.[36]

Under the Local Government Act 2002, the Local Ombudsman for Wales has responsibility for investigating cases of alleged misconduct by a member of a local government body.[37] In 2005–06, Peat found evidence of misconduct in eight cases, in contrast with none the previous year (for an analysis of misconduct complaints, see Table 7.4(c)(ii)). These misconduct cases, in the Ombudsman's opinion, give rise to too many trivial cases. A handful of cases come from a very small number of councils in what appear to be 'tit for tat' campaigns. He found it necessary to issue a warning to all members of two councils about making vexatious allegations – itself a breach of the Code of Conduct.[38]

The caseload of the Welsh Administration Ombudsman in the final year of the office was again low – only 45 cases, with agriculture, planning and health/social care being the main areas of complaint. Similarly with the Health Service Commissioner for Wales cases: 27 of the complaints investigated were upheld, and 13 were not. As elsewhere, complaints about continuing care provision were a major factor, accounting for one-fifth of the Commissioner's caseload (see Tables 7.4(c) and (d)).

With the transition to a unified public service Ombudsman office completed, we shall be able to see what effect, if any, the new format has upon the size and shape of the caseload. It is also too early to take a view on cost-effectiveness. The combined office has a budget of £2.3 million and employs 34 staff.

The Scottish Public Service Ombudsman

In the words of Professor Alice Brown the current Ombudsman, the Scottish Public Service Ombudsman (SPSO) has 'a unique perspective on the delivery of public services'.[39] Since October 2005, its remit, which already covered local government, the health service, social housing and the departments and agencies of the Scottish Executive has included higher and further education institutions.

In her report for 2005–06, Alice Brown highlighted a sharp increase in awareness of the SPSO (99 per cent more enquiries and 56 per cent more complaints than the previous year). In May 2006, the office had announced improved access arrangements, with the launch of freephone numbers for complainants and a revamped website. The latter, reflecting the 'one-stop shop' concept underpinning the concept of a public service Ombudsman, includes a 'Complaint Agency Finder' facility. These additional facilities can be expected to result in a further increase in the SPSO's caseload next year. (See Table 7.5.)

Following local government (54 per cent), the health service (28 per cent) is the next largest source of complaints to the SPSO, with – interestingly – the Scottish Executive and the devolved administration at 7 per cent, lower even than social housing. (see Table 7.5(b)). NHS clinical treatment was the highest subject of complaint in 2005–06, followed by housing repairs and maintenance, and local authority handling of planning applications – not dissimilar from the pattern in England. The pattern of complaints is relatively even across different parts of Scotland: in 2005–06 the Highlands and Islands had the highest propensity to complain adjusted for population, followed by Lothian, and the West of Scotland.[40]

As a result of the introduction of a new investigation and reporting system, the SPSO lays reports before Parliament in most months. The first compendium of reports was laid in December 2005. Each is accompanied by a commentary

Table 7.5 The Scottish Public Service Ombudsman, 2003–06

(a) Caseload, 2003–06

Year	No. complaints received	Annual increase (%)
2003–04	1,293	–
2004–05	1,387	7
2005–06	1,724	24

(b) Analysis of complaints received, 2004–06

Category	No. 2005–06	2004–05
Local authorities	931	925
Health Service	477	239
Social housing	145	131
Scottish Executive	127	89
Further education/higher education (FE/HE) institutions	48	n.a.
Other or outside jurisdiction	17	3

(c) Outcomes, 2005–06

Category	No. NHS	Housing	Executive	FE/HE
Withdrawn	29	8	3	3
Outside jurisdiction	30	13	20	8
Premature	71	68	32	2
Referred back	6	n.a.	n.a.	n.a.
Discontinued	54	10	22	–
Settled without investigation	4	10	3	–
Fully or partly upheld	20	1	4	–
Not upheld	20	4	2	–
Total	242	114	86	8

(d) Finance and staffing

Year	Expenditure	Staff no.
2003–04	£10.49m	31.5
2004–05	£11.06m	34.4
2005–06	£11.85m	39.3

Sources: SPSO Annual Reports and Accounts; Finance Committee, Scottish Parliament, Paper 631, September 2006.

in which the Ombudsman highlights a main theme – in September 2006, for example, it was on health services. Overall, in that month the Ombudsman laid before Parliament a total of 23 cases: 13 health, seven local government, two housing and one Scottish Executive.

As with all Ombudsman schemes, only a small proportion of the SPSO's cases result in a full investigation and finding in favour of the complainant (see Table 7.5(c)). And when the complainant is vindicated by the Ombudsman's findings, it is not always clear what would be the most appropriate remedy. In 2005, Brown called for legislation to allow public bodies to make an apology when a mistake has been made without that apology being treated as an admission of liability or negligence. She has continued to press this proposal and has commissioned research on the impact of such legislation in Australia since its adoption in 2002.

Whether her advocacy will bear legislative fruit in Scotland or the UK remains to be seen. For the moment, the Scottish Parliament seems more interested in halting the growth of commissions and oversight bodies since devolution. In September 2006, its Finance Committee published a report into accountability and governance of commissions and scrutiny bodies with a view to encouraging a more coherent and cheaper system.[41] The SPSO's expenditure in 2005–06 was £11.85 million and it employed 39 staff (see Table 7.5(d)). The SPSO gave evidence to the two Justice Committees which were considering bills to establish a Scottish Commissioner for Human Rights and an Independent Police Complaints Commissioner, arguing that a case might be made to include these functions in the 'one-stop shop' which the SPSO was originally conceived to provide.

A Military Ombudsman?

A very significant development during 2006 was legislative provision for a Service Complaints Commissioner to deal with complaints from members of the armed services or their families. The issue of transparency and independence in the handling of such complaints has been the subject of exchanges between the Commons Defence Committee and the government since 2004.[42] It was given further impetus in March 2006 by the report of the Deepcut Review, in which Nicholas Blake QC argued that 'it will difficult for the Armed Forces to satisfy the public that they have nothing to hide in the running of their discipline and complaints system if there is a perception of unwillingness to accept meaningful independent oversight, which is increasingly seen as a necessary counterweight to the powers and prerogatives of military life'. He concluded that the government's proposals in the Armed Forces Bill did not go far enough to ensure independent supervision and review, and recommended the appointment of 'a Commissioner of Military Complaints (the Armed Forces Ombudsman) who should be a person independent of the three Services as an essential step in improving confidence, transparency and justice'.[43]

In response to Blake's recommendations, the government revised its proposals,[44] and provision for a Service Complaints Commissioner and a related system of service complaint panels was made in the Armed Forces Act 2006.[45] The Act prescribes[46] that the Commissioner is to be an independent person (a member of neither the armed forces nor the civil service, and not to be regarded as a servant or agent of the Crown) appointed by the Secretary of State. The Commissioner is required[47] to produce an annual report to the Secretary of State on the 'efficiency, effectiveness and fairness' with which the system for dealing with service complaints has operated, how he has exercised his functions in respect of complaints made to him, and any other matters he considers appropriate. The Secretary of State is required to lay the Commissioner's report before Parliament, but may exclude from it any material publication of which he considers would be against the interests of national security or might jeopardise the safety of any person.

A Service Complaints Commissioner of this kind is a step towards a British military Ombudsman, such as exists in Germany, Israel, Norway, Australia and Canada.[48] Until the regulations are made, a Commissioner appointed and an annual report or two issued, it will not be clear how independent and effective this new system will be. The debates in Parliament revealed the tension between two sets of deep concerns: those about maintaining the integrity of military discipline and the chain of command and those about the vulnerability of individuals, particularly young recruits and trainees, to injustice and abuse of their rights in closed systems such as military establishments.[49] As the Minister of State, Adam Ingram, acknowledged in his Commons statement in June, the Deepcut Review report highlighted the need for deeper reform, especially the need for independent assurance and oversight. Future events will show whether the provisions of the 2006 Act will meet that requirement.

Tribunals

In the view of Lord Newton of Braintree in his preface to the Council on Tribunals Annual Report, 2006 was 'perhaps the most significant year for the tribunals world since 1958, when the Council itself was set up'.[50] The main reason for this judgement was the launch, in April, of the new Tribunals Service (TS) by the Lord Chancellor, Lord Falconer, in his capacity as Secretary of State for Constitutional Affairs. This reform has consistently had strong support from the Council of Tribunals, with Lord Newton himself serving as a member of the Programme Board overseeing the setting up of the TS, and continuing to serve on its Management Board.

The new service brought together 21 tribunals from across government departments into a single organisation.[51] More than half a million people are users of these tribunals. Early in 2007, two new tribunals will be implemented within the Tribunals Development Group: the Gambling Appeals Tribunal, to hear appeals against decisions of the Gambling Commission under the Gambling Act 2005; and the Claims Management Services Tribunal, to hear appeals from the regulator established by the Compensation Act 2006.

Since April 2006, the TS has been an executive agency of the Department for Constitutional Affairs (DCA). At the same time as its launch, Lord Falconer announced key performance targets for seven tribunals, including those dealing with employment and employment appeals, asylum and immigration, criminal injuries compensation, and mental health review cases,[52] and the DCA published on its website a framework document for the TS, setting out its purpose and accountabilities, and a business plan, setting out its key priorities and objectives for the coming year.[53]

A closely linked development was the publication in July 2006 of the draft Tribunals, Courts and Enforcement Bill intended to provide a new statutory framework for the tribunals system in line with the 2004 White Paper.[54] It will bring the tribunal judiciary together under a Senior President and replace the Council on Tribunals with an Administrative Justice and Tribunals Council with a broader remit.[55] The consultation period ended in September 2006 and the bill itself received its second reading in the Lords on 29 November 2006.

The citizen and the administration

Complaint-handling bodies like Ombudsman offices and tribunals operate at two levels: the systemic and the individual cases. The UK government is currently pursuing a public service reform agenda emphasising choice, diversity and transparency, on the one hand, and the (longer-standing) values of efficiency and effectiveness, on the other. As well as being the agents of that agenda in their dealings with service-delivery agencies, complaint-handling bodies also have to show that they are responding to it when accounting to Parliament, the public and the core executive. In 2006, we have seen examples of both phenomena in the world of the Ombudsman and the newly emerging tribunals system. Change is challenging, and challenges present both opportunities and threats.

Notes

1. PASC, *First Report: A Debt of Honour*, HC 735, 2005–06.
2. HC Debs, 444, 28 March 2006, cc. 681–3.
3. HC Debs, 448, 26 June 2006, cc. 9–10.
4. David Watkins, *The Ex-Gratia Payment Scheme for Former Far East Prisoners of War and Civilian Internees: Investigation into Civilian Eligibility Criteria*, Ministry of Defence, 7 July 2006.
5. HC Debs, 449, 19 July 2006, cc. 26–7WS.

6. See Third Report of the Parliamentary Ombudsman, *Tax Credits: Putting Things Right*, HC 124, 2005–06; Prime Minister's Questions the following day, HC Debs, 447, 22 June 2005, c. 791; PASC, *Minutes of Evidence*, HC 577-i, 2005–06, especially QQ. 10 and 51.

7. PASC, *Second Report: Tax Credits: putting things right*, HC 577, 2005–06, especially paras 12, 19 and 35.

8. PASC, *Fourth Special Report: Tax Credits: Putting Things Right – Government Response to the Committee's Second Report*, HC 1076, 2005–06.

9. Equitable Life ceased taking new business in December 2000. The Financial Services Authority published a review (the Baird Report) in October 2001; the first Parliamentary Ombudsman in June 2003 (HC 809, 2002–03); the Report of the Penrose Inquiry in March 2004 (HC 290, 2003–04), as a result of which Ann Abraham announced her intention of conducting a further investigation in July 2004 (Third Report, HC 910, 2003–04).

10. Parliamentary and Health Service Ombudsman, *Sixth Report: Trusting in the Pensions Promise – Government Bodies and the Security of Final Salary Occupational Pensions*, HC 984, 2005–06.

11. PHSO Press Office, *Guide to the Parliamentary Ombudsman's Report 'Trusting in the Pensions Promise … '*, para. 26, drawing on paras 5:36–5:74 of the full report.

12. PASC press notice 2005–06/28, 15 March 2006.

13. HC Debs, 443, 15 March 2006, c. 1450.

14. HC Debs, 443, 16 March 2006, cc. 1620–4.

15. PASC, *Minutes of Evidence*, HC 1081-i and ii, 2005–06, Q. 70.

16. Department of Work and Pensions, *Response to the Report by the Parliamentary Ombudsman, 'Trusting in the Pensions Promise'*, June 2006.

17. Ibid., paras 59.3 and 59.4.

18. PASC, *Minutes of Evidence*, HC 1081-i, 2005–06.

19. PASC, *Sixth Report: Further Memorandum by the Parliamentary and Health Service Ombudsman*, HC 1081, 2005–06, paras 10 and 11.

20. Text of Speech on PHSO website <www.ombudsman.org.uk/news/speeches.html>; HC Debs, 7 December 2006, c. 512ff.

21. PASC press release, 2005–05/56, 28 July 2006.

22. *Observer*, 6 August 2006.

23. Sir Gus O'Donnell, PASC, *Minutes of Evidence, 16 May 2006*, HC 884-v, 2005–06, Q. 249.

24. PHSO, *Annual Report 2005–06* (London: The Stationery Office, July 2006), p. 55; PHSO, *Resource Accounts 2005–06* (London: The Stationery Office, July 2006), p. 5.

25. PHSO, *Three Year Strategic Plan 2006–09*, July 2006, p. 12.

26. PHSO, *Annual Report 2005–06* (London: The Stationery Office, July 2006), p. 51; PHSO, *Resource Accounts 2005–06* (London: The Stationery Office, July 2006), pp. 2–3.

27. Available at <www.ombudsman.org.uk/news/pga_consultation.html>.

28. Parliamentary Ombudsman, *Fifth Report: Redress in the Round – Remedying Maladministration in Central and Local Government*, HC 475, 2005–06.

29. The statutory test under the Local Ombudsman's founding legislation, The Local Government Act 1974, Part III.

30. The figure in 2004/05 was £1.1 million.

31. Cabinet Office, *Review of the Public Sector Ombudsmen in England*, April 2000. See also PASC, *Third Report: Review of the Public Sector Ombudsmen in England*, HC 612, 1999–2000.

32. Department for Local Government and Communities, *Strong and Prosperous Communities: The Local Government White Paper*, Cm. 6939, October 2006, para. 2.35.
33. Commission for Local Administration in England, *Three Year Corporate Plan, 2007–10*, November 2006, pp. 5–6.
34. Legislation was first promised by the Home Secretary in Cm. 5563, July 2002, para. 6.39. In early 2005 it was included in the Management of Offenders and Sentencing Bill, but this fell when the general election was called.
35. Public Service Ombudsman for Wales (PSOW), *Annual Report 2005/06*, p. 17.
36. Ibid., p. 18.
37. That is, county and county borough councils, community councils, the National Park and Police Authorities.
38. PSOW, *Annual Report 2005/06*, p. 30.
39. Scottish Public Service Ombudsman (SPSO), *A Shared Approach to Building a Better Scotland*, Response to the Consultation Paper, 28 July 2006, p. 1.
40. SPSO, *Annual Report 2005–06*, p. 6.
41. Finance Committee, *Seventh Report: Inquiry into Accountability and Governance*, SP Paper 631, 15 September 2006.
42. See, for example, House of Commons Defence Select Committee, *Third Report – Duty of Care*, HC 63-I, 2004–05, paras 423–27, March 2005; Ministry of Defence, *The Government's Response to the House of Commons Defence Select Committee, Third Report – Duty of Care*, Cm. 6620, July 2005, para. 118.
43. Nicholas Blake QC, *A Review of the Circumstances Surrounding the Deaths of Four Soldiers at Princess Royal Barracks, Deepcut between 1995 and 2002*, HC 795, 2005–06. See specifically paras 12.94–105 and Recommendation 26.
44. Ministry of Defence, *The Government's Response to the Deepcut Review*, Cm. 6851, June 2006; the Minister of State's Statement to Parliament, and subsequent questions and answers, are reported in HC Debs, 447, 13 June 2006, cc. 637–53.
45. Armed Forces Act 2006, Part 14, ss. 334–39.
46. Ibid., s. 366.
47. Ibid., s. 339.
48. A helpful short review of overseas arrangements is provided in the Commons Defence Committee's report, *Duty of Care*, HC 63, 2004–05, paras 413–18.
49. See, for example, the debate in the Lords on the second reading of the Armed Forces Bill, HL Debs Hansard, 14 June 2006, cc. 232ff., and *Duty of Care* (HC 63, 2004–05).
50. Annual Report of the Council on Tribunals, HC 1210, 2005–06.
51. The blueprint for the new service was provided by Sir Andrew Leggatt's report in 2001, *Tribunals for Users*, and the 2004 Government White Paper, *Transforming Public Services: Complaints Redress and Tribunals*, Cm. 6243, July 2004.
52. DCA press notice, 31 March 2006.
53. Available at <www.tribunals.gov.uk/publications/documents/framework_document.pdf> (undated).
54. *Transforming Public Services: Complaints, Redress and Tribunals*, Cm. 6243, July 2004.
55. DCA press notice, 25 July 2006.

8
Parliament:
The House of Commons – Plenty of
Business but Marking Time

Richard Kelly, Oonagh Gay and Philip Cowley

Communicating with the public, both by Parliament and its members, was a feature of 2006. The House of Commons approved what could be a fundamental change in the way in which it considers legislation. Standing committees (now public bill committees) will be able to take evidence from interested parties for many bills, similarly to select committees, before the traditional committee stage of bills. This change was prompted by the Modernisation Committee, which argued that it would make it easier for the public and other stakeholders to engage in the legislative process. More general opportunities for the public to visit and have better information about what is happening in Parliament continued to concern members and the House authorities, and whether the House's organisational structure is appropriate for its objectives in linking Parliament and the public is one of the central questions of a review of the management and services of the House. The opportunities afforded to backbenchers in questioning the government, in raising constituency issues, and in introducing legislation were identified as issues of concern during the year and various inquiries have been started to explore these issues further.

Composition

Three by-elections took place in 2006, all caused by deaths of sitting members: Rachel Squire (Labour), Peter Law (Independent), and Eric Forth (Conservative). They resulted in one defeat for the sitting party. In addition to the by-elections, one further change in the standing of the parties followed Clare Short's decision to resign the Labour whip in October. The changes in the overall composition of the Commons since the general election in May 2005 are shown in Table 8.1.

Table 8.1   The state of the parties

	May 2005	December 2005	December 2006
Labour[a][b]	355	355	353
Conservative[c]	198	198	198
Liberal Democrats[a]	62	62	63
Democratic Unionist Party	9	9	9
Scottish National Party	6	6	6
Sinn Fein	5	5	5
Plaid Cymru	3	3	3
Social Democratic & Labour Party	3	3	3
Ulster Unionist Party	1	1	1
Respect	1	1	1
Independents[d]	2	2	2
Independent Labour[b]	–	–	1
Speaker	1	1	1
Total	646	646	646

Notes: [a] Rachel Squire died on 5 January. Willie Rennie (Lib. Dem.) won the subsequent by-election on 6 February 2006.
[b] Clare Short resigned the Labour whip on 20 October 2006 and now sits as an Independent Labour MP.
[c] Eric Forth died on 17 May. Bob Neill (Con.) won the subsequent by-election on 29 June 2006.
[d] Peter Law died on 25 April. Dai Davies (Ind.) won the subsequent by-election on 29 June 2006.

Voting in the Commons[1]

The year began badly for the government in the Commons, when on 31 January 2006 it suffered two defeats during the Lords amendment stage of the Racial and Religious Hatred Bill. Neither of the backbench rebellions – one consisting of 26 Labour MPs, another of 21 – should have been large enough to bring about a defeat, but the whips had miscalculated, allowing too many Labour MPs to be absent for campaigning in the Dunfermline and West Fife by-election. The embarrassment was made all the worse by the fact that the Prime Minister was present for the first vote but was allowed to leave the Commons before the second – which was then lost by a majority of just one. The government's earlier Commons defeats in November 2005 could be fairly described as a failure of political leadership (with the government failing to acknowledge the scale of discontent on the back benches); those in January 2006 were simply a failure of management.[2]

This brought the number of defeats suffered by the government in the Commons in its first year in office after the 2005 election to four. No other post-war government with a majority of over 60 in the Commons had gone down to as many defeats in an entire Parliament, let alone merely in its first session. Indeed, John Major's Conservatives – much derided at the time for their divisions – suffered just four defeats as a result of backbench dissent on whipped votes in the five years between 1992 and 1997. The third Blair term, therefore, managed to achieve in nine months what it took Major five years, despite having a majority three times the size.

The following month saw the government giving a free vote on the banning of smoking in pubs and clubs, despite Labour's manifesto having contained an explicit pledge to allow smoking to continue in pubs that were not serving food – the so-called 'partial ban'.[3] The retreat from the manifesto came as a result of both Cabinet splits and overwhelming evidence of backbench hostility; the wisdom of the decision was demonstrated when the votes took place on 14 February.[4] Given the chance to stick with the initial 'partial ban', just 29 Labour MPs (including John Reid, the Cabinet minister most closely associated with the policy) did so. A staggering 91 per cent of Labour MPs to vote, including Tony Blair and Gordon Brown, voted to ban smoking in pubs, the opposite position to which they had fought the election under a year before. A second vote, to extend the ban to private members' clubs, saw 84 per cent of Labour's MPs go against the manifesto (again including the majority of Cabinet).[5] The free vote took much of the political sting out of the issue – but it was still a telling example of backbench influence. It is difficult to think of any other example over the last 50 or so years of any government with a nominally secure majority abandoning part of its manifesto in the face of backbench pressure within just a year of its election – and then seeing that manifesto so comprehensively rejected by the party's MPs.

The most controversial series of votes, however, came over the government's Education and Inspections Bill. The bill single-handedly set a whole series of records for backbench dissent. It witnessed the largest overall rebellions of the Blair third term to date; the rebellion over the bill's programme motion (15 March 2006) was the largest since the procedure was first introduced; a rebellion at report stage (23 May) was the largest report-stage revolt since Labour came to power in 1997; the third-reading revolt (24 May) was the largest third-reading rebellion ever endured by a Labour government; and although slightly smaller in absolute terms than the 72 Labour MPs who voted against the second reading of the Higher Education Bill in 2004, as a percentage of the parliamentary party the 69 Education and Inspection rebels constitute the largest rebellion over domestic legislation suffered by the Blair government.[6]

From the moment the proposals surfaced in the government's White Paper, *Higher Standards, Better Schools for All*,[7] it was clear that they attracted considerable opposition from within the Parliamentary Labour Party. In December 2005, backbench critics launched a so-called 'Alternative White Paper', which by January 2006 had just shy of 100 signatories. The good news for the government was that many of those who signed the Alternative White Paper were prepared to negotiate with the government – that was, at least ostensibly, the point of the exercise; they were looking for what one described as a 'dialogue' to help produce a better bill. The fear, as the same MP put it, was that 'it takes two to tango and there is no sign that Ruth [Kelly] and Tony [Blair] are sewing their sequins on'.

By the time the bill was introduced into the Commons, the government had managed to win over some critics, by giving what to most observers seemed to be concessions (described by the government as 'clarifications').[8] But, despite this, the revolt (consisting of 52 Labour MPs) was still large enough to force the government to rely on the support of Opposition MPs to secure the bill's second reading. The same applied at third reading.[9] It was not, to use a phrase that achieved wide currency at the time, a 'Labour bill'. In anticipation of this, as the votes approached, there had been much discussion of the Prime Minister as a potential Ramsay MacDonald figure ('Ramsay MacBlair'). Other Labour Prime Ministers had previously relied on the votes of Opposition MPs in order to achieve their legislation, although the majority of such occasions occurred when the government had a tiny majority; for a Prime Minister with a majority of over 60 to have to rely on Opposition MPs to enact a key plank of his legislative programme was extremely unusual.[10]

As the first session of the third Blair term ended on 8 November, there had been a total of 95 rebellions by Labour MPs since their re-election in May 2005. That equated to a rebellion in 28 per cent of divisions. This was the highest figure for a first session in any post-war government, easily eclipsing what had until recently been the record-holder, the 1992–93 session (a rebellion in 23 per cent of divisions), when John Major struggled so terribly with the Maastricht legislation. For the most part, there was no great surprise about the identities of those Labour backbenchers causing the whips difficulties. By the end of the first session of the Parliament, a total of 114 Labour MPs had voted against their whips. Some 89 per cent of these MPs were known to the whips' office from the previous Parliament. Indeed, they included the top 56 rebels from 2001–05 (and who remain on the back benches), *all* of whom had voted against the whip in the new Parliament. In other words, with a handful of exceptions, the government's difficulties have been caused by the very same people who have been rebelling against the government for years.[11] It was not in any way to diminish the behaviour of the rebels to note that it was entirely predictable.

Modernisation

The legislative process

On 7 September 2006, the Modernisation Committee published a report on *The Legislative Process*. At the heart of the report was a series of proposals to change the way in which standing committees work – in other words, to change the way in which the House of Commons undertakes its detailed scrutiny of the clauses of bills presented to it.

At the launch of the report, Jack Straw, the Leader of the House of Commons and chairman of the Modernisation Committee, argued that the routine programming of bills, which had been introduced following previous Modernisation Committee recommendations, had made the parliamentary process more efficient. He now wanted to make the House more effective in the way in which it scrutinised legislation.[12] In its summary, the committee argued that the revised procedures should make it 'easier for the general public, as well as lobby groups, representative organisations and other stakeholders to influence Parliament's consideration of bills'.[13]

Rather than the purely adversarial standing committees, which operate like a mini-version of the chamber with the government on one side and the Opposition on the other, the committee recommended that it should be the norm for public bill committees to take evidence as well as deliberate on a bill. It identified a number of benefits that could be derived from taking evidence, including:

- informing members about the subject of a bill
- a more consensual process – like select committees, which tended to be positively viewed outside Parliament
- effective engagement with the public in the legislative process. The committee had received evidence that it was difficult to influence the standing committee process.[14]

Standing orders had already allowed for the establishment of special standing committees, which could take evidence, but their use was rare and their procedures quite restrictive. The Modernisation Committee wanted the public bill committee process to be as flexible as possible:

We recommend that public bill committees should hold at least one evidence session, with the minister and officials, in all cases. Beyond that, the general restrictions on the number, duration and timing of oral evidence sessions held by public bill committees should be lifted. Appropriate out-dates should be applied instead on a case-by-case basis in the programme order. The programming sub-committee of the public bill committee should decide on how the committee uses the time available to it, including the division of time between evidence-taking and debate.[15]

Despite the much more limited use of pre-legislative scrutiny in the 2005–06 session (just four bills were published in draft, compared to twelve in 2003–04 and five in 2004–05, the short session before the general election),[16] the Modernisation Committee argued that 'The purpose of a public bill committee is not to replicate the pre-legislative inquiry, nor should it be seen as a substitute for proper pre-legislative scrutiny.'[17]

The Modernisation Committee also called for better explanatory material to accompany not only bills but also their amendments. To these ends it recommended that texts showing how bills would look if particular amendments were agreed should be published and that explanatory statements to amendments in standing committees should be considered. In addition, it recommended that the Library should 'produce a report of the standing committee stage' for most government bills and certain Private Members' Bills, in time to inform the debate at report stage. The committee acknowledged that its recommendations would have resource implications.[18]

On 1 November, the House considered a number of 'House' or procedural issues, including this report. It debated a motion welcoming the report and approving 'in particular the proposals for the committal of bills to committees with powers to take evidence to become the normal practice for *programmed government bills* which start in this House' (our emphasis). The House agreed to the motion and to the necessary changes in standing orders, without a division.[19] Jack Straw acknowledged that the 'new procedures are being introduced – in parliamentary terms – with some speed'. So he indicated that as a 'transitional measure ... evidence-taking would only become the norm for government bills introduced ... after Christmas'.[20] The House also accepted a recommendation from the committee to require more notice of an amendment at committee stage, this time on a division (by 223 votes to 172).[21]

The Modernisation Committee's recommendation that the main programme motion (that is, the total time allocated for committee consideration of a bill) should no longer be taken immediately after second reading was not accepted by the government and therefore not debated, to the disappointment of Theresa May, the Shadow Leader of the House of Commons.[22] Although the proposals were accepted by the House, it is unclear how effective they will be in practice. One sceptical commentator observed:

> Jack Straw's new proposals for the legislative process are much less important than his proposals for MPs' postage budget. They recognised this and gave far more energy to the latter. His serious, well-received proposals for Standing Committees are entirely pointless.
>
>   That a Bill Committee (as they will now be) can call for expert evidence is a little late for pre-legislative scrutiny.
>
>   Also, the government (in the form of its whips) will decide how many evidence sessions will be allowed (because they appoint the Programming Sub-committee).[23]

September sittings and Questions in the recess

In September 2003 and September 2004, the House sat for a two-week period. In other years, the House would have been in recess. The September sittings were not repeated in either 2005 or 2006. Following the government's announcement in November 2005 that the House would not sit in September 2006,[24] a number of Members frequently called for the reintroduction of September sittings. Soon after his appointment as Leader of the House, Jack Straw faced Questions on his plans for September sittings. On 9 May, he said that it was too late to make changes for 2006 as maintenance and holiday plans would already have been made.[25] On 12 October, during Business Questions, he announced that he would give the House an opportunity to decide whether to sit in September in the future.[26]

On 20 July, the Leader of the House announced that, for the first time, he proposed to allow the tabling of Questions during the recess:

> I am pleased to inform the House that later today I intend to table a motion and an explanatory memorandum that will allow for the tabling and answering of named day Questions and, if there is a need, written ministerial statements on specified days during the first two weeks of September. This information will thereafter be printed in the *Official Report*.[27]

On 24 July, the House agreed a motion that allowed members to table named-day Questions on three days in September (4, 6 and 11 September), for answer on three later days (11, 13 and 18 September, respectively) and allowed ministers to give notice of written ministerial statements on the earlier dates and make them on the later dates.[28] When the House returned in October 2006, Straw reported that a total of 732 Questions had been asked by more than 100 members during the summer recess, and that 35 written ministerial statements were made. He linked the answering of Questions in September to the decision about sitting in September, saying that 'I am in no doubt that, if we keep to the current recess arrangements, September Questions are an important element.' But he also announced his intention that the House should debate the issue of September sittings before the end of the Session.[29] He proposed:

> That this House welcomes the introduction of a procedure for the tabling and answering of written Questions and the making of written ministerial statements during the summer adjournment, as adopted by the House on 24 July for the current session; accordingly reconsiders the part of its resolution of 29 October 2002 endorsing the proposal for September sittings; and is of the opinion that the House should not sit during September (except pursuant to the provisions of Standing Order No. 13 (Earlier meeting of the House in certain circumstances)).[30]

On 1 November, the House debated the motion and an amendment from David Winnick that would have committed the House to 'hold regular sittings for a period in September'. The amendment was defeated by 354 votes to

122,[31] and Straw's proposal was then agreed to without a division.[32] Straw subsequently said that 'The House agreed in principle on 1 November that September Questions should become permanent and I will make proposals to achieve that.' He also undertook to consider whether the period for answering questions in September could be extended.[33]

Existing procedures

Despite the action on modernisation and the concerns that Parliament is becoming increasingly irrelevant to the general public, existing long-standing procedures have been used during the course of the year and generated considerable press coverage.

On 11 July 2006, the Speaker agreed to a request for an emergency debate under Standing Order No. 24.[34] The debate, on extradition arrangements with the United States, took place the following day. Unusually, at the end of the debate, the House voted to adjourn and the rest of the day's business was lost.[35] The last time a debate was requested under Standing Order No. 24 was on 20 October 2004. The request was refused.[36] The previous successful application was on 20 March 2002, on troop deployment to Afghanistan.[37]

On 31 October, Plaid Cymru and the Scottish National Party were granted a half-day Opposition Day. They chose to debate Iraq and proposed:

> That this House believes that there should be a select committee of seven honourable Members, being members of Her Majesty's Privy Council, to review the way in which the responsibilities of government were discharged in relation to Iraq and all matters relevant thereto, in the period leading up to military action in that country in March 2003 and in its aftermath.[38]

The motion was defeated with a government majority of 25, and an alternative motion from the government, noting that four inquiries had already taken place but recognising the importance of learning lessons, and stating that an inquiry should not take place while it could divert the attention of troops on the ground, was accepted by a majority of 30.

As reflected in the debate on September sittings, parliamentary Questions are considered to be a very important means by which the House seeks to hold the government to account. However, concerns have been expressed about both the increasing volume of parliamentary Questions and about the quality of answers. On 28 June, Peter Luff (Conservative) instigated an adjournment debate that touched on both issues. He acknowledged that the number of Questions tabled was 'sharply up' (see Table 8.2). He suggested three reasons for this. Firstly, it had become easier to table Questions (partly because of e-tabling). Secondly, he attributed some of the increase to laziness: Questions were being used to attain information, 'not to inquire into aspects of government policy'. Thirdly, he argued that the number tabled served as an informal means of assessing members' activity. He proposed remedies for each of these problems.[39] He also expressed concerns about answers that were 'increasingly late, inadequate or simply spectacularly unhelpful'. He added that, 'In recent months, I have noticed a serious deterioration in the quality and timeliness of answers.'[40]

Table 8.2 Written parliamentary Questions tabled in the first session of the most recent Parliaments

Session	No.
1997–98	53,000
2001–02	73,000
2005–06	95,000

Source: HC Debs, 453, 27 November 2006, c. 824.

In response, Nigel Griffiths, the Deputy Leader of the House, reiterated that the Leader of the House had made clear that 'the government attach a high priority to the obligations on Ministers to respond properly to written Questions'.[41] However, Griffiths accepted – as Robin Cook, when Leader of the House, had before – that the quality of answers had declined as the number of Questions increased. He suggested members seeking information should use other sources, including the Library, first. He argued that league tables did not always reflect performance. He concluded by saying that the Procedure Committee may examine the issue further.[42] And, indeed, on 8 December, the Procedure Committee announced an inquiry into written parliamentary Questions.[43]

Parliament and the public

In 2005, the Hansard Society Commission on the Communication of Parliamentary Democracy (the Puttnam Commission) and the Modernisation Committee's *Connecting Parliament with the Public* formed the background to many debates on how members and Parliament itself communicate with the public. That debate continued during 2006, not only in terms of a communications allowance, which is discussed below, but through the House of Commons Commission and the now annual debate on its annual report. Progress has also been made on a number of recommendations made by both the Modernisation Committee and the Puttnam Commission.

The Modernisation Committee took evidence from Lord Adonis, the Minister for Schools, and from Lord Puttnam and other members of his commission, in March and May, respectively; and the Hansard Society launched *Parliament in the Public Eye 2006: Coming into Focus?* at a conference in Westminster on 2 November 2006. In the latter, Lord Puttnam judged both Parliament and the media's progress against the commission's recommendations to improve the way Parliament is communicated to the public. He concluded: 'To achieve the aims that the Commission set out requires a joint effort. At present I would be inclined to give Parliament a B and the media a C minus.'[44]

During the course of the year, the House of Commons' progress has included the launch of a new voters' guide, *The Voting Times*,[45] which was recommended by the Modernisation Committee;[46] an increase in the number of visits of students, hosted by the Education Unit, and the appointment of outreach officers.[47] After experimental and subsequently permanent changes to the rules on broadcasting Commons' proceedings, more reaction shots and low-level sound rather than silence during divisions were permitted, new interview points were made available, and BBC Parliament was released from its undertaking to cover the Commons, regardless of the proceedings in the House of Lords.[48] A major redesign of the parliamentary website – perhaps the most visible feature of a strategic decision to change the way in which the communication structures of Parliament operated – is being implemented and content improved; and both the Commons and Lords boards of management are now represented on the Parliament-wide Group on Information for the Public.[49] There has also been progress on the new visitor reception building, although its completion is running behind schedule.[50] The Administration Committee and the House of Lords Information Committee are examining the case for a parliamentary visitor and information centre. Their terms of reference are: 'To consider the viability of a parliamentary visitor centre, with particular reference to the Abingdon Green site.'

The administration of the House of Commons

In the 2005 debate on the House of Commons Commission's annual report, there was some criticism of the management of the House. That was to an extent echoed in the Puttnam Commission's call for the House of Commons to have a chief executive to head the House administration. As foreshadowed in the 2005 debate, a review of the implementation of the Braithwaite Report (the previous review of the management and services of the House) was announced by the Commission on the same day as the debate on its 2005–06 report. The Commission appointed Sir Kevin Tebbit, previously a Permanent Secretary at the Ministry of Defence, to conduct the review. He was given the following terms of reference:

> To review the implementation of the recommendations of the report of Mr Michael Braithwaite Report (HC 745, 1998–99) on the management and services of the House of Commons and his subsequent report on the Serjeant at Arms' Department, and in particular to assess:
> – whether the expected benefits have been realised;
> – what further actions are required for the House Service to achieve the objectives laid down in the Outline Strategic Plan for the House of Commons Administration 2006–11;

- whether, in particular, the organisational and staffing arrangements currently in place are adequate to realise the objectives laid down in the Resolutions of the House of 26 January 2005 relating to Connecting Parliament with the Public.[51]

Members

Members' salaries

On 18 May 2006, the House agreed a motion that allowed members' salaries to be increased in two stages,[52] from £59,095 to £59,686 on 1 April, and again to £60,277 on 1 November, giving a 2 per cent increase on the 2005–06 salary. This was necessary because, although the Prime Minister announced that members' salaries would be increased in two stages in line with those of senior civil servants, on 30 March 2006,[53] the resolution on members' salaries agreed on 10 July 1996 only provided for a 'yearly rate' of salary.[54]

In July 2006, Jack Straw announced that the Prime Minister had asked the Senior Salaries Review Body (SSRB) to conduct its triennial review of members' pay and allowances.[55] During the course of the year, there had been calls for considerable increases in members' salaries. In December 2005, it was reported that Members wanted a 22 per cent pay increase to bring their salaries back in line with their comparators,[56] and in December 2006, there were reports of calls for a salary of £100,000.[57] However, Straw's evidence to the SSRB argued that 'pay rises for MPs and ministers should be subject to the same restraints imposed on public sector workers'.[58]

Private Members' business

There have been regular calls for the House to find more time for Private Members' business, and concerns that in the last two sessions only three Private Members' Bills have been passed.[59] During the debates on sitting hours in January 2005, there were suggestions that Private Members' Bills should be considered on Wednesday evenings, but no changes were made and the House has retained the practice of allocating 13 Fridays in each session for Private Members' Bills.

On 23 November 2006, the Modernisation Committee announced two parallel inquiries: 'Strengthening the Role of the Backbencher' and 'Making Better Use of Non-legislative Time'. The terms of reference included the prospect of reintroducing Private Members' motions, a procedure that ceased to operate following the Jopling Review of sittings in the mid-1990s.[60]

Communications allowance

On 1 November 2006, the House agreed to the principle of establishing a communications allowance by 290 votes to 199. It asked the Members' Estimate Committee to bring forward more detailed proposals:

> That this House welcomes the principle of establishing, from 1st April 2007, a separate Allowance for Members of Parliament to assist in the work of communicating with the public on parliamentary business and instructs the Members Estimate Committee to prepare a detailed proposal for such an allowance.[61]

In introducing the motion on the allowance, the Leader of the House outlined the increasing amount of correspondence members had to deal with; recent reports (such as the Puttnam Commission and the Power Inquiry[62]) recommending that Parliament and members should improve their communications with their constituents; and the concerns of the Committee on Standards and Privileges over the rules concerning the existing stationery and communication facilities.[63] He explained that the motion did not commit the House to a form or level of allowance, but he indicated that, if agreed, the rules would 'indicate what the boundary between political work and parliamentary work should be'.[64] The new allowance would have a knock-on effect on the current provisions for members' postage and stationery:

> at present there is no limit on prepaid stationery and envelopes … it has been not implicit but explicit that part of any change … is that there would be a limit on prepaid stationery and envelopes, and I hope that would meet the convenience of the House.[65]

He confirmed that there would be a cap on the amount of postage and stationery members could use, if the communications allowance was introduced. He had received a suggestion that the allowance should be set at £10,000 but the actual value would be a matter for the Members' Estimate Committee and would depend on the size of the cap.[66]

Some concerns were expressed about the proposals. Theresa May, the Shadow leader, pointed out that members had very different ways of communicating with their constituents and would have very different requirements when the allowance was introduced; hence, rather than detailed rules for the new allowance, she preferred an overall budget 'which allows the Member of Parliament to choose how they communicate'.[67] Speaking in a personal capacity, David Heath, the Liberal Democrat spokesman, questioned 'how some Hon. Members manage to spend quite as much as they do on their postage allowance within the rules of the House, as I understand them.'[68] Chris Mullin expressed concern about the difficulties that would be encountered by candidates facing incumbent MPs who had a communications allowance that contributed to the 'recent growth in thinly disguised party propaganda'.[69]

Parliamentary Standards

The Committee on Standards and Privileges has had to deal with a steady stream of complaints since the new Code of Conduct, approved in July 2005, empowered the Parliamentary Commissioner for Standards to investigate misuse of House services and facilities. The whole tenor of complaints to the Commissioner has changed compared to a decade ago, when allegations concerning the failure to register significant gifts and financial interests were prominent. Most allegations now concern misuse of stationery and inappropriate use of House allowances. In his annual report for 2005–06, the Commissioner noted with satisfaction how the pressure for system change had moved to the arena of ministerial conduct, and reported on progress towards achieving a 'one-stop shop' for the registration of Members' financial interests. The Electoral Administration Act 2006 allowed the Electoral Commission to cease the registration of gifts and benefits given to members in their political capacity, and instead to rely on the publicly available Register of Members' Interests. There are tricky aspects to this alignment, not least enforcement mechanisms, which the Standards and Privileges Committee must consider with the Electoral Commission.[70] It also launched a consultation into the rules for All-Party Groups, following a *Sunday Times* exposé,[71] and made proposals for minor revisions of the detailed Guide to the Rules.[72] Nevertheless, there were two reports dealing with financial interests. The Standards and Privileges Committee criticised George Galloway's failure to register his Legal Fund, and dealt in July 2006 with John Prescott's initial failure to register his stay at the US ranch of Philip Anschutz, owner of a company that forms part of the consortium responsible for the redevelopment of the Millennium Dome.

The committee stepped into the fierce political debate over the Ministerial Code by recommending an element of independent investigation whenever specific allegations are made against ministers. This is a different role from that of independent adviser on ministerial interests given to Sir John Bourn, Comptroller and Auditor General, in March 2006.[73] The committee complained in the final paragraph of the Prescott Report that 'it is in our view difficult for the public to understand the distinctions between the Parliamentary and Ministerial Codes, and who is responsible for the enforcement of each'.[74] The Commissioner welcomed the appointment of Sir John, as a fellow Officer of the House of Commons, in his annual report, but noted the need for close liaison, since the boundary between the parliamentary and the ministerial was not always distinct.

The appointment of Sir John as ministerial adviser raises a number of parliamentary issues. Sir John, as Comptroller and Auditor General, is classified as Officer of Parliament, appointed by resolution of the House, following a recommendation from the chairman of the Public Accounts Committee. Tony Blair reacted to the furore over allegations that honours had been awarded on the basis of financial contributions to political parties by establishing a new position of independent adviser on ministerial interests, but decided without any public debate to use Sir John as the most appropriate individual.[75] The Public Administration Select Committee (PASC) welcomed this development as an acceptance of the 'principle that an Officer of the House can undertake this sort of role. It is a precedent that should be built on'.[76] PASC sought to establish parliamentary involvement in an independent investigation, while reserving 'to the Prime Minister the right to judge whether the facts amount to a breach of the Ministerial Code and what the consequences should be'.[77] It remained unhappy with the limitations placed on Sir John's role, which was 'inappropriately weighted in favour of an additional layer of advice over that of Permanent Secretary; and lack[ed] a genuine investigatory dimension'.[78]

The extent of parliamentary involvement in the conduct of political parties has also been a feature in 2005–06 in respect of the relationship between the Speaker's Committee and the Electoral Commission (EC). Parties' concerns about the bureaucracy involved in implementing the Political Parties, Elections and Referendums Act 2000 have spilled over into concerns about the scope and behaviour of the Electoral Commission, as regulator.

The Committee on Standards in Public Life began a review of the account-ability role of the EC on 15 February 2006.[79] Oral evidence indicated problems with the structure and operation of the Speaker's Committee, which oversees the strategic plan and budget of the commission. The precedent for the committee is the Public Accounts Commission, which fulfils a similar role for the National Audit Office. However, the EC operates in a high-profile, politically controversial arena and is more likely to suffer robust criticism of its effectiveness. The committee's representative, Peter Viggers, argued that the committee's proceedings could not be held in public, for fear of prejudicing the impartiality of the Speaker:

> The Office of the Speaker is such that it would not be appropriate for the Speaker to contribute to a debate in public. That is not the way the Speaker's office works. Therefore, by its own nature, the Speaker's Committee meets in private. The minutes are very full and accurate. I do not think that the Speaker's Committee has a specific role. I do not think it would be appropriate for it to seek to obtain a role in promoting the broader dialogue of political process. I think that responsibility lies elsewhere.[80]

Other witnesses suggested that the lack of transparency and full administrative support for the Speaker's Committee was inhibiting effective accountability. The devolved governance arrangements for the UK have not been recognised within the accountability framework for the commission. Sam Younger, the EC chairman, expressed his desire for a more general relationship with Parliament which would enable the work of the commission to undergo appropriate scrutiny. He did not express any public criticism of the more limited role of the Speaker's Committee, but said that the EC was happy for the meetings to be held in public. The inquiry reported early in 2007 and presaged some major changes.

Finally, another Officer of the House, the Parliamentary Ombudsman, has had difficulty in her relationship with the executive. Ann Abraham won support from PASC for her stance on compensation for those who lost pension payments after following information in official leaflets. PASC expressed concerns that the attitude of departments was changing towards the office, as they rejected with impunity independent assessment of their actions and findings of maladministration. This went to the heart of the Ombudsman system – and of parliamentary scrutiny of the executive.[81]

Conclusions

The House's efforts to improve its communications with the public and members' desire to improve their communications have not always been straightforward. The visitor reception building's opening has been delayed; the introduction of a new communications allowance proved controversial; and the House's organisational structure is subject to review. New procedures for considering bills have been introduced, but were not used until early 2007 so their implications have yet to be seen; and Questions were answered during the summer recess for the first time. However, existing procedures have also been used effectively and in ways that have drawn the public's and the media's attention to the chamber of the House of Commons. The government was defeated a couple of times but also amended bills considerably as a result of backbench pressure. A Queen's Speech dominated by Home Office measures suggests similar pressures are likely in 2007.

Notes

1. This section was provided by Philip Cowley.
2. The defeats of November 2005 are discussed in R. Kelly et al., 'Parliament: The House of Commons – Turbulence Ahead?', in M. Rush and P. Giddings, *The Palgrave Review of British Politics 2005* (Basingstoke: Palgrave Macmillan, 2006), pp. 106–8.
3. *Britain Forward Not Back*, p. 66. Private Members' clubs were to be allowed to decide for themselves on whether or not to be smoke-free.
4. Some within government attempted to justify this on the grounds that they would implement the manifesto, but then allow MPs a free vote on whether to take the issue 'further' and that therefore this was not the abandonment of a manifesto commitment. Yet MPs were being allowed a free vote to remove rights – the rights of non-food-serving pubs to decide whether to be smoke-free or not – which had been explicitly promised in the manifesto. To 'go beyond' the manifesto was therefore to reject the manifesto.
5. The issue also caused difficulties for the Conservatives. Also allowed free votes, the first vote – on a ban in pubs – saw them split 81:94 against. The second vote – on Private Members' clubs – saw a split of 47:125. Andrew Lansley (Opposition Health spokesman) made much of splits within the government over the issue, but his own troops were far more divided than those of the government.
6. The record for third-reading revolts was previously held by the rebellion over the National Service Bill on 22 May 1947, which involved 37 Labour MPs.
7. Cm. 6677, October 2005.

8. Just under half (48 per cent) of the signatories to the Alternative White Paper went on to vote against the Education and Inspections Bill at second reading; 37 per cent voted for the government, with the remainder either abstaining or being absent.
9. The bill would have failed to receive its second reading if the Conservatives voted against it; by third reading, and with a smaller revolt, the Conservatives alone would not have been decisive to kill the bill, although the combined votes of the Conservatives and the Democratic Unionist Party would have been sufficient to deny the government a majority.
10. See P. Cowley and M. Stuart, 'Delivering Labour's Legislation Thanks to the Tories – As Most Other Labour Premiers have Done', available from <www.revolts. co.uk>.
11. The correlation between the number of votes cast by rebels against the government during the first session of the 2005 Parliament and between 2001 and 2005 was extremely high, at 0.93.
12. Modernisation Committee press notice, *Modernisation Committee Publishes New Proposals for the Legislative Process*, 7 September 2006, session 2005–06, No. 12.
13. Modernisation Committee, *First Report: The Legislative Process*, HC 1097, 2005–06, p. 3.
14. Ibid., paras 53–8.
15. Ibid., para. 71.
16. Draft Coroners Bill, draft Legal Services Bill, draft Tribunal Courts and Enforcement Bill, and draft clauses of the Terrorism Bill; see also House of Commons Library, *Pre-legislative Scrutiny*, SN/PC/2822, <www.parliament.uk/commons/lib/research/ notes/snpc-02822.pdf>.
17. Modernisation Committee, *The Legislative Process*, para. 73.
18. Ibid., paras 75–7, 81–3, 90, 115.
19. HC Debs, 451, 1 November 2006, cc. 304–404.
20. Ibid., c. 308.
21. Ibid., c. 407.
22. Modernisation Committee, *The Legislative Process*, paras 46–9; HC Debs, 451, 1 November 2006, c. 321.
23. Simon Carr, *Independent*, 2 November 2006.
24. HC Debs, 439, 10 November 2005, c. 470.
25. HC Debs, 446, 9 May 2006, c. 167.
26. HC Debs, 450, 12 October 2006, c. 449.
27. HC Debs, 449, 20 July 2006, cc. 455–6.
28. Ibid., 24 July 2006, c. 707.
29. HC Debs, 450, 12 October 2006, c. 449.
30. HC Debs, 451, 1 November 2006, c. 414.
31. Ibid., c. 415.
32. Ibid., c. 418.
33. HC Debs, 453, 27 November 2006, cc. 823–4.
34. HC Debs, 448, 11 July 2006, cc. 1294–5.
35. Ibid., 12 July 2006, cc. 1396–450.
36. HC Debs, 425, 20 October 2004, c. 894.
37. HC Debs, 382, 19 March 2002, c. 169 and 20 March 2002, cc. 328–73.
38. HC Debs, 451, 31 October 2006, c. 163.
39. HC Debs, 448, 28 June 2006, cc. 349–53.
40. Ibid., cc. 344–5.

41. Ibid., c. 356.
42. HC Debs, 448, 28 June 2006, cc. 358–60.
43. Procedure Committee press notice, *New Inquiry: Written Parliamentary Questions*, 8 December 2006, session 2006–07, No. 2.
44. Lord Puttnam, 'Introduction', in Gemma Rosenblatt (ed.), *Parliament in the Public Eye 2006: Coming into Focus? A Review of the Hansard Society Commission on the Communication of Parliamentary Democracy* (London: Hansard Society, 2006), p. 10.
45. *The Voting Times*, <www.parliament.uk/votingtimes/index.html>.
46. HC Debs, 450, 19 October 2006, c. 333WH.
47. House of Commons Commission, *Twenty-eighth Report of the House of Commons Commission – Financial Year 2005–06*, HC 1234 2005–06, paras 163–8.
48. HC Debs, 447, 20 June 2006, cc. 1725–6W; HC Debs, 454, 19 December 2006, c. 1791W.
49. John Pullinger, 'Organisational Change within Parliament – Comment', in Rosenblatt, *Parliament in the Public Eye 2006*, pp. 20–3.
50. House of Commons Commission, *Financial Year 2005–06*, paras 178–80; HC Debs, 454, 19 December 2006, cc. 1791–2W.
51. HC Debs, 450, 19 October 2006, c. 1359W.
52. HC Debs, 446, 18 May 2006, cc. 1152–64.
53. HC Debs, 444, 30 March 2006, cc. 96–9WS.
54. HC Debs, 281, 10 July 1996, c. 533.
55. HC Debs, 449, 25 July 2006, cc. 102–3WS.
56. BBC News, 4 December 2005, <http://news.bbc.co.uk/1/hi/uk_politics/4496440.stm>.
57. *Guardian Unlimited*, 4 December 2006, <www.guardian.co.uk/uk_news/story/0,,1963741,00.html>.
58. *Daily Telegraph*, 6 December 2006; see also Government evidence to the SSRB review, <www.commonsleader.gov.uk/output/page1812.asp>.
59. For further details of these bills see the House of Commons Information Office, *The Success of Private Members' Bills*, Factsheet L03 (revised November 2006), <www.parliament.uk/documents/upload/l03.pdf>.
60. Modernisation Committee press notice, *Modernisation Committee Launches New Inquiries*, 23 November 2006, session 2006–07, No. 1.
61. HC Debs, 451, 1 November 2006, cc. 411–14.
62. Hansard Society, *Members Only: Report of the Hansard Society Commission on the Communication of Parliamentary Democracy* (London: Hansard Society, 2005); Power Inquiry, *Power to the People* (London: Rowntree Trust, 2006).
63. HC Debs, 451, 1 November 2006, cc. 310–12.
64. Ibid., cc. 312–13.
65. Ibid., c. 313.
66. Ibid., c. 317.
67. Ibid., c. 327.
68. Ibid., c. 336.
69. Ibid., cc. 349–50.
70. Parliamentary Commissioner for Standards, *Annual Report 2005–6*, HC 1480, 2005–06.
71. Standards and Privileges Committee, *Ninth Report: Lobbying and All Party Groups*, HC 1145, 2005–06.

72. Standards and Privileges Committee, *Sixteenth Report: Review of the Guide to the Rules Relating to the Conduct of Members: Consultation Document*, HC 1869, 2005–06.
73. For the statement from the Prime Minister see HC Debs, 444, 23 March 2006, c. 33WS.
74. Standards and Privileges Committee, *Thirteenth Report: Conduct of John Prescott*, HC 1553, 2005–06.
75. For further details see House of Commons Library, Standard Note No. 3750, *The Ministerial Code*.
76. PASC, *Seventh Report: The Ministerial Code: The Case for Independent Investigation*, HC 1457, 2005–6, para. 22.
77. Ibid., para. 25.
78. Ibid., para. 41.
79. The committee published its Issues and Questions paper on 15 February 2006, and this is available at <www.public-standards.gov.uk/publications/11thinquiry/review_elec_com_iq.pdf>.
80. Evidence relating to the inquiry of the Committee on Standards in Public Life into the Electoral Commission is available at <www.public-standards.gov.uk/11thinquiry/transcripts_evidence.aspx>.
81. PASC, *Sixth Report: The Ombudsman in Question: The Ombudsman's Report on Pensions and its Constitutional Implications*, HC 1081, 2005–06. See above, pp. 84–5.

9
Parliament:
The House of Lords – Negotiating a Stronger Second Chamber

Meg Russell and Maria Sciara[1]

Since 1999, when the majority of hereditary peers were removed from the House of Lords, there has been a feeling that Britain's second chamber is increasing in confidence and strength. This belief particularly pervades the political community, and is also beginning to be discussed by scholars.[2] While continuing to be unelected the chamber now primarily comprises members appointed on their merits, rather than by accident of birth. It is also far more politically balanced than it was before 1999. This has given it a greater sense of *legitimacy* – although its unelected nature means this continues to be questioned.[3] Between the chamber's reform and the end of 2006 it had inflicted over 350 defeats on the Blair government. The greater confidence of the Lords leads some politicians to conclude that it has been dangerously strengthened and that any new reform should be targeted at reining it back. But for others the priority is to democratise the chamber and give it an even more legitimate role in the policy process.

Various events fuelled debates about the legitimacy, strength and reform of the Lords during 2006. One was allegations early in the year that money given to the Labour and Conservative parties had been exchanged for peerages and thus seats in the upper house. This threatened to taint not only the parties but also Parliament, and helped revive calls for Lords reform. Such calls also received a boost from jostling for position by Labour figures anticipating the succession to Tony Blair. However, while this may have provided comfort to those wanting to democratise the Lords, there were also contrary moves. A new joint committee was established to consider the conventions governing the Lords – the clear motivation being government views that increasingly confident peers are stretching the boundaries of existing convention, and that something must be done to stop it. And although a new reform package was promised, this was delayed, and no action ultimately taken. While debates about reform raged amongst the political and media classes to little effect, events in the Lords showed further gradual change. The chamber continued to grow, ending the year with almost 750 members entitled to sit. The centuries-old tradition of the Lord Chancellor acting as presiding officer ended and peers elected their first Lord Speaker. The number of government defeats was again high, with significant concessions made on key bills, and growing signs of the Commons and the Lords acting in partnership to extract concessions from the executive. Although small and piecemeal, these real-life events may reflect trends which prove to be of more lasting significance than any rhetoric about reform. Slowly, the Lords is finding a new place in British politics, and becoming a more influential and more mainstream institution.

Allegations of 'cash for peerages'

The biggest Lords-related news story during 2006 was a negative one which ran most of the year, centring on allegations of 'cash for peerages'. A list of proposed appointees was leaked to the press in November 2005, with rumours suggesting that the House of Lords Appointments Commission (responsible for vetting the propriety of party nominees, as well as choosing independent members) was concerned about some of the names. In April, one, Dr Chai Patel, broke his silence, to demand details of the objections to his nomination. It was already known that some nominees were major party donors. But Dr Patel revealed that he had funded Labour through a £1.5 million loan, avoiding the need for the party to declare the contribution to the Electoral Commission. It turned out that three other Labour nominees, and one Conservative nominee, had similarly made loans to the parties. To make matters worse, Labour Party Treasurer Jack Dromey revealed that he knew nothing of the transactions in his party. Shortly afterwards, a police investigation began considering whether the Honours (Prevention of Abuses) Act 1925, which forbids the sale of honours, had been breached.

These events did little to boost the image of the House of Lords, though the main damage was sustained by the parties. Various party advisers and ministers, including the Prime Minister himself, were questioned by the police, and at one point party fundraiser Lord Levy was arrested. The affair cast doubt on the appointments process to the Lords, and whether this includes adequate checks – though ironically it was the new system the government put in place in 2000 which had brought these difficulties to light. There is little new about allegations of 'cash for peerages': the 1925 Act followed similar allegations on a far larger scale under Lloyd George. What is different now is that there is an Appointments Commission to vet nominations, which seems prepared to question the Prime Minister's judgement.

Concern about appointments boosted those campaigning for an elected upper house, though – as discussed below – little concrete happened. It also raised questions about how the appointments process could be improved. The Appointments Commission remains non-statutory, its role in political nominations is limited to advising on the propriety of names put forward by Number 10, and there are no clear criteria for choosing party nominees. The two largest parties have no system of internal democracy for selecting their candidates for peerages, though the Liberal Democrats now involve their party conference and the Greens ballot their members. The Prime Minister continues to choose the nominees for the governing party, as well as deciding the timing and party balance of creations.

Questions about the Prime Minister's patronage powers will not easily go away. They were examined by the House of Commons Public Administration Select Committee (PASC) which announced an inquiry into the scrutiny of political honours in March. Although this was almost immediately put on hold at police request (as public witness sessions could prejudice the criminal investigation), PASC decided to publish an interim report in July.[4] This recommended 'making it explicit that nominations to the peerage entail appointment to the legislature rather than the award of an honour',[5] greater transparency within parties over how nominees are chosen, a statutory basis for the Appointments Commission giving it a clear role and powers, and consultation on the criteria for future nominees. Such proposals would help boost the integrity (and thus legitimacy) of the Lords while not fundamentally changing its composition. Unfortunately, this means they were not readily embraced either by government or most Lords reformers. But if large-scale reform is further delayed, the proposals may yet be returned to.

Compositional changes

Overall, Labour continues – for only the second year – to be the largest party in the Lords. But the balance of power remains with the Liberal Democrats, Crossbenchers and 'others', as shown in Table 9.1.

The controversy over appointments resulted in a delay in announcing a new peerage list at the start of the year. This was finally published in April minus the five names of the original major lenders. It comprised seven Labour, seven Conservative, five Liberal Democrat and four 'Crossbench' names. This latter included, for the first time, three nominees from the Northern Ireland Democratic Unionist Party, which had long argued for seats, along with former Ulster Unionist Party leader David Trimble. It remains an anomaly that these political members join the Crossbench group, consisting largely of independents, rather than sitting in their own right. The one Green member of the Lords (whose existence is one of the lesser-known facts about the British Parliament) chooses to sit under his own party label. There were strong rumours that this lone representative, now aged 78, was to gain a party colleague in the new round of appointments. However, if this opportunity was real it was rather spectacularly missed when the party's chairman put his own name forward without permission of its executive. His nomination was withdrawn, and the party balloted members on a replacement, selecting London Assembly member Jenny Jones. However, there was no Green name on the final list.

Table 9.1   Composition of the House of Lords, 1 January 2007

Affiliation	Life peers	Hereditary peers	Serving Law Lords	Bishops	Total	Losses in 2006	Gains in 2006	Net change
Conservative	159	47	0	0	206	5	7	+2
Labour	207	4	0	0	211	4	8	+4
Lib. Dem.	73	5	0	0	78	0	5	+5
Crossbench[a]	153	33	12	0	200	8	14	+6
Bishops	0	0	0	26	26	1	2	+1
Other[b]	12	2	0	0	14	0	0	0
Total	618	91[c]	12	26	735	18	36	+18

[a] Including nine Ulster Unionist Party members, three Democratic Unionist Party members and one Plaid Cymru member, who by convention sit as Crossbenchers.
[b] This group largely comprises members who have left one of the main parties, and it includes the one Green Party member.
[c] There was one vacancy, due to the death of Lord Mowbray and Stourton in December.

Sources: Calculated from House of Lords Information Office figures and Hansard. Note that all figures in this table are based on dates that members take the oath and therefore do not precisely match published House of Lords figures which are based on dates that writs of summons are issued.

Table 9.2   Arrivals and departures from the House, 1999–2006

	Total at start of period[a]	Losses	Gains[b]	Net change
1999, Nov onwards	669	4	4	0
2000	669	18	42	+24
2001	693	28	47	+19
2002	712	25	5	−20
2003	692	28	14	−14
2004	678	24	53	+29
2005	707	23	46	+23
2006	730	18	36	+18
Total at 1 Jan 2007	748	168	247	+79

[a] Including members on leave of absence (who are excluded from Table 9.1)
[b] Based on dates that members take the oath.

Source: Project House of Lords database, derived from Hansard and House of Lords website.

As well as these arrivals there were 13 other entrants to the chamber over the year.[6] With only 18 deaths and retirements, the size of the chamber continues to grow, and is now 79 higher than it was when reform greatly reduced the membership in November 1999. The pattern of gradual growth since then is shown in Table 9.2, and does not appear sustainable in the longer term. One difficulty is that (with the exception of bishops) members of the Lords cannot retire.[7] This problem was highlighted in July by Lord Phillips of Sudbury (Lib. Dem.), when he announced his desire to leave the House. He introduced the Life Peerages (Disclaimer) Bill, which would have allowed a peer to renounce their position, and require the Prime Minister to appoint a replacement from the same political party. However, it had no chance of becoming law.

Reform

Labour's 2005 manifesto had promised three things on reform: the removal of the remaining hereditary peers, a further free vote on Lords composition (following the inconclusive votes of 2003), and action on the powers of the House. The Blair government had not initially questioned the chamber's powers, but in the face of growing Lords activism had started to consider this necessary. It proposed a review of conventions by a joint committee, and limits on the time bills could spend in the Lords to 60 sitting days. By the start of 2006, no progress had been made on any aspect of reform. The 'cash for peerages' scandal resulted in a flurry of interest, and there was much talk, but other than the review of conventions (discussed separately below) no further progress had been made at the year's end.

Aside from 'cash for peerages', the unofficial contest for a new Labour leader and deputy leader made many senior figures keen to demonstrate their radicalism by talking up Lords reform. This is seen as one of Tony Blair's policy failures, which could be exploited by challengers in his own party, as well as by David Cameron. As early as April, Peter Hain called for a 'great reforming bill' to deal with the House of Lords.[8] In November Hilary Benn spoke out for an 80 per cent elected house.[9] Both Cabinet ministers declared themselves as deputy leadership candidates. Even Alan Milburn (who unlike them had voted for an appointed House in 2003) came out for a directly elected second chamber.[10] Gordon Brown, expected to take over from Tony Blair, has long hinted that he would like to introduce elections to the Lords. However, Blair himself suggested in September that Lords reform remained one of the '39 steps' he wished to complete before leaving office.[11]

Despite this rhetoric, past failures probably taught the government to proceed cautiously. Behind-the-scenes negotiations between the parties, and with Labour backbenchers, were initially led by the Lord Chancellor, Lord Falconer. When Jack Straw became Leader of the House of Commons in May he then took over responsibility for Lords reform. Straw was previously sceptical about elections to the upper house, having voted against all elected options in 2003. However, he expressed a willingness to compromise, and in a speech in July suggested that a 50:50 elected/appointed mix was likely. In the autumn a leaked paper from the cross-party talks indicated that this was now the government's preferred position, and a White Paper along these lines was widely and imminently expected. However, its publication was delayed and it had not appeared by the end of the year. The Queen's Speech, rather than promising a bill, merely stated that the government would 'work to build a consensus on reform of the House of Lords' and would 'bring forward proposals'.[12] Given the political difficulties the delay was not surprising: both main parties remain split on the issue and complaining about Blair's inaction is much easier than devising a widely acceptable solution. In particular the proposal of a 50:50 chamber probably suits no one, and notably was defeated without a division in the Commons votes in 2003. The leaked proposals attracted criticism from senior figures in all three parties – some for including too many elected members, and others for including too few. The delay to the votes (initially promised for spring) at least saved both main parties from the embarrassment of displaying their splits on the floor of the House of Commons, as happened on the previous occasion.

A new leader, or even the existing one, may seek to restart Lords reform again in 2007. But the task is so complex that intentions are not enough. Essentially, the job is to find a compromise that democratises the chamber without making it any stronger. This appears both logistically and tactically impossible. The more confident the chamber becomes in blocking government legislation, the more interest there is on the Labour side in limiting its powers. For many in the party, Lords reform has always been about ensuring that governments can govern unimpeded, rather than about adding further democratic checks.[13] But with respect to the Lords' powers the government was forced during the year to distance itself from its specific manifesto commitment to limit the chamber's consideration of bills to 60 days. Evidence by the senior parliamentary clerks to the Joint Committee on Conventions demonstrated that almost half of bills take more time in the House than this.[14] Jack Straw told the committee that the government had 'no immediate plans to legislate in this way and we wish to await the proposals of this Committee before making any decisions'.[15] However, he also stated that without agreement over the conventions it would be 'extremely difficult to reach agreement on future composition'.[16] This suggested that progress would now be more difficult than ever.

A *Times* poll in April showed the public also split and confused about Lords reform: 75 per cent believed that 'The Lords should remain a mainly appointed house because this gives it a degree of independence from electoral politics and allows people with a broad range of experience and expertise to be involved', while 72 per cent believed that 'At least half of the members of the House of Lords should be elected so that the upper chamber of Parliament has democratic legitimacy.'[17] This internally inconsistent set of positions may also sum up the views of the political class.

Wrestling with the conventions

Contemporary anxieties about the Lords were neatly encapsulated during 2006 by the establishment in May of the Joint Committee on Conventions.[18] Although the government is reluctant to admit that the Lords is more legitimate as a result of the 1999 reform, this was a clear indication of its concern about the chamber's growing assertiveness. Not only have recent years seen high numbers of government defeats in the Lords but also, as evidence to the committee from the Clerk of the Parliaments showed, there is a tendency to more rounds of 'ping-pong' between the two Houses before legislation is agreed. Although comparison over time is difficult, given the lack of historic data and the different behaviour of the Lords under Conservative governments, Table 9.3 shows that the number of times the Lords insisted on its amendments was particularly high in the 2001–05 Parliament. In 2000, the Lords also rejected a piece of secondary legislation for the first time since 1968, and further such defeats have been threatened. Just before this, the Conservative leader in the chamber, Lord Strathclyde, had pronounced previous conventions 'dead' following reform.[19] More recently, the Liberal Democrats have repeatedly questioned the Salisbury convention that a manifesto bill should not be rejected outright by the Lords.[20]

Table 9.3 Number of bills per Parliament where the House of Lords has insisted on its amendments, 1974–2005

Parliament	Number of insistences[a]				Total
	1	2	3	4	
1974–79	2	1	1	0	4
1979–83	0	0	0	0	0
1983–87	1	0	0	0	1
1987–92	0	1	0	0	1
1992–97	1	0	0	0	1
1997–2001	3	1	0	1	4
2001–05	12	3	0	2	17
Total	19	6	1	3	29

[a] I.e. number of times the bill has returned to the Lords and been defeated again, after the initial defeat.

Source: Figures drawn from the Clerk of the Parliament's evidence to the Joint Committee, HL 265-II, 2005–06, pp. EV 97–8.

The Joint Committee's terms of reference required it to consider 'the practicality of codifying the key conventions of the relationship between the two houses of Parliament which affect the consideration of legislation'.[21] In particular it was asked to consider the Salisbury convention, and conventions regarding secondary legislation, the notion that government legislation should be considered 'in reasonable time', and the 'ping-pong' process.

Given the constitutional limbo between one reform and the next in which the Lords finds itself (a situation indeed prevailing for most of the twentieth century), the committee's work had a certain surreal quality. It was unclear at times whether Lords' conventions were being discussed in the past, present or future tense, and evidence sessions included much reflection on questions such as when a convention is a convention and whether it is possible for conventions to be codified at all. While widely accepted conventions (such as the confidence vote applying in the Commons alone) were barely mentioned, the committee concentrated on matters that were so contentious they seemed impossible to be agreed upon, and could therefore probably no longer be considered conventions.

Aside from providing rich material for scholars of philosophy or law to pore over, the committee's work served other useful purposes. The evidence from the clerks provided interesting data, and the parties were pressed to state their positions. The Liberal Democrats maintained their view that reform of the chamber has rendered the Salisbury convention obsolete, but also proposed that no bill (whether in the manifesto or not) should be rejected outright by the Lords.[22] In its report in November the committee concluded that conventions by their nature must remain 'flexible and unenforceable', but suggested that some understandings might be reached between the chambers by mutual resolution. These could include manifesto bills not being subject to 'wrecking' amendments, government legislation being considered by the Lords in 'reasonable time' and both chambers being given notice before considering each other's amendments.[23] Even the terms of these agreements, however, would remain necessarily ill-defined. The committee also stated, in a conclusion troubling for the government, that current conventions could not necessarily be expected to hold if the chamber were reformed in future to include elected members.

Reform in action: the Lord Speaker

Although wholesale Lords reform did not happen, 2006 nevertheless saw real reform of another kind. In 2003 the government announced its intention to abolish the office of the Lord Chancellor, who historically acted as presiding officer in the Lords. Although strong opposition to the proposals resulted in the post of Lord Chancellor being retained, the final settlement – in the Constitutional Reform Act 2005 – allowed the post now to be held by a member of the Commons. As the Lords was potentially left with no presiding officer, a select committee was set up to consider the role and powers of a Speaker for the Lords.

In July 2005, the House agreed a resolution that it should 'elect its own presiding officer' and 'consider further how to implement this resolution with full regard to the House's tradition of self-regulation'.[24] The committee then provided concrete proposals. It concluded that the Lords should not have a 'House of Commons type speaker'.[25] To respect the established culture of self-regulation, the new Lord Speaker, like the Lord Chancellor, should therefore have no power to, for example, select amendments, call on peers in debates, or intervene when members speak for too long or stray from the point. There was some debate over whether the Speaker should take over the role performed by the Leader of the House (a government minister) of deciding the order of speakers at question time. Even this was considered a step too far, though the Speaker, rather than the Leader, will now rule on the admissibility of Private Notice (that is, urgent) Questions. In addition, the Lord Speaker will have a role representing the House at home and overseas.

At the Motion for Approval debate in January 2006, Lord Strathclyde, the Conservative Leader in the House, moved an amendment to combine the Speaker's position with that of the already existing Chairman of Committees. This proposal reflected concern about whether two posts (and two salaries) were justified – however, it was dropped due to lack of support. Another amendment to transfer the Leader's duties during questions to the Speaker was defeated on a free vote, and it was agreed to proceed on the basis of the committee's report.

The election of the first Lord Speaker took place at the end of June by secret ballot, using the alternative vote system, by which candidates are ranked in order of preference and those with fewest votes eliminated on each round.[26] Each of the nine candidates provided a 75-word statement describing why they wanted the position. On 4 July it was announced that Baroness Hayman, who was the clear leader on the first ballot, had defeated Lord Grenfell (a Deputy Speaker) by 263 votes to 236 in the final round.[27] Baroness Hayman is a former Labour minister, but upon election she announced that she would give up the whip and she now sits as an unaligned peer.

On the surface, it appears that little has substantively changed. It has been emphasised that self-regulation, rather than firmly chaired debate, should remain. As the committee noted, many feared that 'any change in the role currently performed by the Lord Chancellor would be a "slippery slope"' away from these traditions.[28] Consequently, the former presiding officer's responsibilities have largely been transferred unchanged. However, it is too soon to predict what the medium- to long-term consequences of this reform will be. The position of Lord Speaker has the potential to be moulded by its occupier, as well as by wider events. Formally, the extent to which she can take an active role is limited and she remains subservient to the House. However, as peers become more assertive the role may become a more active one, adding to the cultural changes that have already affected the chamber since its reform in 1999.

The legislative evidence

As data is gathered from the passage of bills over several parliamentary sessions, a picture of a stronger House of Lords is slowly emerging. The number of government defeats in the chamber in 2006 is shown in Table 9.4. In 2005–06, there were 62 defeats, compared with 56 in the similar long post-election session of 2001–02 and 39 in 1997–98. It is difficult to draw definitive conclusions from such trends, as each session is different and the political context constantly changes. Post-2005, the Blair government is less popular, and its majority in the House of Commons is reduced. Accordingly, one might expect to see the balance tilt from the Lords to the Commons, in terms of keeping the government in check. However, an interesting pattern of partnership between the chambers is instead emerging, and became clearer in 2006. This challenges the popular assumption that the two chambers are in competition and instead shows that they can unite against the executive, particularly when policy is contested by government backbench MPs. This is reinforced by the fact that 78 per cent of peers and 75 per cent of Labour

Table 9.4   Government defeats in the House of Lords, 2006

Subject	Calendar year 2006	2005–06 session total
2005–06 session business		
Charities Bill	–	1
Civil Aviation Bill	4	4
Companies Bill	1	1
Company Law Reform Bill [HL]	5	5
Compensation Bill [HL]	1	1
Criminal Defence Service Bill [HL]	–	1
Electoral Administration Bill	2	2
Equality Bill [HL]	–	1
Government of Wales Bill	6	6
Identity Cards Bill	11	12
National Lottery Bill	1	1
NHS Redress Bill [HL]	2	2
Northern Ireland (Miscellaneous Provisions) Bill	2	2
Police and Justice Bill	8	8
Racial and Religious Hatred Bill	–	1
Road Safety Bill [HL]	4	8
Terrorism Bill	4	4
Violent Crime Reduction Bill	1	1
Motions and other business	–	1
2006–07 session business: no defeats by year end		
Total	52	62

Note: [HL] = bills originating in the House of Lords.

MPs believe the chamber is more legitimate since its 1999 reform.[29] The indications are, therefore, that this may have significantly boosted the strength of Parliament as a whole.

A kind of partnership had already been demonstrated over the Terrorism Bill in late 2005, when MPs inflicted their first defeats on the Blair government, over the period for which police could detain suspected terrorists. Although the bill had not yet been to the second chamber, this could be seen as a preemptive strike by the Commons, knowing that the Lords would certainly have amended the bill.[30] The other main issue of concern to MPs was that of 'glorification' of terrorism, where the government had avoided defeat by one vote.[31] Peers voted by a large margin to remove all references to 'glorification'; but, following minor concessions by the government, MPs were persuaded to overturn the Lords amendments. At this stage, the Conservatives in the Lords dropped their opposition and the 'glorification' clause was accepted. Without continued Commons support peers were not prepared to press the point.

On the Racial and Religious Hatred Bill the partnership was more effective. Here the key sticking point between ministers and Parliament was the definition of 'incitement' to religious hatred.[32] In 2005, the government faced public campaigns, rebellions in the House of Commons and the largest Lords defeat of the 2005–06 session. Peers did not seek to remove the clause, but to clarify that ridicule, insult or abuse would not be sufficient grounds to prove incitement. The government's offer of a 'freedom of expression' clause did not go far enough to placate either peers or MPs. When the bill returned to the Commons in February as amended by the Lords, the Conservative spokesperson, Dominic Grieve, proposed that 'the Government can have their legislation ... in the form that the Lords have wisely altered and it can then go forward'.[33] Similarly, Labour's Tony Wright suggested that 'the Lords delivered to us a Bill which, if it did not completely square the circle, did it as well as it was humanly possible'.[34] Such claims are normally mere debating points, but to everyone's surprise a majority of MPs agreed. The Commons inflicted two defeats by voting not to overturn the Lords amendments.[35] On this occasion, the two Houses' interests remained aligned, and in partnership they achieved their preferred policy positions.

The Identity Cards Bill, like the Terrorism Bill, demonstrated a less visible partnership, but nonetheless put the government under significant pressure. Despite its controversial nature, the bill had a relatively smooth passage through the Commons. In the Lords, the largest points of contention were the costs of the scheme and the extent of compulsion of the cards. On the latter point the peers sought to turn the Salisbury convention on its head, by arguing that they, not the government, were defending the election manifesto.[36] This had stated that ID cards would be introduced 'initially on a voluntary basis as people renew their passports', but the bill required all passport applicants to apply for a card.[37] Consequently, there were four rounds of 'ping-pong' on the bill, driven by a coalition of Conservative and

Liberal Democrat peers. This continued despite insufficient support for their position in the House of Commons each time the amendments returned. The minister, Baroness Scotland, argued that 'the Government, with the support of the elected House, will continue to resist them strongly' should the Lords persist, and they eventually backed down.[38] What went less noticed, however, was that an early Lords defeat, removing the right for government to make ID cards compulsory for all by means of secondary legislation, was reluctantly accepted by ministers, without being put to the Commons. Following the problems over the Terrorism and Racial and Religious Hatred Bills, and given the wording of the manifesto, the government chose not to take the risk. Again, the prospect of MPs and peers united in opposition was enough to extract major policy concessions, made easier by lack of media attention and thus embarrassment to the government.

Two other defeats towards the end of the session, on the Police and Justice Bill, saw peers achieve mixed success in extracting policy concessions. One responded to the public controversy following the extradition of the 'NatWest Three', with peers opposing the lower threshold of evidence required to extradite British citizens to the US. However, there proved to be insufficient support for their position in the Commons, and this opposition was dropped. The peers did win a major victory, however, over government plans to merge the five criminal justice inspectorates. Their amendment was moved by Lord Ramsbotham, former Chief Inspector of Prisons (Crossbench), and supported by both the opposition parties, the other 32 Crossbenchers voting, and 11 Labour rebels. It was consequently a large defeat (by 113 votes) and one which looked difficult to reverse. This led ministers to drop the proposals immediately rather than seeking to overturn the Lords' position and facing prolonged 'ping-pong'. It demonstrated the force that united opposition, and Crossbench experts, in the House of Lords can have.

Conclusion

The events of 2006 continue to suggest that the House of Lords is growing in influence, enhancing Parliament's negotiating power with the executive. It is not yet possible to say definitively that 1999 was a turning point in the development of the second chamber's role; there are too many short-term factors at play. In 2006, a key factor was the waning popularity of the government, stimulating its parliamentary opponents and helping them unite and inflict defeats via the House of Lords. This might have been the case even without reform, but this is doubtful. In any case, two things are clear. First, the government itself believes that the House of Lords is changing, and it is worried about the chamber's strength. This was shown by the threats to reduce the time for the consideration of legislation, and the attempt to agree conventions stating that the chamber should act with restraint. Second, it is increasingly clear that little can easily be done to weaken the chamber again. Opposition parties are unlikely to consent to formal weakening, except perhaps where this is coupled with democratisation. But it is widely recognised that introducing elections would further increase the chamber's confidence and authority, and thus its de facto strength. Agreement on more reform thus looks very difficult.

Two wider points can be made, given these developments. First, a chamber does not necessarily have to be elected in order to be strong – it can be enough to act with a certain level of public and elite political support. Based on the characteristics of second chambers generally considered by scholars, little has changed about the House of Lords since 1999 – it remains unelected and has the same powers as before.[39] Indeed, some even argued that the reform would make the chamber weaker.[40] Instead, what we see is that the departure of the hereditaries and, crucially, the new party balance, have boosted the Lords' sense of legitimacy and given it more confidence to challenge the government. This remains even despite allegations of cronyism in Lords appointments. Second, a stronger upper house does not necessarily mean a weaker lower house – indeed, possibly quite the reverse. Although ministers try to present arguments as Lords versus Commons, the far more interesting dynamic is that of Parliament versus executive. The existence of the Lords as a serious longstop has given a greater confidence to MPs to extract concessions from ministers, and the greater rebelliousness of the Commons also acts to boost the power of peers. This intercameral partnership, if it continues and grows, could represent a real shift of power within the British Westminster system.

Notes

1. This work was supported by the Economic and Social Research Council, grant no. RES-000–23–0597.
2. See M. Russell and M. Sciara, 'The House of Lords in 2005: A More Representative and Assertive Chamber?', in M. Rush and P. Giddings (eds), *The Palgrave Review of British Politics 2005* (Basingstoke: Palgrave Macmillan, 2006), pp. 122–36; P. Cowley, 'Making Parliament Matter?', in P. Dunleavy, R. Heffernan, P. Cowley and C. Hay (eds), *Developments in British Politics 8* (Basingstoke: Palgrave Macmillan, 2006).
3. For a discussion see M. Russell and M. Sciara, 'Legitimacy and Bicameral Strength: A Case Study of the House of Lords', paper to 2006 Conference of the Political Studies Association specialist group on Parliaments and Legislatures, University of Sheffield. Available at: <www.ucl.ac.uk/constitution-unit/research/Parliament/house-of-lords.html>; A. Kelso, 'Reforming the House of Lords: Navigating Representation, Democracy and Legitimacy at Westminster', *Parliamentary Affairs*, 59 (2006), 563–81.
4. PASC, *Fourth Report – Propriety and Honours: Interim Findings*, HC 1119, 2005–06.
5. Ibid., para. 30.
6. Seven were independent members announced by the Appointments Commission in May. Others included the new Archbishop of York, John Sentamu; the retiring Bishop of Oxford, Richard Harries; and Retiring NHS Chief Executive, Nigel Crisp. The latter two were prime ministerial nominees and sit as Crossbenchers.

7. Though they can go on temporary 'leave of absence'. The figures in Table 9.1 exclude the handful who have done so.
8. Appearing on GMTV, 23 April, reported by the Press Association.
9. *Guardian*, 20 November 2006.
10. 'Milburn Looks to Leadership', <http://news.bbc.co.uk/hi/uk_politics/5346572. stm>.
11. 'Blair sets out the 39 steps he hope will secure his legacy', *The Times*, 27 September 2006.
12. HL Debs, 687, 15 November 2006, c. 3. The White Paper, *The House of Lords: Reform* was published in February 2007 as Cm 7027.
13. See P. Dorey, '1949, 1969, 1999: The Labour Party and House of Lords Reform', *Parliamentary Affairs*, 59 (2006), 599–620.
14. Joint Committee on Conventions, *Conventions of the UK Parliament*, HL 265-II, 2005–06, pp. EV 95-7.
15. Ibid., p. EV 11.
16. Ibid., p. EV 13.
17. See <www.populuslimited.com/pdf/2006_04_04_times.pdf>.
18. The committee comprised 11 peers and 11 MPs – 11 Labour, 6 Conservative, 3 Liberal Democrat and 2 Crossbench, and was chaired by Labour's Lord Cunningham, a trusted former minister.
19. Speech to the thinktank Politeia, 30 December 1999.
20. See Russell and Sciara, 'The House of Lords in 2005', pp. 123–4.
21. Joint Committee on Conventions, *First Special Report*, HL 189, 2005–06, para. 2.
22. The party's written evidence to the committee stated that 'the House should not vote down entire Government Bills at Second Reading, as to do so would run contrary to its role as a revising chamber' and 'the House should not reject whole Bills at Third Reading either, but we strongly believe that the House must maintain its unfettered right to amend at Third Reading'. HL 265-II, 2005–06, p. EV 66.
23. Joint Committee on Conventions, *Conventions of the UK Parliament*, HL 265–I, 2005–06, pp. 76–9.
24. HL Debs, 673, 12 July 2005, c. 1002.
25. Report of the Committee on the Speakership of the House, *The Speakership of the House of Lords*, HL 92, 2005–06, para. 8.
26. This is the same as the electoral system used in hereditary by-elections. It is a more streamlined system than that agreed in 2001 for electing the House of Commons Speaker, which requires repeated voting.
27. The other candidates were Lord Boston of Faversham (Crossbench), Lord Elton (Con.), Baroness Fookes (Con.), Countess of Mar (Crossbench), Lord Redesdale (Lib. Dem.), Lord Richard (Lab.) and Viscount Ullswater (Con.).
28. HL 92, 2005–06, para. 14.
29. Surveys of Peers and MPs carried out for the project, in February 2005 and February 2004 respectively. For peers the response rate was 57 per cent (n = 374 on this question, including 103 Labour). For MPs the response was 30 per cent (n = 107 on this question amongst Labour MPs). For further analysis see Russell and Sciara, 'Legitimacy and Bicameral Strength'.
30. Particularly in the light of the marathon argument between the government and the Lords on the Prevention of Terrorism Bill earlier in the year: see Russell and Sciara, 'The House of Lords in 2005'.
31. See HC Debs, 438, 2 November 2005, cc. 832–938.

32. This had previously been considered by the Lords and rejected twice in the Anti-Terrorism, Crime and Security Bill in 2001. Consequently the clause was dropped.
33. HC Debs, 442, 31 January 2006, cc. 215–6.
34. Ibid., c. 229.
35. See P. Cowley and M. Stuart, 'Rebelliousness in a Westminster System: Labour MPs under the Blair Government', Seventh Workshop of Parliamentarians and Parliamentary Scholars, Wroxton College, Oxfordshire, 29–30 July 2006.
36. Some similar arguments took place on the Health Bill, where the government whipped its peers to vote for a total ban on smoking in public places though the manifesto had claimed that a partial ban would be introduced. On this occasion Lord Stoddart of Swindon complained that 'Yesterday, [on the Terrorism Bill] we were being told that we must honour manifesto commitments; today, we are being told to ignore a manifesto commitment. The Government cannot have it both ways' (HL Debs, 679, 1 March 2006, c. 324). However, this aroused less opposition from peers than the Identity Cards Bill, as the tougher measures had been imposed overwhelmingly on the government by MPs.
37. *Britain Forward Not Back*, Labour Party, 2005.
38. HL Debs, 679, 6 March 2006, c. 546.
39. For example, Arend Lijphart in his *Patterns of Democracy* (New Haven: Yale University Press, 1999) argues that what matters are formal powers and the extent to which the two chambers are 'congruent' in membership, but that unelected chambers 'lack the democratic legitimacy, and hence the real political influence, that popular election confers' (p. 206).
40. M. Flinders, 'Majoritarian Democracy in Britain', *West European Politics*, 28 (2005), 62–94. Flinders' argument, based on Lijphart, is that the composition of the two chambers is now more similar following the departure of the hereditaries, and that the Lords must therefore be weaker after reform.

10
The Law and Politics: Clashing Rights and Interests

Sue Prince

Amid the clash of voices in 2006, respect for individual human rights did not attract the consensus view it might have done had circumstances been different. The government introduced new terrorism legislation to bypass House of Lords' rulings, which had undermined existing statutory provisions on the subject. The Conservative Party argued that existing rights protected the interests of terrorists and prisoners over and above those of ordinary citizens. Elsewhere, momentum was growing for the codification of certain powers held by the executive under the royal prerogative, and the role of the Attorney General also came under consideration.

Terrorism and the law

The difficulties of upholding the rule of law and seeking to prevent acts of terrorism were a major problem for the government in 2006. The Human Rights Act 1998 (HRA) reinforces the principle of the rule of law because interference with human rights has to be prescribed by, or be in accordance with, the law. Certain rights, such as the prohibition of torture or degrading treatment or punishment under Article 3 of the European Convention on Human Rights (ECHR), are considered absolute and do not permit any derogation by a state. However, with regard to the right to liberty under Article 5 of the ECHR there are clear circumstances where an individual's rights might be waived in favour of the protection of the public, such as when someone is detained after conviction by a court or when they are detained pending trial. The rights provided under Article 5 are therefore not absolute and, in 2001, the government issued a derogation from Article 5 to pass legislation allowing for extended powers to detain suspects on charges related to terrorism.[1] But it has fallen foul of the courts on this legislation.[2] The problem is that although the government can detain an individual while it is considering deportation it is not possible under Article 3 of the ECHR to deport someone to a country where they might be tortured. Additionally, under Article 5 of the ECHR it is not possible to detain someone indefinitely without charging them with a crime. The government enacted the Prevention of Terrorism Act 2005 (PTA) to replace section 4 of the Anti-Terrorism Crime and Security Act 2001, which had been subject to a declaration of incompatibility in 2004. This statute enabled the Home Secretary to issue 'control orders', with the consent of the court, which make those suspected of terrorism-related offences subject to house arrest or electronic tagging.[3] The Act created two types of control order in sections 1–4 of the Act, the first being non-derogating control orders, which do not derogate from the rights protected under Article 5 of the ECHR.[4] These do not deprive the subject of their liberty but only restrict their right to privacy, to a (purportedly) limited degree. Derogating control orders, under section 4 of the Act, however, deprive the individual of their liberty by, for example, placing them under strict house arrest. No derogating orders have yet been made under the Act.

In August 2006, in *Secretary of State for the Home Department* v. *MB*,[5] a non-derogating order was the subject of litigation in the courts. The Home Secretary, suspecting MB of having been involved in terrorism-related activities, issued a control order to prevent him travelling to Iraq on the grounds that he might become involved with insurgents there. Under the terms of his control order, as well as surrendering his passport MB had to report daily to a police station.

MB challenged the order in court on the basis that it was incompatible with the ECHR because section 3 of the PTA did not provide a fair procedure for challenging control orders as it allowed the government to rely on 'closed material' in support of its application. A substantial part of the case against him rested on the allegation that he was involved in terrorism-related activities, details of which were contained in this closed material. MB was not even allowed a summary of the information. The rules governing the use of closed material state that disclosure of such information is not allowed if it is contrary to the interests of national security, and therefore contrary to the public interest – but it is the court which decides whether the closed material can be used.[6]

At first instance, Sullivan J made a 'declaration of incompatibility' under section 4 of the Human Rights Act, holding that the relevant sections of the PTA did not comply with the demands of procedural fairness required by the right to a fair trial under Article 6 of the ECHR. In the media, the Home Secretary, John Reid, criticised the judge and said that the judgment was full of 'misunderstandings and errors'.[7] The Court of Appeal, upholding the appeal, considered that the judge was in error in this case. The judges said that a thorough analysis of the case law of the European Court of Human Rights showed that the superior court had previously considered that the use of closed material was acceptable and that the non-disclosure of relevant evidence does not offend against an absolute right.[8] In certain cases, therefore, it is possible to derogate from the absolute need to provide full disclosure of evidence where it is in the interests of national security, as long as adequate safeguards apply to limit any prejudice that may arise from the non-disclosure.

In a further case in the Court of Appeal, the same deference to the executive was not apparent, as the court upheld a 'declaration of incompatibility' under section 4 of the HRA, also originally decided by Sullivan J. The case likewise concerned 'non-derogating' control orders. At first instance, in *Secretary of State for the Home Department* v. *JJ and Others*, Sullivan J found that the restrictions placed upon six men curtailed their liberty to such an extent that any freedom was 'non-existent for all practical purposes'.[9] All were suspected of terrorist-related activities and the terms of the control orders were such that each was required to remain within his residence at all times, save for a period of six hours between 10.00 a.m. and 4.00 p.m. Each lived in a small one-bedroom flat and any visitors had to be identified to the Home Office; the flats themselves were subject to unannounced spot checks by the police. Even when they were allowed to leave the flats, the men were restricted to visiting a very small and defined area. They were not allowed to make any plans to meet anyone and all visitors to their homes had to be identified to the police before being allowed to visit. Such a deprivation of freedom was found in the court to be incompatible with the right to liberty under Article 5 of the ECHR. Again, the government clashed with the judiciary. The Home Secretary said, following the decision, that the measures were necessary to protect the public and that they were proportionate to the level of the threat posed by the men.[10]

A requirement for proportionality as an aspect of the rule of law requires that any interference by a law with a human right must be as limited as possible. In the Court of Appeal, Lord Phillips said that the restrictions imposed by the control orders made the 'most serious inroads on liberty'.[11] The court maintained that the deprivation of liberty forced upon these men was contrary to the government's duties under Article 5 of the ECHR. It did not quash the control orders but instead required the Home Secretary to modify the existing obligations so that they were lawful. The Home Secretary reacted to the judgment by reducing the period of house arrest for the men from 18 hours a day to 14 hours. He has also applied for the case to be reviewed in the future by the House of Lords.

A further case exacerbated the acerbic relationship between the government and the judiciary, sparking what was described as a 'constitutional crisis'.[12] The Home Secretary refused leave to remain in the UK to nine Afghan nationals who had hijacked an aircraft in Afghanistan in 2001 and forced the pilot to fly to Stansted Airport, near London, where eventually they surrendered to the police. The men had carried firearms and explosives with them on the flight. They were convicted of serious criminal offences and served most of their prison sentences before these were set aside on a technicality. The men applied for asylum in Britain on the grounds that they were members of an organisation which was a political opponent of the Taliban in Afghanistan and there was a strong possibility that they would be tortured or killed had they been returned to their own country. The Home Secretary rejected their claims for protection under Article 3 of the ECHR, arguing that the political climate had now changed in Afghanistan and it was safe for the men to return. On appeal, the Immigration Appeal Tribunal found, based upon human rights reasoning, that there would not be sufficient protection for the men should they be returned to their homeland and that their involvement in the hijacking would put them at great risk of being killed. The Home Secretary originally delayed making a decision and then decided to apply his new discretionary leave policy, which had been revised in the summer of 2005, and under which he could decide it was inappropriate to grant leave.[13] In this case it was because the crime of hijacking posed a great threat to life and it was in the public interest to deter individuals from such activities. At first instance, the judge held that it was aspects of this policy of the Home Secretary that were unlawful, since it gave him too much discretion to refuse to apply the decision made by the Immigration Appeal Tribunal.[14]

The Court of Appeal reinforced this earlier decision and held that such unfettered discretion exercised by a minister was not sufficiently clearly defined and accessible to be lawful, and for that reason it offended not only Article 5 of the ECHR but also the principle of the rule of law.[15] For the actions of the Home Secretary to have been lawful the court stated that they would have to have been bestowed by Parliament.

Brooke LJ, in his reasoning in the Court of Appeal, commenting on the furore over the case, said: 'Judges and adjudicators have to apply the law as they find it, and not as they might wish it to be.'[16] The difficulty for the judiciary is that it is applying the law on legal principles based upon justice and fairness, but these same principles are not necessarily still seen as a universal priority by the media or the government, both of whom seem prepared to allow individuals to forgo explicit individual rights in order to counter the threat of terrorism.[17] Clashes between judges and ministers are not new, but the crucial difference now is that the Human Rights Act increasingly extends judicial review into the political arena.

Other changes in the law suggest that further clashes between the executive and the judiciary are probable. For example, wide powers given to police officers under section 44 of the Terrorism Act 2000 allow the stopping and searching of individuals at random and there have been a number of allegations of abuse of this power.[18] The sheer number of searches heightens the likelihood of legal challenges: for instance, the City of London Police report that, between July 2005 and June 2006, they have conducted about 11,500 searches.[19] Challenges are even more likely under the provisions of the Terrorism Act 2006 making it a criminal offence to encourage or glorify terrorism or to commit acts preparatory to terrorism. These measures aroused considerable debate in Parliament,[20] but the government argued that they were necessary to help law enforcement agencies counter the threat of terrorism in the UK.[21] The Joint Committee on Human Rights stated that the proposals, when in bill form, were incompatible with Articles 5 and 10 of the ECHR,[22] but the Act remains to be tested in the courts.

Reviewing the Human Rights Act

In June, the Conservative Leader, David Cameron, accused the government of 'hyperactive legislating' in the areas of criminal justice and national security. He argued that the fundamental challenge to government is striking the right balance between security and liberty and that it was actually the Human Rights Act 1998, originally introduced to protect individual liberty, which undermines the ability of society to protect itself. He said the HRA had introduced 'a culture that has inhibited law enforcement and the supervision of convicted criminals'.[23] Instead, he advocated a modern 'British Bill of Rights', which would be clearer and more precise than the ECHR. His ideas echoed a militant campaign in the *Sun* to 'end the human rights madness' and tear up 'crazy' human rights laws.[24]

The Lord Chancellor, Lord Falconer, was quick to defend the provisions of the ECHR and the HRA itself and asserted that they did not 'remotely reduce the ability of the state to provide proper protection for its citizens', but gave a legal basis on which the state provided protection.[25] The human rights organisation Justice welcomed debate on human rights issues, pointing out that the ECHR was actually drafted by British lawyers after the Second World War, under the auspices of the Council of Europe, to lay the foundations of a Europe-wide system of human rights.[26]

In July, the government's review of the HRA stated that the Act had been widely misunderstood by the public but the government was fully committed to its implementation. The review dismissed the Conservative Party's proposal to withdraw from the ECHR,[27] and went on to identify two fundamental problems with introducing a 'British Bill of Rights' and repealing the HRA. The first was that entrenching such a statute would threaten the cardinal principle of the British constitution, that of parliamentary sovereignty. Entrenchment would mean that the ultimate arbiter on rights would not be Parliament but non-elected judges.

The second problem was that, under Article 25 of the ECHR, citizens would be able to take their disputes to the European Court of Human Rights in Strasbourg so long as Britain remained a signatory. The right of individual petition to the court has existed since 1966. In addition, the fact that Britain has been a signatory to the ECHR for so long means that the principles inherent in the Convention are now embedded within the fabric of British law. The review concluded that the HRA has not significantly altered the constitutional balance between Parliament, the executive and the judiciary, and advocated more guidance and training within government departments and agencies, as well as an increase in public education to build general confidence in the Act.[28]

In fact, the HRA has generated a substantial body of case law. The review identified that approximately 2 per cent of cases determined by the courts came within the 'human rights' classification, with the majority raising new issues of principle and covering a wide range of civil and criminal litigation. The judges, however, have adopted a conservative approach, apparently loath to apply the remedies provided in the HRA. Although section 3 of the HRA requires the judiciary to interpret legislation so that it is 'read and given effect in a way which is compatible with the Convention rights', the courts have only applied this section on 12 occasions since 2000.[29] Section 4, which allows the courts to make a 'declaration of incompatibility', requiring Parliament to revisit the matter and decide whether to amend the legislation concerned, has only been used by the courts in exceptional circumstances. The courts have upheld declarations on 16 occasions since the enactment of the HRA.[30] Lord Steyn has suggested that the limited number of cases in which these remedies have been utilised may be due to a general judicial unwillingness to 'flout the will of Parliament', combined with the natural inclination of British judges to give a technical 'literalistic interpretation' to legislation rather than the more purposive, and European, approach required when a right is being considered. This is as yet an unfamiliar approach for the British judiciary.[31]

In addition to the government's review, Parliament's Joint Committee on Human Rights conducted an inquiry into the HRA itself. It said that criticisms of the HRA did not justify a wholesale review of the Act, but that it was partly the fault of government that the statute was being undermined:

We must ... draw to Parliament's attention the extent to which the government itself was responsible for creating the public impression that ... it was either the Human Rights Act or misinterpretations of that Act which caused the problems. In each case, very senior ministers, from the Prime Minister down, made assertions that the Human Rights Act, or judges or officials interpreting it, were responsible for certain unpopular events when ... these assertions were unfounded. Moreover, there was no acknowledgement of the error, or withdrawal of the comment, or any other attempt to inform the public of the mistake ... [I]n our view, public misunderstandings of the effect of the Act will continue so long as very senior ministers fail to retract unfortunate comments already made and continue to make unfounded assertions about the Act and to use is as a scapegoat for administrative failings in their departments.[32]

The Joint Committee stated that such events only served to highlight how far Britain had to venture before a 'human rights culture' was effected.[33] It reiterated that this remained an important goal for the UK. Such an aim could not be left to the remit of the courts but had to be integrated into the delivery of all public services. The establishment of the Commission for Equality and Human Rights was an important element in this challenge.[34]

Proceedings arising from the HRA and the ECHR are clearly an area in which clashes between the executive and the judiciary can be expected to arise. It will be interesting to see how politicians generally respond to those clashes and in particular whether David Cameron persists in his intention to substitute a 'British Bill of Rights' for the 1998 Act.

The royal prerogative

For several years there have been attempts to codify the powers exercised by the government when it is acting under the royal prerogative. Last year, the latest in a series of Private Members' Bills on the subject, tabled by Clare Short, failed to muster enough support in the House of Commons.[35] This year, the Liberal Democrat, Lord Lester of Herne Hill, made a further attempt with a Constitutional Reform (Prerogative Powers and Civil Service) Bill seeking to make the executive more accountable to Parliament by requiring the government to exercise powers under the royal prerogative only with the support of the legislative branch. This would have covered the powers to sign treaties and to go to war, though not in exceptional circumstances, such as where immediate action by the government was required. It also excluded those powers exercised exclusively by the monarch. The bill was passed by the Lords and appeared to have the support of some senior ministers, including the Chancellor of the Exchequer, Gordon Brown, who said that there was a clear case for greater accountability of the executive and a 'greater role for Parliament in decisions of peace and war'.[36] In the Lords it was argued that the bill would be a victory for parliamentary sovereignty. However, while the constitutional supremacy of Parliament was acknowledged, it was pointed out that, in reality, the executive usually controlled the House of Commons and that the question needs to be considered as to whether this should continue to be the case.[37] Moreover, it was argued that it would be difficult for Parliament to debate such issues effectively without adequate disclosure of national security matters governments are usually reluctant to divulge.[38] In the Commons, the bill ran out of time and the issue will therefore need to await further future political will to address it. A consequence of amending the British constitution in this way would be a major increase in judicial review in this area, which has up to now been developing on an incremental basis.[39] Further debate on these issues will be helped by the report of the House of Lords Constitution Committee which reviewed the role of the powers of royal prerogative and considered for itself the advantages and disadvantages of codification.[40]

The Supreme Court

The Lord Chancellor relinquished his historic position as Speaker of the House of Lords in July, and the functions of the Lord Chancellor as a Lord of Appeal under the Appellate Jurisdictions Act were abolished by secondary legislation.[41] The original intention had been to remove the Lord Chancellor from many of his responsibilities three years ago, but there were so many complex powers and duties associated with the office that it proved harder to accomplish than anticipated. In fact, the Constitutional Reform Act 2005 contained 407 provisions relating to the different functions of the Lord Chancellor,[42] and further legislation was necessary to deal with other changes – for instance, 80 were made in The Lord Chancellor (Transfer of Functions and Supplementary Provisions) (No. 2) Order 2006. Lord Goodhart noted that these provisions illustrated the 'absurdity of the attempt by the Prime Minister on 12 June 2003 to abolish the historic office of Lord Chancellor by press release'.[43]

The Supreme Court Implementation Programme, operating under the Constitutional Reform Act 2005, presented the plans for the new Supreme Court, to be based in the Middlesex Guildhall, London, to the Lord Chancellor in March.[44] The court is planned to be operational from October 2009.[45] Until then, when they become Justices of the Supreme Court, the Law Lords will remain as a committee of the House of Lords.

The role of the Attorney General

The Constitutional Reform Act 2005 established a division of powers between the Lord Chancellor and the Lord Chief Justice, partly due to the need for a clear separation of functions previously performed by the Lord Chancellor, both as a Cabinet minister and as head of the judiciary. The mixture of legal and political duties has also caused problems this year for the government's chief legal adviser, the Attorney General, Lord Goldsmith, who has ministerial as well as legal responsibilities, and is currently a de facto member of the Cabinet.

The government spent a great deal of 2006 embroiled in allegations that several individuals had been offered peerages in return for loans to the Labour Party. The Honours (Prevention of Abuses) Act 1925 was passed following a similar scandal involving David Lloyd George in the early 1920s. The Act makes the granting of a dignity, or an honour, an offence if done as a result of a valuable gift or money.

The conflict between the Attorney General's political and legal responsibilities was the subject of much discussion with regard to his advice on the legality of the invasion of Iraq. It again became an issue at the end of 2006, when Lord Goldsmith announced that an investigation by the Serious Fraud Office (SFO) was being discontinued 'in the national interest'.[46] He announced that the SFO were to drop their investigation into corruption at the defence company, BAE Systems, which was taking place under the Anti-Terrorism, Crime and Security Act 2001. The investigation had concerned possible irregularities involved in a massive arms deal called the 'Al Yamamah contract' between the British and Saudi governments, which had been in operation over the last twenty years. The contract, to equip, arm and train the Saudi air force was the largest ever British export agreement. In a statement in the House of Lords, Lord Goldsmith said that it might have been difficult to effect a prosecution and, most importantly, 'It has been necessary to balance the need to maintain the rule of law against the wider public interest.' He said that to continue the investigations would impact upon national security, especially in respect of British-Saudi co-operation on the 'war on terror'.[47] Saudi suggestions that the contract might be in jeopardy had clearly raised serious commercial issues for the government, but fed the strong suspicion that it had succumbed to pressure to discontinue the investigation. Such a situation makes the position of the Attorney General difficult, given his duty to uphold the rule of law in the face of non-legal concerns or interests. As Attorney General, Lord Goldsmith is responsible for approving prosecutions in complex or politically sensitive cases. He has stated that his decisions are 'apolitical'.[48] It was doubts about similar claims of personal impartiality that led to reform of the Lord Chancellor's position.

Freedom of information

The Freedom of Information Act 2000, which came fully into force in 2005, gives individuals and organisations the possibility of accessing information held by public authorities. One of the major problems identified by the Constitutional Affairs Committee has been the excessive amount of delay in responding to requests which undermines the effectiveness of the Act itself.[49] However, the Department of Constitutional Affairs reported that over 90 per cent of requests for information between January and September 2006 had been processed within the deadline or were allowed a permitted deadline extension.[50] In 2005, 38,108 requests were received, of which 92.1 per cent were processed by the end of the year. Just over half the requests were to Departments of State, with most made to the Ministry of Defence, followed by the Home Office, Transport, Work and Pensions, and the Cabinet Office. Of the requests made to other bodies, nearly two-fifths (37.9 per cent) were to the Health and Safety Executive and a further third (33.8 per cent) to the National Archives.[51]

An independent review of the implementation of the Act, published in October, determined that the average number of requests for information from central government should be approximately 36,000 per year at a cost of £24.4 million.[52] Of these, about 35 per cent might be refused on the basis of exemptions. The wider public sector receives about 87,000 requests, at a total cost of £11.1 million. The majority of these requests are to local authorities. The report assessed the costs of processing individual information requested under the Act and concluded that it would be beneficial to introduce a charge for certain types of information requested.

The government is currently considering curtailing the access to information under the Act by regulating the type of requests that can be rejected. The government claims that the number of requests is taking up too much time and is expensive in staff time. Requests could therefore be turned down on the basis that they are 'too expensive to answer'.[53] The Campaign for the Freedom of Information has suggested that restrictions on the grounds of expense would increase the number refused by 4,400.[54]

The Extradition Act 2003

The Extradition Act 2003 implemented a system of fast-track extradition, which does not require any court proceedings before an individual is extradited to the United States. In the indictment of *Government of US* v. *Bermingham, Mulgrew and Darby*, a case linked to the Enron bankruptcy, three former executives of NatWest Bank were alleged to have committed fraud and were extradited to the United States to face trial. The case attracted extensive media coverage and parliamentary concern in Britain in the months leading up to their extradition.[55] The human rights pressure group Liberty argued that the Act violated the requirements of a right to privacy under Article 8 of the ECHR.[56] It reported that 47 requests have been made by the US government to extradite individuals from the UK, while the British government has only made 12 similar requests and is arguing for amendments to the law.[57] Notwithstanding campaigns by the unusual combination of business and civil liberties groups (see Chapter 5, this volume), attempted legislation in the Lords and an emergency debate in the Commons, the extradition went ahead.

Conclusion

The relationship between the government and the judiciary has deteriorated in 2006, with the continuing clash between the protection of individual rights and the protection of the interests of society. Restrictions on individual liberties are enacted by Parliament, only to be declared incompatible with human rights legislation by the judiciary. The consequent attacks by ministers and the media on the judiciary are no longer received in silence. The Lord Chief Justice, Lord Phillips, referred in July to the unjustified as well as 'personal and intemperate media attacks on members of the judiciary'.[58] Blaming the judiciary for poorly drafted legislation is a dangerous game which draws the judges increasingly into the political arena, and, even more seriously, runs the risk of undermining public confidence in the rule of law. The real problem is how to manage the tension between individual rights and the public interest, while also upholding the rule of law.

Notes

1. Anti-Terrorism Crime and Security Act 2001 and the Human Rights Act 1998 (Designated Derogation) Order 2001, No. 3644.
2. *A and others* v. *Secretary of State for the Home Department* [2004] UKHL 56.
3. This was a response to the *A* case, since the government considered it was no longer lawful to hold suspected terrorists at Belmarsh High Security Prison, ibid.
4. Section 2, Prevention of Terrorism Act 2005.
5. [2006] 3 WLR 839.
6. Under CPR, Parts 76.1 (4); 76.28 and 76.29.
7. *Evening Standard*, 5 July 2006.
8. See the cases of *Chahal* v. *UK* (1996) 23 EHRR 413, *Tinnelly and Sons* v. *UK* (1998) 27 EHRR 249, and *Rowe and Davis* v. *UK* (2000) 30 EHRR 1.
9. (2006) 103(28) L.S.G. 27, para. 69.
10. *Guardian*, 29 June 2006.
11. [2006] 3 WLR 866, para. 872.
12. *Guardian*, 29 June 2006.
13. Home Office Asylum Policy Instruction on Discretionary Leave.
14. *R (on the application of S)* v. *Secretary of State for the Home Department* [2006] EWHC 1111.
15. *R (on the application of S)* v. *Secretary of State for the Home Department* [2006] EWCA Civ 1157, para. 34.
16. Ibid., para. 50.
17. *Sun*, 11 May 2006.
18. *Daily Telegraph*, 31 January 2006.
19. City of London Police Stop and Search Mechanisms (Management Information Unit, August 2006).
20. HC Debs, 439, 9 November 2005, cc. 310–437. See also HL Debs, 676, 5 December 2005, cc. 421–69, 485–504; 7 December 2005, cc. 619–80, 700–36; 13 December 2005, cc. 1118–98, 1213–45; and 20 December, cc. 1631–70.
21. *Daily Telegraph*, 17 February 2006.
22. Joint Committee on Human Rights, 'Counter-Terrorism Policy and Human Rights: Terrorism Bill and Related Matters', HL 75-I/HC 561-I and HL 75-II/HC 561-II, 2005–06.
23. D. Cameron, 'Balancing Freedom and Security – A Modern British Bill of Rights' (Centre for Policy Studies, 26 June 2006).
24. *Sun*, 12 May 2006 (35,000 *Sun* readers voted in a poll to scrap the Act, with only 233 readers voting to keep it (13 May 2006)).
25. Lord Falconer of Thoroton, 'Democratic Renewal: Reform of Parliament and Public Life', Speech to the Hansard Society, London, 16 May 2006.
26. Justice, statement 26 June 2006.
27. Withdrawal is permitted from the ECHR but there would be political ramifications which would be likely to have ramifications for Britain wanting to influence the development of human rights in other jurisdictions. In addition, the ECHR

underpins much EU legislation so it would not be possible for Britain to remove itself totally from the Convention without affecting its position in the EU as well.

28. 'Review of the Implementation of the Human Rights Act' (Department of Constitutional Affairs, July 2006).

29. Ibid., p. 17. The relevant cases were *R* v. *A (No 2)* [2002] 1 AC 45; *R* v. *Offen* [2001] 1 WLR 253; *Cachia* v. *Faluyi* [2001] 1 WLR 1966; *R* v. *Lambert* [2002] AC 545; *R* v. *Carass* [2002] 1 WLR 1714; *Sheldrake* v. *DPP* [2004] QB 487; *Goode* v. *Martin* [2002] 1 WLR 1828; *R (Van Hoogstraten)* v. *Governor of Belmarsh Prison* [2003] 1 WLR 263; *R (Sim)* v. *Parole Board* [2003] 2 WLR 1374; *R (Middleton)* v. *Her Majesty's Coroner for the Western District of Somerset* [2004] 2 WLR 800; *Beaulane Properties* v. *Palmer* [2006] Ch 79; *Culnane* v. *Morris* [2006] 2 All ER 149.

30. The following cases do not include those that were overturned on appeal: *R (H)* v. *London North and East Region Mental Health Review Tribunal (Secretary of State for Health intervening)* [2002] QB 1; *International Transport Roth GmbH* v. *Secretary of State for the Home Department* [2003] QB 728; *R* v. *McR* (2002) NIQB 58 unreported; *R (Wilkinson)* v. *Commissioners of Inland Revenue* [2003] 1 WLR 2683; *R (Anderson)* v. *Secretary of State for the Home Department* [2003] 1 AC 837; *R (D)* v. *Secretary of State for the Home Department* [2003] 1 WLR 1315; *Blood and Tarbuck* v. *Secretary of State for Health* Declaration by consent (2003, unreported); *Bellinger* v. *Bellinger* [2003] 2 AC 467; *R (on the application of FM)* v. *Secretary of State for Health* [2003] ACD 389; *R (Uttley)* v. *Secretary of State for the Home Department* [2003] 1 WLR 2590; *R (on the application of Hooper)* v. *Secretary of State for Work and Pensions* [2003] EWCA Civ 875; *R (on the application of Wilkinson)* v. *Inland Revenue Commissioners* [2003] EWCA Civ 814; *A and others* v. *Secretary of State for the Home Department* [2004] UKHL 56; *R (on the application of Morris)* v. *Westminster City Council & First Secretary of State* [2005] EWCA Civ 1184; *R (Gabaj)* v. *First Secretary of State* (2006, unreported); *R (on the application of Baiai)* v. *Secretary of State for the Home Department* [2006] EWHC 823 & [2006] EWHC 1454.

31. *Ghaidan* v. *Godin-Mendoza* [2004] 2 AC 557, 575.

32. Joint Committee on Human Rights, *Thirty-second Report: The Human Rights Act: The DCA and Home Office Reviews*, HL 278/HC 1716, 2005–06, para. 41.

33. Ibid., para. 138.

34. This body will act as a champion for human rights provision from autumn 2007.

35. Armed Forces (Parliamentary Approval for Participation in Armed Conflict) Bill, Bill 16, 2005–06.

36. *Guardian*, 27 February 2006.

37. HL Debs, 679, 3 March 2006, c. 444.

38. Ibid., c. 452.

39. Inter alia, *Council for Civil Service Unions* v. *Minister for the Civil Service* [1984] 3 WLR 1174; *R* v. *Sec of State for Foreign & Commonwealth Affairs, ex parte Everett* [1989] 1 All ER 655; *R (on the application of Abbasi)* v. *Sec of State for Foreign & Commonwealth Affairs and Sec of State for the Home Dept* [2002] EWCA 157; *CND* v. *Prime Minister* [2003] ACD 36.

40. Committee on the Constitution, *Fifteenth Report: Waging War: Parliament's Role and Responsibility*, HL 236-I-II, 2005–06.

41. Schedule 1, Lord Chancellor (Transfer of Functions and Supplementary Provisions) (No. 2) Order 2006 abolishes the functions of the Lord Chancellor as a Lord of Appeal under the Appellate Jurisdictions Act.

42. HL Debs, 680, 20 March 2006, c. 91.
43. Ibid., c. 92.
44. Section 148, Constitutional Reform Act 2005.
45. HL Debs, 679, 1 Mar 2006, c. WS30.
46. HL Debs, 687, 14 December 2006, cc. 1711–13.
47. HL Debs, 1711, 14 Dec 2006.
48. *Guardian*, 6 November 2006.
49. Committee on Constitutional Affairs, *Seventh Report: Freedom of Information – One Year On*, HC 991, 2005–06.
50. 'Freedom of Information Act 2000, Statistics on implementation in central government, January to March, April to June, and July to September 2006', <www.dca.gov.uk/foi/stats>. The figure for 2005 was 87 per cent (DCA, *Freedom of Information Annual Report, 2005*, 2006).
51. DCA, *Freedom of Information Annual Report, 2005*, 2006, Appendix, Tables 1–2.
52. Independent Review of the Freedom of Information Act, prepared for the DCA (Frontier Economics, October 2006).
53. *Guardian*, 27 November 2006. For details of the government's proposals see its response to the Constitutional Affairs Committee, *Seventh Report*, HC 991, 2005–06 at <www.dca.gov.uk/foi/reference/ConstitutionalAffairsCommittee.htm>.
54. <www.cfoi.org.uk/foi161006pr.html>.
55. *The Times*, 22 February 2006.
56. Liberty, press release, 30 November 2006.
57. Ibid.
58. Lord Phillips, Lord Mayor's Dinner for Judges, 18 July 2006.

11
Public Policy: Ploughing On

Andrew Hindmoor

Shortly after confirming that he would resign before the next general election, the Prime Minister indicated that he would use his final years in office to secure New Labour's policy legacy and that this would mean accelerating the pace of reform. Over the last 12 months, political attention has frequently focused on the increasingly public clashes between Blair and Brown over the precise date for the handover of power. But it is clear that while the episodic breakdowns in this relationship have damaged Labour's standing in the opinion polls, they have not impeded policy development. This chapter documents significant changes in education, health and pensions policy in 2006. In this respect, the most interesting feature about the relationship between Blair and Brown is not that their personal relationship has become so poor but that their policy relationship remains so close.

Brown came close to a public fight over the details of pensions policy and in 2006 there were persistent reports that he had privately expressed scepticism about the creation of trust schools. Some commentators have also suggested that Brown's often-repeated commitment to raising average spending in state schools to the level found in independent ones reveals a point of disagreement with a Prime Minister whose favoured pledge has been to raise health spending in Britain to the European average. But this is hardly proof of major ideological or even substantive policy differences. There is as yet no real evidence that Brown will, if he succeeds Blair, follow a substantially different policy agenda or that his control of the Treasury has prevented Blair from pursuing particular policy goals. Indeed, it is Brown's management of the economy which has underpinned policy development.

Economic policy

Throughout the political ups and downs of New Labour's time in office, the economy has performed consistently (although rarely spectacularly) well.

However, by the end of 2005 a number of commentators were suggesting that the economy was edging its way into trouble. In December, the Chancellor was forced to admit that the annual rate of economic growth had fallen from nearly 4 per cent in 2004 to just 1.7 per cent in 2005. Rising fuel prices and a stagnant housing market were blamed and a strong recovery predicted. Yet there were reasons to be less sanguine about British economic performance.

- During a speech in May 2006, the Governor of the Bank of England, Mervyn King, observed that UK house prices still seemed 'remarkably high' relative to rental prices and average income. In the housing boom of the late 1980s, the ratio of average house prices to income was 5.2. In 2005, the ratio stood at 6.2. A sudden collapse in the housing market in south-east England in the 1980s was one of the causes of a sharp recession. The implication of Mervyn King's analysis was that the Bank of England was worried about history repeating itself.
- The UK has become particularly vulnerable to a fall in housing prices and/or a rise in interest rates because personal savings are so low and debt is so high. Between 1997 and 2004, the rate of savings on post-tax income fell from 10.0 per cent to 4.4 per cent while total personal debt climbed to an average 150 per cent of annual income. Savings fell and debt rose partly because people were able to borrow money against rises in the value of their homes, but this means that even a temporary collapse in the housing market will risk leaving people suddenly exposed to unmanageably large debts.
- A number of reports published in 2006 showed that private sector productivity and investment remained depressed. In the 1990s, impressive rates of American economic growth were fuelled by rising productivity and investment attributed to the diffusion of information technology. In the 2000s, it would appear that British economic growth has been sustained by increased public expenditure and surging consumer spending. Business investment remained depressed because profits, already hit by Treasury 'stealth taxes', were increasingly being used by companies to pay higher shareholder dividends, fund takeovers and cover shortfalls in pension commitments. As Figure 11.1 demonstrates, by the end of 2004, business investment in the UK, measured as a percentage of gross domestic product (GDP), had fallen below that of the US, France and Germany.
- Overall public expenditure rose from around 38.0 per cent to 42.5 per cent of GDP between 1999 and 2006. Some of this increase was funded by higher indirect taxes but, as growth began to falter in 2005, much of it was paid for through borrowing. By the time of the 2006 budget, the cyclically adjusted budget deficit had risen to 3 per cent of GDP. In a period in which economic growth was faltering, most commentators

judged this level to be unsustainable. Recognising this, the Treasury indicated that the Comprehensive Spending Review scheduled to report in the summer of 2007 would be more fiscally conservative. But if economic growth has previously depended upon increased public expenditure, removing this prop from the economy when growth is already faltering may prove dangerous.

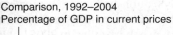

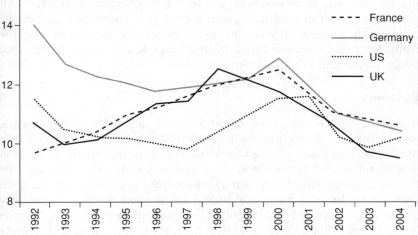

Figure 11.1   UK business investment, 1992–2004

Source: 'UK Productivity and Competitiveness Indicators 2006', Department of Trade and Industry, Economics Paper No. 17. Available at <www.dti.gov.uk/files/>.

In these uncertain circumstances it was perhaps no surprise that the March 2006 budget was a relatively low-key affair. The principal measures unveiled by Gordon Brown were a headline-grabbing freeze on the duty on champagne and cider, the sale of the Tote and the government's stake in British Energy and Westinghouse, increases in child tax credits, the elimination of vehicle excise duty on the least-polluting cars, additional money to enable free off-peak travel for pensioners, and various pieces of investment for the 2012 Olympics. In total, and going on the Treasury's own figures, the budget was forecast to cost more than it raised in 2006–07 and to raise more than it cost in 2007–08 and 2008–09. However, when measured against total revenue and expenditure, the overall sums involved – an outlay of £380 million in 2006–07 and an additional £415 million and then £705 million in the following years – are relatively insignificant.

In previous years when the economy has been thought to be in trouble, most notably in the aftermath of the 1998 Asian financial crisis, it has always recovered to leave Gordon Brown's economic halo intact. This also seemed to be the case in 2006. In the second quarter of 2006, average house prices, far from falling, showed a modest rise. During the same period, retail sales grew by 2.1 per cent: a rise only partly attributable to sales of alcohol and food during the World Cup. Finally, and perhaps most significantly, the independent Office for National Statistics (ONS) published research showing that the overall level of growth between 2002 and 2006 was likely to have been much higher than previously believed. Growth may have fallen in 2005 but it did so from a higher level and to a smaller extent than previously thought. So rapid was the turnaround in economic expectations that, by August 2006, the Bank of England, concerned that inflation was tracking outside its expected range, announced a quarter-point rise in interest rates.

Pensions

In 2002, the government created a Pensions Commission, chaired by the former Director General of the Confederation of British Industry (CBI), Adair Turner. Initially, it was given the task of examining voluntary pension provision but soon had its remit extended to look at state provision. The commission was created in response to three growing problems. The first was the relatively low rate of personal savings for pensions. In 2001, the Treasury introduced a pension credit intended to protect those pensioners with the lowest income. But because this credit is means-tested and so progressively withdrawn as savings and income rise, it has had the largely unanticipated effect of reducing people's incentive to save. Second, voluntary provision was being increasingly undermined by the decision of many private companies to close their final earnings company pension schemes to new employees – and in the case of some firms, the first being Rentokil, to existing ones as well. Quite why company pension schemes have fallen into such a state of apparent disrepair at a time when the stock market has generally performed well is a contentious question. Supporters of the government suggest that firms have sought to minimise their contributions at a time when executive pay has grown exponentially. Critics argue that the government is now paying the price for a decision Gordon Brown took in 1997 to abolish corporate tax relief: a decision which was the subject of a stinging report by the Parliamentary Ombudsman in March 2006.[1] The closure of pension schemes is a major problem because, if left unaddressed, it will significantly reduce the income of future pensioners. The third problem was an expected rise in the number of people of retirement age. The number of people aged over 65 when measured as a proportion of those of working age is expected to grow from 27 per cent to 45 per cent over the next 30 years.

The Pensions Commission published its final report in November 2005. Much as expected, it made three principal recommendations. First, that the retirement age be raised from 60 to 68 over the course of the next two decades. Second, it recommended creating a national savings scheme in which employees would be automatically enrolled but subsequently free to opt out. Employees would be required to pay 5 per cent of their salary into this scheme, to be topped up by a 3 per cent contribution from employers. Inspired by equivalent schemes in Australia and New Zealand, the commission's expectation is that many of the people who do not join a personal pension scheme will nevertheless remain within one upon which they have already been enrolled. Third, the commission argued in favour of raising the basic level of the state pension by linking payments to average earnings rather than average prices. This, it estimated, would raise public expenditure by something like 1.5 per cent of GDP.

Before the report's publication, these proposals were, to varying degrees, all challenged by the Treasury. It argued that the commission had underestimated the likely costs of restoring the link between pensions and earnings. It was also clear that the Treasury (and the Chancellor in particular) did not take kindly to the commission's clearly stated criticisms of its pension credit scheme. With the Prime Minister apparently having been persuaded by the commission's arguments, the stage seemed set for a major political battle. Then, in April 2006, Brown suddenly and unexpectedly accepted the principle of linking pensions to earnings and told reporters that 'we are 90 to 95 per cent there with Turner'. A month later the government published its formal response to the Pensions Commission. It not only agreed to raise the retirement age but accelerated the commission's proposed timetable for doing so. It accepted the proposal to create a national pensions scheme and, finally, agreed to restore the link between pensions and earnings, albeit at a slightly later date than the commission had proposed.[2]

Energy, nuclear power and climate change

Two events pushed energy policy toward the top of the policy agenda in 2005/06. First, in its annual Climate Change Report the government for the first time admitted in public what ministers had privately been conceding for over a year: that Britain would not meet its self-imposed target to reduce the emission of greenhouse gases. In the Kyoto protocol, most developed countries (minus America and Australia) agreed to cut emissions of greenhouse gases – principally but not exclusively carbon dioxide – by 12 per cent relative to 1990 levels by 2012. In a moment of environmental leadership New Labour pledged to go further and cut emissions by 20 per cent: a commitment repeated in the party's 2001 and 2005 manifestos. As Figure 11.2 shows, British emissions did indeed fall between 1990 and 1998. This was, however, largely the result of power companies switching from coal- to gas-fired power stations. Since that time, overall emissions have remained largely unchanged. The government still seems likely to meet its Kyoto target but is now almost certainly not going to meet its self-imposed one.

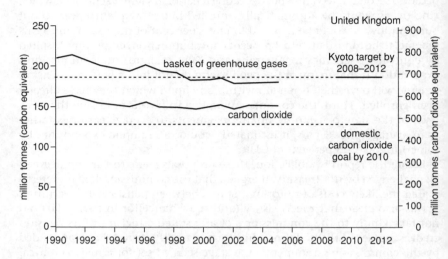

Figure 11.2   Emissions of greenhouse gases, 1990–2012

Note: Estimates for 2005 are provisional. Updated August 2006.

Source: Defra e-digest Environmental Statistics – <www.defra.gov.uk/environment/statistics/index.htm>.

The pressure on the government to review its policy on climate change then increased following the publication of a review of the economics of climate change by Sir Nicholas Stern, a former Permanent Secretary at the Treasury, in October 2006.[3] In an extremely dense 700-words/page which nevertheless attracted a great deal of publicity, Stern argued that the costs of reducing levels of global warming now (estimated to be the equivalent of around 1 per cent of global GDP) would be far less than the costs of dealing with the consequences of global warming in the future (estimated to be the equivalent of up to 5 per cent of global GDP). On this basis, Stern recommended greater use of carbon taxes and emissions trading schemes, and greater investment in low-carbon emissions technology and energy-saving.

The second event pushing energy up the policy agenda was the price dispute between Russia and the Ukraine over the amount the latter paid for its natural gas. On 1 January 2006, the Soviet company Gazprom with, it must be presumed, clear state backing, cut its supplies to the Ukraine. As a result, the Ukraine diverted some of the gas meant to go to Western Europe for its own use. Although Gazprom resumed supplies on 4 January, the incident reduced available supplies to a number of European countries (but not Britain) by up to 30 per cent. This created a wave of concern about the way in which Russia might in the future use its control of valuable energy supplies as a foreign policy weapon.

By the time of the Russia–Ukraine dispute, Tony Blair had already signalled his concerns by announcing a review of energy policy. Although presented as an opportunity carefully to review policy two years after the publication of a White Paper on energy policy, it was widely and probably correctly denounced as a sham exercise intended simply to confirm and to give greater legitimacy to the Prime Minister's preference for nuclear power.

Nuclear power's proponents – including, it would seem, the Prime Minister – argue that not only is this method of generating power safe and cost-effective but that it does not require imports from potentially hostile countries and is environmentally friendly. Although the environmental credentials of nuclear power are vigorously contested, the basic facts are relatively straightforward. After all carbon costs have been taken into account, a modern lightwater nuclear reactor generates around 16 tonnes of carbon dioxide per megawatt hour of electricity produced. The equivalent figures for gas and coal are 356 tonnes and 891 tonnes respectively. However, critics can point to the fact that nuclear power still generates significantly more carbon dioxide than renewable energies. Furthermore, they can also argue that the economics of nuclear power are uncertain and that governments across the world have singularly failed to find an effective way of dealing with nuclear waste.

In August 2006, the government's Committee on Radioactive Waste, the latest body to be charged with finding a solution to this problem, recommended building underground bunkers to store long-term waste at an estimated cost of around £10 billion.[4] It also argued that, in order to encourage communities to volunteer themselves as the sites of these bunkers, it would be necessary for the government to offer them additional public investment. Although widely derided at the time, the proposals represented a significant step forward in so far as they at least addressed the issue of incentives. Yet as the committee itself accepted, construction of a storage bunker is unlikely even to commence before 2030.

The energy review was eventually published in July 2006 and, as widely expected, found in favour of nuclear power, the key part of the document stating that new 'nuclear power stations would make a significant contribution to meeting our energy policy'.[5] The report promised to consider ways in which the government might simplify the licensing and planning processes associated with the construction of nuclear sites. These issues are to be made the subject of a future but as yet unscheduled White Paper. The debate about nuclear power is already proving to be a hugely divisive one. While many backbench Labour MPs have already expressed their implacable opposition to the construction of any new nuclear power stations, some environmentalists have reluctantly conceded that they may have to form a part of any solution to the problem of global warming. As it currently stands, however, the debate is a confused and misleading one:

- First, nuclear power and renewables are routinely presented as alternatives to each other. Indeed, it was widely reported that the Prime Minister only commissioned the energy review once he had decided that renewable energy did not provide a viable long-term alternative to coal or gas. Yet the most substantive parts of the energy review actually relate not to nuclear power but to renewable energy. In 2002, the government introduced an obligation on generators of electricity to use a certain proportion of renewable energy. The review proposed raising the level of this obligation from 15 per cent to 20 per cent by 2027. Set against this, the conclusion that nuclear policy stations 'would make a significant contribution' actually seems quite flimsy.
- Second, newspaper coverage of the energy review suggested that the government wants nuclear power to replace coal and gas as Britain's principal energy source. Yet it seems much more likely that the government is actually scrabbling to preserve the status quo. In 2005, nuclear power generated 7.8 per cent of Britain's electricity. Coal produced 17.1 per cent, oil 33 per cent, gas 40 per cent and renewables (principally hydro, solar and wind power) 0.6 per cent. However, over the next few decades the majority of existing nuclear power stations will reach the end of their natural lives and will need to be decommissioned. On current projections, nuclear's share of the energy market will then fall to around 4 per cent. Any new nuclear programme may therefore simply result in the preservation of existing market share.
- Third, in one important sense, the energy review simply confirmed existing government policy. In France, where nuclear power is the principal source of energy, successive governments have had to provide significant subsidies to private firms to construct and run nuclear stations. Indeed, there is no country in the world in which private firms have taken on the costs and risks of building a power station in the absence of some government support. Yet the energy review confirms what has been the single most important part of British energy policy since the late 1980s, the commitment to the free market. It quite clearly states that 'it will be for the private sector to initiate, fund, construct and operate new nuclear power plants and to cover the full costs of decommissioning and their full share of long-term waste management costs'. We should not therefore conclude that just because the government now believes that nuclear power can make a 'significant contribution' to energy policy that any new power stations will necessarily be built.
- Fourth, in a report published in April 2006, the Commons Environmental Audit Committee showed that, no matter what decisions are taken over

the next year, it is extremely unlikely that any new nuclear power stations will be built and put online before 2020.[6] In the meantime, the most important energy decisions will be those taken by electricity companies who must soon decide whether to replace existing but increasingly obsolete coal-fired power stations with coal or gas replacements. A recently introduced European Directive requiring that coal-fired stations be fitted with expensive chimney-scrubbing equipment means that most companies are probably going to choose gas on economic grounds. This will have a positive environmental pay-off in that gas produces significantly less carbon dioxide than coal but will increase Britain's dependence upon imports from Russia.

Migration

Voters have increasingly come to regard immigration (and the related but distinct issue of asylum) as one of the most important policy issues facing the country. A poll conducted for ITV in September 2006 showed that only 4 per cent of people believed that the government had immigration under control, that 80 per cent believed that immigrants took jobs from British workers, and that 60 per cent believed that immigration had eroded British culture. Two particular events fuelled public debate about migration in 2006: an influx of largely temporary migrant workers from Eastern Europe and the Home Office's failure to deport foreign prisoners prior to or upon their release from prison.

In May 2004, Cyprus, Malta, and eight Eastern European countries – Poland, Hungary, the Czech Republic, Slovakia, Slovenia, Estonia, Lithuania and Latvia – joined the European Union. At this time, most of the existing members chose to exercise their negotiated right to impose temporary restrictions upon the arrival of migrant workers from these Eastern European countries. Britain, Ireland and Sweden – later to be joined by Spain and Portugal– were the only countries which allowed for the free movement of workers. Initial Home Office research indicated that perhaps 13,000 workers would move to Britain and that the majority would stay less than a year. In fact, by August 2006, an estimated 600,000 workers had arrived (although, as expected, a majority stayed less than 12 months).

The scale of this influx provoked howls of outrage from the Conservative Party and eventually, and less predictably, from sections within the Labour Party. John Denham, a former Home Office minister and now chair of the Home Affairs Committee, suggested that migrant labour had resulted in many people's wages in his constituency of Southampton being halved. Frank Field, a former Social Security minister, suggested that migration from Eastern Europe was undermining the government's welfare-to-work programme because it gave employers the easy option of recruiting young, healthy and cheap labour from Eastern Europe, rather than having to take the risk of hiring someone who had been unemployed for several years or who suffered from a minor disability. Under increasing political pressure, ministers began to indicate in the summer of 2006 that they would impose some formal limits upon the arrival of migrant labour from Romania and Bulgaria when those countries joined the European Union in 2007. This decision was then confirmed in October 2006 when it was announced that only 20,000 low-skilled workers will be allowed into the country to work in agriculture and food processing.

A report published by the European Commission in May 2006 offered a more sober assessment of the causes and consequences of Eastern European migration.[7] Its three principal findings were as follows. First, that the introduction of quotas and such arrangements by other countries had surprisingly made almost no difference to the overall numbers of workers arriving from Eastern Europe. In countries like Austria, which put in place strict controls on the arrival of workers, those arriving from Eastern Europe simply worked illegally, claimed to be self-employed, or acquired papers showing that they had been transferred from a company in their home country. Second, that there was absolutely no discernible relationship between the number of migrant workers arriving from Eastern Europe and the level of unemployment in their host country. Third, that because nearly all of the migrants found work and paid taxes, they made a net contribution to the economy of the countries concerned.

The second migration-related issue related to the release of foreign prisoners. In April 2006, it emerged that more than 1,000 foreign prisoners had been freed without being considered for deportation, five of whom had been convicted of committing sex offences on children. When it then became clear that the National Audit Office had warned the Home Office about this problem in July 2005, the Home Secretary, Charles Clarke, came under a great deal of pressure to resign. Having initially refused to countenance his resignation, the Prime Minister then removed him from office in May 2006. Within three weeks, his replacement, John Reid, described large parts of the Home Office as 'inadequate, dysfunctional and not fit for purpose'.

After a hastily conducted policy review, the Home Office published a new policy paper on immigration in July 2006, with the reassuring title *Fair, Effective, Transparent and Trusted: Rebuilding Confidence in Our Immigration System*.[8] Large parts of it drew heavily upon previously announced or already introduced policy initiatives, such as the points-based immigration system introduced in March 2006. It did, however, contain some new proposals, including the introduction of exit as well as entry controls and measures to strengthen the numbers, powers and visibility of the Borders Service. On prison releases, it proposed amending existing laws to make deportation of non-British citizens the legal presumption and to remove the requirement for prisoners to consent to their transfer to another country.

Health

Total NHS expenditure, measured as a proportion of GDP, rose from 4.2 per cent to 6.5 per cent between 1999 and 2005. Yet, despite this unprecedented rise in public spending, the story attracting most policy interest in 2006 was growing financial deficits within the NHS. In October 2005, a survey indicated that three-quarters of medical directors working in acute care hospitals believed that their trust was facing a financial shortfall. In December 2005, it was estimated that the overall NHS deficit for that year would be over £600 million. By March 2006, this estimate had been increased to over £800 million and newspapers were reporting that some hospitals had started to make cutbacks in non-emergency care. In the same month, the Chief Executive of the NHS, Sir Nigel Crisp, announced his unexpectedly early retirement.

What does the existence of these deficits tell us about the NHS? During a speech to the Health Network in April 2006, Tony Blair argued that the government's reforms to the NHS had 'exposed the deficits [but that they] did not create them' and suggested that they might actually show that the government's reforms were working.[9] Since 2004, the NHS has been moving toward a financial system in which hospitals are paid according to the volume (and effectiveness) of treatments undertaken at a set of fixed, national, prices. In this quasi-market system, hospitals have a strong incentive to increase their efficiency by, for example, specialising in particular areas of treatment. One almost inevitable consequence of this method of payment is that hospital trusts whose treatment costs exceed these prices will accumulate deficits. The government argues that these deficits will be eliminated in the medium term as trusts are forced to reduce their costs and that the existence of the deficits shows that its reforms are beginning to bite.

The alternative view is that the deficits have arisen because money is still being wasted within the NHS. The usual argument here is that too much money has been spent on managers and bureaucrats and not enough on doctors and nurses. In 2006, two more sophisticated and interesting arguments were advanced. The first was that too much money had been wasted in the first part of the decade on building large and extremely expensive hospitals, paid for through the Private Finance Initiative (PFI).[10] Huge deficits finally emerged in 2006 because this was the period in which hospital trusts had to start to repay these debts. Although the Treasury continued to defend both the hospital construction programme and the PFI, the government conceded some ground to its critics on this issue in a January 2006 White Paper. *Our Health, Our Care: A New Direction for the NHS*[11] seemed to accept that too much had been spent on large centralised hospitals and not enough on smaller local clinics dealing with preventive care. Promising a 'radical and sustained shift in the way in which services are delivered', the White Paper announced, among other things, the construction of local 'polyclinics' in which social services work alongside medical staff in buildings, with extended opening hours and sufficient facilities to perform minor surgery.

A second argument about waste was that over half of the additional NHS expenditure has gone on improved salaries for doctors and nurses.[12] The government argued that higher salaries were the necessary and predictable price of attracting more staff. But Sir Derek Wanless, whose government-commissioned report on NHS expenditure in 2002 was used by the Treasury to justify spending increases, admitted in an interview he gave in April 2006 that the cost of salaries had, in practice, far outstripped his projections, rendering many of his earlier arguments and assumptions about the value of higher public health spending redundant.

Confronted with arguments about wasted money, ministers have emphasised the extent to which waiting lists and mortality rates from cancer and heart disease have fallen over the last few years. Yet, given the resources lavished upon the NHS, it would have been very surprising if there had not been a significant improvement in these figures. In trying to judge whether money has been wasted, the key question is therefore about productivity: about changes in the relationship between expenditure inputs and treatment outputs. This was the subject of a complex report by the ONS in February 2006.[13] By measuring productivity in three different ways it came to three different conclusions about the performance of the NHS:

- Perhaps the most obvious way of measuring productivity is in terms of the ratio between expenditure inputs and outputs, measured by the number of operations performed, the number of patients treated, and so on. Although total output has risen by around an average of 28 per cent a year between 1995 and 2004, overall productivity has, on this measure, fallen by between 0.6 per cent and 1.3 per cent a year.
- One problem with this crude input–output measure is that it fails to take account of changes in the quality of care, measured through, for example, survival rates and adjusted life expectancy. Taking these factors into account, the report estimated that NHS output has actually risen by between 4.8 per cent and 5.5 per cent a year since 1995. Set against the level of spending input, productivity has, on this measure, either risen by 0.2 per cent a year or has fallen by an average of 0.5 per cent.
- In 2005, an independent review into the way in which productivity statistics are compiled argued that it may sometimes be appropriate to adjust the relative value of particular goods and services as the economy becomes more prosperous.[14] The principle involved is a controversial one, but the basic argument is that health is intrinsically more valuable in a richer economy than it is in a poorer one. By adjusting NHS output in line with increases in real earnings over the period between 1995 and 2004, it can be shown that productivity has risen by an average of between 0.6 per cent and 1.6 per cent.

Education and admissions

For many Labour MPs, the comprehensive school system still ranks alongside the creation of the NHS as one of Labour's great triumphs. Playing to this audience, the then Shadow Education Secretary, David Blunkett, won thunderous applause during the 1995 Labour Party Conference when, in what was to prove a rather unfortunate parody of George Bush Senior's promises on taxation, he proclaimed: 'read my lips: no selection by examination or interview' in schools. At the time, this was rather naively interpreted by some party activists as a declaration of war upon grammar schools. In practice, New Labour has steadily extended the principle of selection.

Shortly after taking office, the government made it clear that it had no interest in forcing grammar schools to become comprehensives. Then, a few years later, it began to press the claims of two new kinds of schools, specialist schools and city academies. Over the next few years, the government hopes to complete its project of turning most comprehensives into specialist schools. As their name implies, these schools specialise in teaching particular subjects, be it languages or information technology, and are allowed to select up to 10 per cent of their intake on the basis of their ability in that particular subject. City academies, which have been created in the inner cities to replace failing comprehensives, are usually backed by private sponsors and have greater freedom from their local education authority when it comes to paying and recruiting teachers, setting the curriculum and, crucially, selecting pupils.

Fewer than 50 schools have been recreated as city academies. Yet having been dazzled by some research showing that academic performance in these schools has improved at a faster rate than it has in the rest of the state sector, the government has now sold itself on the idea of turning as many comprehensive schools as possible into 'trust' schools which, like city academies, will operate largely independently of local education authorities, attract private sponsors, and be free to set budgets, recruit, dispose of assets, and select pupils. Shortly after the police launched a formal investigation into claims that potential sponsors of city academies were being bribed with the promise of peerages, the government made clear its intention to legislate for the creation of trust schools. Having previously tolerated the retention of grammar schools and the creation of specialist schools and city academies, the resulting Education and Inspections Bill sparked widespread disquiet within the Labour Party.

By December 2005, a majority of English and Welsh Labour backbenchers had expressed support for an 'Alternative White Paper', which proposed placing the existing Code of Admissions on a statutory footing to prevent trust schools from practising selection. Speaking in apparent support of the nascent rebellion, the Deputy Prime Minister, John Prescott, expressed his fears about the emergence of a 'two-tier' schooling system, while the former leader, Neil Kinnock, warned that the government's proposals would lead to a 'dreadful shattering' of the comprehensive system. Adding to the government's problems, the Conservatives – who had made it clear that they would support the legislation so long as the Prime Minister did not concede any ground to his critics – suggested that trust schools would be little different from the grant-maintained schools it had introduced in the early 1990s and which the incoming Labour government had abolished in 1997. According to the former Conservative Education Secretary, Kenneth Clarke,

> if it looks like a dog and barks like a dog, it probably is a dog. Labour members are never more ridiculous than when they go blue in the face trying to convince us that the supposed trust schools are not grant-maintained schools.[15]

By January 2006, the government had decided that it had no alternative but to make concessions in order to retain the support of most Labour MPs. Responding to a critical report by the Education and Skills Select Committee,[16] the government agreed to outlaw the use of interviews as a part of the admissions process; to require schools to 'act in accordance with' rather than simply 'take note' of the existing admissions code; and to create local admissions forums with the power to object to an independent adjudicator about individual school admissions practices.[17] Together with additional amendments requiring a school's assets to be returned to the local authority in the event of a school closure and one which allowed the best-performing local education authorities to apply to open new 'community' (that is, non-trust) schools, these concessions were sufficient to secure approval for the legislation. Having previously boasted of how he did not have 'a reverse gear', the passage of this bill revealed a Prime Minister willing to compromise with his party.

Conclusion

In the final few years of John Major's administration a seemingly never-ending litany of personal and political scandals seemed to be all that was left of a government which had run out of energy, backbench support and policy ideas. After nearly as long in office, New Labour has become equally as scandal- and accident-prone. In 2006 Charles Clarke was forced out of office and two other members of the Cabinet, Ruth Kelly and Tessa Jowell, came under a great deal of pressure to resign: the former because of her handling of the appointment of convicted child sex offenders to teaching posts, and the latter because of the financial affairs of her husband. And throughout this period some of the Prime Minister's closest political friends were being questioned by police about the sale of peerages.

Yet in policy terms, the pace of change has been unrelenting. In the case of health policy, 2006 was the period in which earlier policy reforms began to bite. In education policy (the creation of trust schools), migration (the imposition of controls on Romanian and Bulgarian workers), energy policy (the cautious embrace of nuclear power) and pensions policy, the last year has seen not only significant developments but also reversals in previously stated policy positions.

Notes

1. Parliamentary Health Ombudsman, *Sixth Report: Trusting in the Pensions Promise – Government Bodies and the Security of Final Salary Occupational Pensions*, HC 984, 2005–06. See above, pp. 84–5.
2. *Security in Retirement: Towards a New Pensions System*, Cm. 6841, May 2006.
3. See <www.treasury.gov.uk/independent_reviews?stern_review_economics_climate_change/sternreview_index.cfm>.
4. See <www.corwm.org.uk/content-0>.
5. See <www.dti.gov.uk/energy/review/page31995.html>.
6. See <www.publications.parliament.uk/pa/cm200506/cmselect/cmenvaud/584/584i.pdf>.
7. Commission of the European Communities, *Report on the Functioning of the Transitional Arrangements Set Out in the 2003 Accession Treaty*. See <http://ec.europa.eu/employment_social/news/2006/feb/report_en.pdf>.
8. See <http://press.homeoffice.gov.uk/pressdocuments/ind-review-250706/IND-REIA.pdf?version=1>.
9. See <http://ec.europa.eu/employment_social/news/2006/feb/report_en.pdf>.
10. See Nick Bosanquet, Andrew Haldenby and Henry de Zoete, 'Investment in the NHS – Facing up to the Reform Agenda', *Reform*, July 2006. See <www.reform.co.uk/filestore/pdf/Investment%20in%20the%20NHS,%20Reform,%202006.pdf>.
11. Cm. 6737, February 2006.
12. See, for example, John Appleby, *Where's the Money Going?* (London: King's Fund, 2006), available at <www.kingsfund.org.uk/resources/briefings/wheres_the.html>.
13. Office for National Statistics, *Public Service Productivity: Health*, February 2006, available at <www.statistics.gov.uk/articles/nojournal/PublicServiceProductivity-Health(27_2_06).pdf>.
14. *The Atkinson Report on Measuring Government Output and Productivity*, January 2006. A press release summarising the main findings can be found at <www.kingsfund.org.uk/resources/briefings/wheres_the.html>.
15. HC Debs, 443, 15 March 2006, c. 1500.
16. Education and Skills Committee, *Fifth Report: Secondary Education*, HC 86, 2004–05.
17. Education and Skills Committee, *Third Special Report: Government Response to the Committee's Fifth Report of 2004–05*, HC 725, 2005–06.

12
Devolution:
Relative Stability and Political Change

Jonathan Bradbury

The experience of devolution in Scotland and Wales has increased the complexity of territorial politics in the UK. At the same time, it has also made for greater political stability, relative to the persistent pressures for change before devolution. The political dominance of the Labour Party at both UK and Scottish/Welsh levels has been of undoubted importance in this. In addition, the very centrality of devolution to political debate in Northern Ireland, even while suspended, has also helped to bolster a greater civil peace there. Overall, despite the misgivings of constitutional unionists and hopes of nationalists that devolution would provide a pathway to independence,[1] thus far it has proved to be a very British reform, modifying rather than transforming the state.[2] There have, of course, been question marks over whether such a mixture of enhanced diversity and relative stability will endure. As the divergence of Scottish, Welsh and Northern Irish politics increases, a politicised Englishness emerges and the institutions of UK territorial management are found deficient.[3] These more divergent pressures for political change have thus far been latent but have the potential to transform the politics of UK devolution.[4]

This chapter addresses the key developments in party politics, government and constitutional debate in Scotland, Wales and Northern Ireland in 2006. In each case, the assessment suggests the continuation of an underlying combination of diversity and relative stability in UK territorial politics. Nevertheless, the year was notable for questions about Labour's control of devolution in Scotland and Wales, while problems within devolved government, and renewed constitutional debates, created the potential for considerably greater instability in the politics of devolution. In Northern Ireland, the stakes were raised as the UK and Irish governments insisted on either the restoration of power-sharing devolution or its rapid abolition. At the end of the year the hopes were stronger for the unlikely achievement of the former, thus consolidating devolution, albeit on an asymmetrical basis, as the institutional focus of territorial politics across the UK. Even so, sceptics were conscious that it hung in the balance, plunging Northern Ireland too into a more uncertain future.

Scotland

In Scotland, devolution had developed on a basis that many had expected. The previously dominant Labour Party had accepted the reality of coalition government with the Liberal Democrats. Policies had then been forged on the basis of Scottish Labour manifestos and Liberal Democrat insistence on policies such as electoral reform in local government and an alternative to tuition fees for university students. The constitutional question had been so heavily debated by the Scottish Constitutional Convention that there was little initial momentum for further development. As time went on, these adaptations in Scottish politics faced pressures. The 2003 Scottish Parliament elections left the Labour–Liberal Democrat coalition with a much reduced majority of six. Jack McConnell, the Labour leader and First Minister, was criticised for lacking vision; and policy performance was frequently found wanting. In 2005, even the constitutional question was reopened, with all the opposition parties raising the issue of fiscal powers and the Scottish National Party (SNP), the Scottish Socialist Party (SSP) and the Greens pressing for independence. The Arbuthnott Commission also opened up debate over the Parliament's mixed-member electoral system. Yet overall, continuity was retained. Labour sought to ginger-up its policy performance during 2005 and McConnell declared that Labour would consider the case for more powers. There was a sigh of relief in Labour circles when the Arbuthnott Commission generally backed the Parliament's existing electoral system with relatively minor adjustments.

In this context, 2006 stands as a year which largely offered up yet more cold comfort for Labour. Party fortunes increasingly suggested momentum for both the SNP and the Liberal Democrats. The SNP's increased majority in the Moray by-election in April, following the death of Margaret Ewing, foreshadowed a period in which the party received growing support. ICM polls in October[5] and November both recorded rising support for the SNP. The November poll predicted that in an immediate Scottish Parliament election the SNP would win 34 per cent of the constituency vote against Labour's 29 per cent, and 31 per cent of the list vote against Labour's 26 per cent. It suggested that the SNP would have 43 seats, five ahead of Labour.[6] The Liberal Democrats also gained momentum. In February, despite the bad publicity surrounding the UK party's leadership contest, the Liberal Democrats overturned a Labour majority to win the Westminster by-election in Dunfermline and West Fife with a swing of 16.24 per cent. The November poll predicted that the Liberal Democrats would win 25 seats in a Scottish Parliament election, a gain of eight. These figures would deprive the Labour–Liberal Democrat coalition of its majority and give the SNP considerably more potential to lead a government, leaving the Liberal Democrats as likely power-brokers.

These advances were partly the product of problems in other opposition parties. Previously the SNP had feared that the advance of the Scottish Socialist Party would completely fragment the left-wing/nationalist protest vote against Labour. Yet the year spelled disaster for the SSP. The former leader, Tommy Sheridan, mounted a libel action against the *News of the World* over allegations of his infidelity, visits to a Manchester sex club and drug-taking. Among those testifying against him were other SSP Members of the Scottish Parliament (MSPs), including the leader, Colin Fox, who said that Sheridan had confessed to the sex club visits at a party meeting. The hearings featured a public airing of the party's internal splits between pro- and anti-Sheridan factions. Although he won his libel action and damages of £200,000, the party split and Sheridan launched a new party, Solidarity, in September. He was joined by one other SSP MSP, reducing the SSP to four MSPs. All approached the 2007 elections with little confidence of retaining their seats.[7]

At the same time, the Liberal Democrats were helped by the fact that the Conservative Party received no discernible bounce from David Cameron's UK-wide leadership. This was despite some efforts to atone for perceived previous sins. In September, in a speech in Glasgow, Cameron reasserted his party's strong commitment to the union but apologised for the 'egregious errors' committed by the Thatcher government in using Scotland as a policy laboratory and not treating it with enough respect, notably on the poll tax.[8] The party, nevertheless, continued to flatline in Scotland. The one other party that appeared to hold its own was the Greens, leading to speculation that, were an SNP–Liberal Democrat-led coalition to emerge after the 2007 elections, it might be with the help of Green Party support.

Yet it is clear that much of the change in party fortunes rested on a rising tide of criticism of Labour. Undoubtedly, Labour's unpopularity in Scotland derived in part from the party's general slide across the UK. The party had been long in office and was often seen as out of touch. Some UK Labour policies were also clearly unpopular, notably the decision to go to war in Iraq and the subsequent disasters facing military deployments. But closer to home there were also problems. The performance of Scottish Enterprise in facilitating economic development attracted criticism both in the media and in the Parliament. Labour-led policies at the UK level of allowing post office closures, and at the Scottish level of seeking an increase in the number of specialist schools, excited opposition, even from the Liberal Democrats.[9]

Debates occurred over one of the Parliament's flagship 'distinctive' policies, free personal care for the elderly. Concerns about the implementation of the policy by local authorities were raised in March. The executive defended funding levels and pointed to the 40,000 people who had received free personal care at home and the further 9,000 who had had their care subsidised in care homes. Nevertheless, the Health Committee, reporting on the issue in September, drew attention to the variations in waiting times across local authority areas, with some being as high as four months. In 24 areas there were notable delays in the delivery of help in washing and dressing. There were particular concerns that councils were delaying patient assessments because of inadequate funding, leading in turn to opposition party accusations that the executive had significantly underestimated the cost of the policy, making public benefit from it a 'postcode lottery'.[10]

The issue of constitutional change also climbed the political agenda. In October, the Liberal Democrats adopted the Steel Commission report, suggesting that instead of the Parliament receiving its finance from a Westminster block grant it should raise its own revenue. This marked out a clear commitment by one of the parties in office to an extension of the Parliament's fiscal powers and it becoming a financially responsible institution.[11] The Fraser of Allender Institute, linked to the Conservative Party, claimed similarly that fiscal responsibility would discipline 'spendthrift' ministers. The October ICM poll indicated possible public support for even more radical change, putting support for independence at 51 per cent with 37 per cent against. The ICM poll in November put Scottish support for independence at 52 per cent.[12]

In response, despite earlier suggestions that the party might adopt a reformist position, Labour decided to defend stoutly the constitutional status quo. In a major speech in October, Jack McConnell argued that politicians really should concentrate on debating how best to use the wealth of powers the Parliament already had, rather than obsessing about more powers. He also defended Scottish devolution in principle as giving Scotland 'the best of both worlds – the best of what's Scottish, the best of what's British as well'. He stressed the positive reasons for the British link – the cross-border ties that so many Scots had – as well as referring to the inappropriateness of advancing nationalism in a global context in which it was increasingly associated with inter-ethnic conflict. He believed the constant debate of independence would leave Scotland in a 'collective state of inertia'.[13] At the Scottish Labour Party Conference in November, McConnell received the support of Tony Blair, who more broadly denounced the SNP for peddling a 'politics of grievance', as well as John Reid. Gordon Brown reiterated his regular theme of the strong cultural links between Scotland and England, and the economic and political interdependence of Scotland with the UK that made independence 'bad for economics' and 'bad for the solidarity that should exist across borders'.[14]

How significant were these developments and debates? Some might say very significant. The party system was possibly in for a major shock, ending Labour ascendancy and ushering in a fragmented and polarised multi-party system. The capacity of politicians under devolved government to deliver competent and innovative government was being seriously questioned. At the very least, it looked like a period of serious reflection on the constitutional settlement was underway; at the most, constitutional unionists had their first genuine sighting of the independence abyss over which Scotland stood. McConnell's attempts to sound like a passionate and principled defender of devolution within the UK were also undermined by SNP accusations that he was a puppet of the UK Chancellor, Gordon Brown, and by the intervention of UK Labour politicians in the debate about Scotland's future.

On the other hand, Labour had many grounds for being sanguine. It had faced similar levels of unpopularity before in 1998, and still come through well in the 1999 elections. It could argue that the Scottish Executive had increased investment in health care and education, unemployment was falling and that initiatives like the smoking ban represented major advances for public health. A period of sustained campaigning could have a considerable impact on an actual election result. In 1998, opinion polls had also registered a narrow majority in favour of independence, only for levels of support to fall and stabilise thereafter. There was no certainty of an upward trend. Support for independence was strongest among young and working-class voters, historically the least likely social groups to vote. Party representation of a pro-independence vote had also fragmented since 1998 in that, while the SNP was the leading pro-independence party, it was by no means the only significant one. Indeed, there remained fears in the SNP that their leader, Alex Salmond, would still actually fail to be re-elected to the Parliament because of the party's fortunes in the constituency and region where he was standing. A key issue remained the extent to which the SNP could put itself forward as being a viable alternative for government rather than just be a short-term recipient of protest votes. Even if the SNP did well, the Liberal Democrats' opposition to a referendum on independence meant that the party probably would retain a greater affinity with Labour. The potential for continuity remained evident even as uncertainty over post-devolution politics in Scotland grew stronger.

Wales

In Wales, devolution had bedded down with a number of key defining characteristics. The Assembly had been Labour-run in one form or another since 1999. Public policy had been marked by Welsh Labour approaches to issues such as health and education that sought 'clear red water' between government at the Wales and UK levels. Labour initiatives also included the 'bonfire of the quangos' announced in July 2004. However, political developments since the 2003 Assembly elections created additional complexities. Pre-eminent among these was that when Peter Law, the Assembly Member (AM) and MP for Blaenau Gwent, became an Independent in 2005, the Labour administration had lost its majority. The Opposition parties also criticised Labour for its rejection of a clear commitment to primary legislative powers for the Assembly and the Richard Report's proposal of an STV (single transferable vote) electoral system. Even so, the mooted grand coalition of the other parties could only really agree on oppositionist strategies to harass Labour; the differences in fundamental principles between Conservative, Liberal Democrat and Plaid Cymru, as well as the electoral competition between them, made an agreed agenda for government seemingly impossible. Labour's delivery on policy goals such as hospital waiting lists and waiting times improved; and Labour's 2005 Government of Wales Bill, though criticised, did, nevertheless, devolve more powers.

But, as in Scotland, 2006 provided further challenges to Labour. A key event was the Blaenau Gwent by-election held in June, occasioned by the death of Peter Law. His widow and former agent stood as independent candidates for the Assembly seat and Westminster seat respectively. Despite concerted Labour campaigning, including numerous visits by Labour leader Rhodri Morgan, the independent candidates triumphed again. Labour emphasised the local factors at play in the election, and the impact of a general public malaise in politics. Privately, however, party strategists on all sides reacted. Encouraged by the result, there were Conservative-Liberal Democrat discussions about a possible multi-party coalition following the 2007 elections, while Labour's defensiveness led to Labour overtures to the Liberal Democrats about a possible renewal of partnership government between them, last seen in 2000–03.

Within the Assembly, its minority position left Labour open to defeat at any time. This vulnerability was underlined when, in October, the Opposition parties combined to vote down Labour's £14 billion budget. This was followed by intensive party negotiations over changed allocations. Even so, in early December, there was apparent unity among the opposition parties to vote down the budget unless a further £17.9 million was found for schools. Nick Bourne, the Conservative leader, talked up the possibility of an alternative non-Labour coalition taking over. However, Plaid Cymru's leader, Ieuan Wyn Jones, facing a revolt from his own AMs, who were reluctant to join a coalition with the Conservatives, went back into talks with Labour. The provision of a further £9.3 million for schools as a result of Gordon Brown's Pre-Budget Report, plus £2 million from the reserves, led to Plaid Cymru AMs abstaining in the eleventh-hour vote on 13 December. This episode exposed the limited credibility of a non-Labour, all-party coalition in the short term, even suggesting that, after the 2007 election, a coalition between Labour and Plaid Cymru, 'Labour's little helpers', might be possible. But it still conveyed the difficulties of Labour getting their business through.[15] More broadly, policy achievements became a political football with the 2007 elections firmly in mind. Opposition leaders sought to portray Labour as tired and devoid of new ideas, playing on the age of the First Minister, Rhodri Morgan. A major policy failure was Labour's inability to deliver on the 2003 manifesto pledge to provide free care for the disabled. In a manner similar to the Scottish Executive's shortcomings over free care for the elderly, Labour had underestimated levels of demand and did not have sufficient resources.

Against this, Labour ministers emphasised the gap between people's generally negative perceptions of public services in Wales and their generally positive experience of services when they personally accessed them. In a speech in September, Morgan stated that Labour had run an administration not characterised by endless ministerial change and policy initiatives but one focused on delivery of agreed aims by ministers put into ministerial positions for several years to see policies through to completion. He emphasised new job creation, service improvements and major construction projects such as the Millennium Centre in Cardiff.[16] Looking to the future, a second round of EU funding, which would help new investment projects, was secured for 2007–13. In October, following successful pilot schemes, it was decided that the Welsh Baccalaureate would be rolled out across Wales as a replacement for the A level. In November, following a review of local government in Wales by Sir Jeremy Beecham, the introduction of local service boards to shake up local government performance was announced. However, it remained open to question whether such policy developments filtered through to the Welsh public.

A key matter in the development of devolution in Wales was the successful passage of the Government of Wales Bill, introduced in December 2005. It did three things. First, it changed the legal status of devolution. The Government of Wales Act 1998 had stipulated that the devolution of secondary legislative powers was to the Assembly as a corporate body. It was at the Assembly's behest that its powers were then delegated to a Cabinet working closely with the Assembly committees. The 2006 Act stipulated that devolution was now to the Crown's ministers in the Welsh Assembly government, each of whom were members of the Assembly and accountable to it, but legally separate from it. This consolidated a convention separating the government and the Assembly that had been operating since 2001. Second, the Act also introduced a small but significant reform of the electoral system. Originally, under the mixed-member electoral system, candidates were allowed to stand both for constituency and regional lists. The 2006 Act banned this so-called 'dual candidacy', so that candidates had to choose.

Finally, and perhaps most importantly, the 2006 Act addressed the powers of the National Assembly. The Act assumed a general convention that Westminster legislation would give the Assembly maximum discretion in its secondary legislative powers in any new act. More specifically, it gave effect to the idea that there would be a new procedure by which Westminster, at the Assembly's request, could pass Orders in Council allowing the Assembly to modify any existing primary legislation as it applied to Wales, thereby granting new secondary powers to the Assembly. Looking to the future, the Act created a mechanism for triggering a referendum on whether the Assembly should have primary legislative powers. It would require the support of two-thirds of Assembly members as well as the support of Westminster before it could be held.[17]

At face value, such changes might be taken as suggesting that the development of Welsh devolution re-inspired territorial instability in the UK. However, mechanisms to enhance secondary legislative powers were justified primarily in terms of the functional requirements of good government. A key episode that had originally raised this imperative was the foot-and-mouth crisis in 2001, when UK government had expected the National Assembly to take charge of the situation in Wales but the Assembly had found that it did not actually have the powers to do it. The incremental development of devolution was further evidenced by the passage of the 2006 Transport (Wales) Act and the implementation of the 2005 Railways Act, which gave the Assembly the strategic powers to create an integrated transport strategy as well as the specific railways powers to oversee local services. In October, the UK government unveiled further plans to give the Assembly more powers over local government, changing, for example, council boundaries and the way by-laws operate. Even the clearly implied eventual aim of moving to primary legislative powers was intended simply to give Wales parity with Scotland. Consequently, the Government of Wales Act 2006 and the accompanying development of the Assembly's powers had a strong sense of consolidating devolution in a country that, in 1997, had voted for an Assembly by only a 0.6 per cent majority.

Of course, such developments were not without their critics. The measure banning dual candidacy in National Assembly elections was controversial. This had been justified by Labour members on the grounds that list members generally were constituency candidates who had lost but nevertheless still ended up elected, and then engaged in unfair competition as sitting list members by nursing constituency seats for future contests. Opposition parties criticised Labour for manipulating the electoral system to protect Labour constituency incumbents[18] and then delayed the bill in the House of Lords, hoping to secure the withdrawal of the dual candidacy clause. They eventually caved in, so as not to lose the bill as a whole. Meanwhile, Plaid Cymru and the Liberal Democrats argued that it would have been better to have a clearer timetable for introducing primary legislative powers. There also remained questions about how smoothly the new Orders in Council arrangements would work and whether its operation would simply exacerbate the lack of clarity in the Assembly's powers.

Overall, Labour still essentially shaped the political, governmental and constitutional agenda in Wales. Nonetheless, during 2006 there appeared to be more indicators of change in Welsh politics than hitherto. Symptomatic of this was talk of a change in the leadership of the Welsh Labour Party should Labour suffer losses in the 2007 Assembly election. Rhodri Morgan had personified Labour's re-grasping of control of the devolution project after the turmoil of Alun Michael's leadership and the 1999 election result. Yet his failure to make an impact in Blaenau Gwent and talk about his age suggested that Labour might be starting to look to a new leader. Jane

Davidson, the Education Minister, received some favourable comment, but the two most likely contenders began to emerge in the form of Carwyn Jones, the Rural Affairs Minister, and Andrew Davies, the Minister for Enterprise, Innovation and Networks. Jones sought to project a Welsh Labour appeal, strongly in favour of further devolution. He attracted support from a number of non-Labour pro-devolution sources. Davies, in contrast, was seen as the establishment candidate: a more experienced minister, positive but pragmatic on constitutional powers and defined by a Gordon Brown-like commitment to business friendly policies and aspirations for social justice.[19] The calm still persisted in Welsh politics; Morgan's Welsh Labour politics still largely defined the difference that devolution made in Wales. However, growing hopes among Opposition parties that they might finally see a swing of the political pendulum, and the nervousness in the Labour Party about its future direction, suggested a storm might be brewing.

Northern Ireland

In Northern Ireland, despite the Assembly's suspension, its elected members still drew two-thirds of their salaries and served their constituents. This was a measure of the hope still placed in devolution as a basis for the normalisation of politics. At the dawn of the year the prospect seemed remote. While the sectarian violence between unionist/loyalist and nationalist/republican communities remained much reduced, voting behaviour in both the 2003 Assembly and 2005 UK elections had seen a polarisation of political sentiment.[20] If a deal were to be done, it would have to be between the hardline Democratic Unionist Party (DUP), led by Ian Paisley, and Sinn Fein, led by Gerry Adams, rather than the more moderate Ulster Unionist Party (UUP) and Social and Democratic Labour Party (SDLP) that had previously led their political communities. This appeared highly unlikely, given Sinn Fein's desire to achieve the full implementation of the Belfast Agreement and the DUP's desire for a new agreement more acceptable to unionism.

2004 and 2005 had both given some cause for optimism. Sinn Fein was in favour of power-sharing devolution; its strategy being to achieve an electoral and governmental position both north and south of the border from which they could press for reunification. The DUP had been expected to be obstructionist. Yet Paisley surprised many commentators by being open to negotiation and, in December 2004, the two parties appeared close to a deal on the 'Comprehensive Agreement', brokered by the UK and Irish governments.[21] However, the deal collapsed because of the DUP's unmet demand for a conclusive decommissioning of Irish Republican Army (IRA) weapons, proven with photographic evidence, as well as an end to all of its criminal activities. During 2005, an IRA statement in July and confirmation of a final act of IRA decommissioning by the Independent International Commission on Decommissioning (IICD) in September removed much of the basis for the DUP's scepticism over arms. Nevertheless, the IICD report acknowledged that IRA criminal activities continued. The year closed with Northern Ireland seemingly as far away from breaking the impasse over returning to devolution as ever.

In this context, 2006 was striking for the concerted efforts of the UK and Irish governments to bring the matter of restoring the Assembly to a resolution one way or the other. In April 2006, Tony Blair and Bertie Ahern, the Irish Taoiseach, visited Northern Ireland and stated that the Belfast Agreement now had a potentially limited time span. The Northern Ireland parties were told that the Assembly would meet for a maximum of three six-week periods in which they had a final opportunity to work towards a return to power-sharing devolution. They were set a deadline of 24 November 2006. If they succeeded, then the next Assembly elections scheduled for May 2007 would be postponed for one year to allow the new administration to consolidate its support. If they failed, the Assembly would be abandoned and the salaries and allowances payable to Members of the Assembly would cease. There would, however, not be a simple resumption of direct rule from London. Instead, there would be an increase in UK–Irish government co-operation in the government of Northern Ireland.[22] This was an attempt to coerce the more reluctant DUP to accept power-sharing for fear of something worse in the form of increased Irish government involvement in the affairs of Northern Ireland.

The Assembly reconvened on 15 May, but all attempts to make progress failed. On 22 May, Gerry Adams nominated Ian Paisley as First Minister and Martin McGuinness, the deputy leader of Sinn Fein, as Deputy First Minister, but Paisley refused to be nominated. On a different tack, Peter Hain, the Secretary of State for Northern Ireland, set up a 'Preparation for Government Committee' within the Assembly, but even then little headway was made. The key opponents to a deal were the DUP, which criticised Sinn Fein on two issues. First, the DUP attacked the criminal activities of the IRA and Sinn Fein's association with it. Second, it also attacked Sinn Fein's refusal to participate in the new Police Board or district policing partnerships as well as on its failure to give general support to the Police Service of Northern Ireland (PSNI). There were also significant differences over the devolution of policing and justice powers; Sinn Fein supported it, but the DUP balked at the idea that the former convicted IRA bomber, Gerry Kelly, was likely to become a justice minister if this happened.

When it became apparent that talks between the parties at Stormont were failing, the UK and Irish governments arranged more intensive negotiations at St Andrews in Scotland in October. Momentum for a deal was provided by a further report from the Independent Monitoring Commission (IMC) on 4 October, stating that the IRA had dismantled some of its most important structures. It no longer had either the capacity or the desire to go back to a sustained paramilitary campaign. Although IRA members were still involved in criminal activities there were signs that the leadership was 'clamping down' on this issue. The UK and Irish governments welcomed the report, but other reactions were mixed. Sinn Fein and the SDLP urged the DUP to accept the fact that the IRA's war was over and that republicans wished to pursue a constitutional course. Nevertheless, Paisley stated that IRA change had only occurred because of his party's pressure and there remained the key problem of 'the IRA's criminal empire'.[23]

Three days of talks at St Andrews did not deliver a deal but did produce an 18 page document detailing a timetable towards securing it. At the root of the document remained the revisions to the Belfast Agreement agreed in principle in December 2004. The party leaderships on both sides were required to gain the endorsements of their parties to the agreement by 10 November. In addition, Sinn Fein was required to call a conference of its supporters to endorse the PSNI. If this was achieved, 'preparations for government committee' would be established involving the party leaders, and Paisley and McGuinness would be elected as First Minister and Deputy First Minister by 24 November. Some form of popular endorsement, albeit unspecified, would then be arranged for March 2007. If all of this were successfully completed, devolution would be re-established on 26 March 2007. It would then be up to the Assembly to decide when Westminster should devolve policing and justice powers to its control at Stormont. If, however, the parties failed to keep to the timetable, devolution would be abandoned and the UK government would indeed pursue direct rule with increased Irish involvement.[24]

The St Andrews talks produced some optimism. On the one side, Adams talked of putting community divisions into the past. Paisley typically commented that 'the days of gunmen in government are over. We will meet the requirements but IRA/Sinn Fein have got to meet these requirements. When they do we will really be in the way for peace.'[25] Nevertheless, both sides had difficulties. The Sinn Fein leadership faced problems in gaining broader party support for a positive approach to the PSNI. Dissident republican paramilitaries sought to undermine a deal. Back in April, Denis Donaldson, the former Sinn Fein official who had confessed to being a British spy, was found murdered in a remote cottage in the Irish Republic. Following the St Andrews talks there were firebomb attacks on property in central Belfast. Similarly, the DUP leadership faced potentially insuperable difficulties in gaining support from their members for going into government with Sinn Fein. The UK Unionist Party, led by Robert McCartney, talked of huge disquiet in the DUP and the prospect of the DUP losing members and voters to his party. Within days, meetings were cancelled amidst DUP accusations that the UK government had softened on the insistence that Sinn Fein support the PSNI.[26]

Consequently, by 10 November Sinn Fein had only been able to give the St Andrews Agreement qualified support, and the DUP neither backed nor rejected it, reiterating the need for Sinn Fein to support the police. The UK government continued to name 26 March 2007 as the absolute deadline for the reconvening of devolution, but simultaneously gave the two parties more time to make the key decisions to allow that to happen. Hence a Northern Ireland Act was passed in November giving effect to the St Andrews Agreement. The Assembly was to stay in existence as a transitional body until 30 January, with elections to a new Northern Ireland Assembly on 7 March. Continuing devolution beyond 26 March would require the DUP and Sinn Fein, assuming they remained the two leading parties, to nominate First and Deputy First Ministers, who would take a pledge of office requiring support for the rule of law, the police and the courts. However, on 24 November the DUP and Sinn Fein only needed to indicate their preparedness to nominate First and Deputy First Ministers in March. This would allow the DUP to prepare their supporters for power-sharing and Sinn Fein to hold a special conference over policing.

The meeting of the Assembly on 24 November proved to be highly controversial. As speeches were being made, the loyalist terrorist, Michael Stone, attempted to enter Stormont with a bag of explosives, with the expressed intention of assassinating Gerry Adams and Martin McGuinness, exposing the deep frustrations of loyalist opinion over unfolding events. Inside the chamber, Adams expressed his desire to nominate McGuinness as Deputy First Minister. However, Paisley said only that his party would honour the St Andrews Agreement if Sinn Fein honoured its obligations to support the rule of law, the police and the courts. The Speaker, Eileen Bell, interpreted this as an expression of support for nominating ministers in principle, allowing the timetable towards March elections to unfold. This led to uproar; and DUP representatives later said that no such expression had been made. However, when the Assembly reconvened on 27 November, Paisley accepted this inter-pretation, and DUP representatives backed him.[27]

There clearly remained much to settle. Even though Paisley had kept the door open for a return to devolution, further progress depended on Sinn Fein publicly and categorically supporting the forces of law and order. But, even if Sinn Fein did so, it also depended on the DUP's continued commitment. There were good grounds for being sceptical. Observers of the collapsed deal of 2004 remained wary of Paisley's skill in being seen to be prepared to do a deal, before claiming that what had undermined progress was duplicity either by the UK government or Sinn Fein. It was questionable in late 2006 whether Paisley had really prepared his party base for such a deal. If the winds within unionism were clearly blowing against a deal, then Paisley's backdown was very likely.

These problems were not seen as insuperable. Discipline within Sinn Fein had proven in the past to be strong. The party was already deeply committed to a strategy of accepting a partitioned Ireland in the short term, and using the legitimation of their politics and electoral success both sides of the border as the political route to a united Ireland. Support for policing within Northern Ireland was a big hurdle to cross, but not impossible. As for Ian Paisley, he might simply be driving the hardest bargain possible by exploiting all of Sinn Fein's readiness to compromise before finally saying yes. There were, of course, ultimately significant misgivings in the unionist community over accepting direct rule with an Irish component as the alternative. But such optimistic assumptions remained to be tested.

Overall, the political future of Northern Ireland remained in the balance at the end of the year. There was still a considerable way to go before power-sharing devolution could be re-established. The lack of mutual trust at an elite level could yet prevent agreement. Of course, not least of the parties' concerns were their electorates and how to carry them with them. Even if power-sharing government were re-established, a DUP–Sinn Fein administration would face severe difficulties in functional effectiveness, given their mutual loathing and suspicions that each party primarily served its own community rather than Northern Ireland as a whole. Even so, signs of political progress buttressed the relative community peace, and a power-sharing government had the potential to buttress it even further. Politicians had got back to where they had been in December 2004 and were possibly moving towards a restoration of power-sharing. However, it was also clear that, if they faltered, devolution could be abandoned indefinitely, to be replaced by direct UK rule, but now with a strong though undefined Irish component.

Conclusion

Two narratives compete in interpreting the politics of devolution across the UK. The first suggests that the 'suspended revolution' in UK territorial politics is being progressively realised.[28] More diverse party systems, strongly differentiated from the UK system, grow more not less likely. Tensions over the use of devolved powers lead to demands for more not less policy innovation and divergence. Constitutional debates have re-emerged that now threaten to move the debate in Scotland on from a Parliament to independence; in Wales, from an Assembly to a Parliament; and in Northern Ireland, from devolution based on the 'moderate' parties to devolution based on the 'extreme' parties, that inter alia provides a platform for Sinn Fein's ambitions for a reunited Ireland.

The need for yet further transformation was raised by a growing debate on the English question. Amidst general criticism of the UK Labour government passing key education and health legislation only with the help of Scottish Labour MPs, the Conservative Party confirmed its general position of being in favour of correcting the so-called West Lothian question. This involves Scottish MPs being able to vote on issues affecting only England, whereas in Scotland these issues are now dealt with by the Scottish Parliament. The Conservatives suggested a policy of limiting the voting rights of Scottish MPs on matters not relating to Scotland. The question of an English Parliament was also raised more seriously within a broader debate about rebalancing the UK after devolution. Even in Scotland, Canon Kenyon Wright, the ex-convenor of the Scottish Constitutional Convention, suggested that this was the way forward for England.[29] In November, an ICM poll suggested that 68 per cent of English voters and 58 per cent of Scottish voters thought that England should have its own Parliament.[30]

The alternative narrative is that there remain stronger forces for continuity than change. Arguably, much of the drift in public opinion in Scotland and Wales over party support, and in Scotland towards independence, reflects mid-term feelings against Labour rather than strong support for other parties or constitutional options. There remains much to play for in the 2007 elections. The momentum of political change may also be arrested. In Scotland, Gordon Brown and Jack McConnell's concerted stance in arguing for Scottishness *and* Britishness suggests the possibility of a novel alternative dynamic. In Wales, most political debate has for the time being turned to how the Assembly's new powers may be implemented. In Northern Ireland, the outcome of the St Andrews talks is unclear and the future of the Assembly is uncertain. Deadlines have proved flexible in the past, suggesting that a stark choice between power-sharing of the extremes or direct rule with Irish involvement may yet be postponed.

In March 2006, Lord Falconer, the UK Secretary of State for Constitutional Affairs, strongly defended Labour's devolution reforms as a revision of territorial relations to sustain the UK, and criticised attempts to discriminate against MPs from outside England as destabilising to the Union.[31] Ministers clearly felt that they were under some pressure. Nevertheless, the fact that they were prepared to defend their approach so robustly is a reflection of the willingness of the centre to apply political resources when required. Broadly, this clear defence of the revised union, and Brown and McConnell's more clearly asserted Britishness may be a foretaste of a strategy to assert clearer central authority in UK territorial management in a post-Blair UK. This may be inadequate, leaving devolution still lacking a clearly articulated set of principles. Nevertheless, it is an approach that the Conservative Party at the centre and political actors at the UK periphery will watch with great interest.

Ultimately, whether devolution and its development are followed with as much interest by the voters may be a deciding factor. As 2006 drew to a close, low turnouts below 50 per cent and 40 per cent in Scotland and Wales respectively were predicted for the May 2007 elections. Amidst popular indifference, the winds of political change may blow stronger than ever.

Notes

1. See, for example, A. Aughey, *Nationalism, Devolution and the Challenge to the United Kingdom State* (London: Pluto Press, 2001) and Tom Nairn, *After Britain* (London: Granta, 2000).
2. C. Jeffery and D. Wincott (eds), *Devolution in the United Kingdom: Statehood and Citizenship*, special edition of *Publius, the Journal of Federalism*, 36 (2006).

3. C. Jeffery, 'Devolution and the Lopsided State', in P. Dunleavy, R. Hefferman, P. Cowley and C. Hays (eds), *Developments in British Politics 8* (Basingstoke: Palgrave Macmillan, 2006).
4. J. Bradbury, 'Territory and Power Revisited: Theorising Territorial Politics in the United Kingdom after Devolution', *Political Studies*, 54 (2006), 559–82.
5. *Scotsman*, 1 November 2006.
6. *Scotsman*, 27 November 2006.
7. *New Statesman*, 25 September 2006.
8. David Cameron, 'I will never take Scotland for granted', speech in Glasgow, 15 September 2006.
9. G. Lloyd and D. Peel, 'Reconstructing Regional Development and Planning in Scotland and Wales', in J. Bradbury and J. Mawson (eds), *Devolution, Regionalism and Regional Development: The UK Experience* (London: Routledge, forthcoming); *Scotsman*, 1 November 2006.
10. Scottish Parliament: Health Committee, 10th Report 2006, *Care Inquiry.*
11. Scottish Liberal Democrats press release, 23 October 2006.
12. *Sunday Telegraph*, 26 November 2006.
13. Jack McConnell, John P Mackintosh Lecture, 31 October 2006.
14. *Daily Telegraph*, 25 November 2006. See also Gordon Brown, speech to the Labour Party Conference, 25 September 2006.
15. *Western Mail*, 6 December 2006 and 14 December 2006.
16. Rhodri Morgan, speech to the Institute of Welsh Politics Conference, Cardiff, 19 September 2006.
17. See *Better Governance for Wales*, Cm. 6582, June 2005; the Government of Wales Act 2006.
18. J. Bradbury and J. Mitchell, 'The Constituency Work of Members of the Scottish Parliament and the National Assembly for Wales: Approaches, Relationships and Rules', *Regional and Federal Studies*, 17 (2007) pp. 119–47.
19. Lee Waters, 'Life after Rhodri', *Agenda, Journal of the Institute of Welsh Affairs* (2006), 10–13.
20. See J. Kampfner, 'Divided in Peace', *New Statesman*, 20 November 2006, pp. 30–3.
21. Northern Ireland Office, *Proposals by the British and Irish Governments for a Comprehensive Agreement*, Belfast, 2004.
22. Northern Ireland Office press release, 6 April 2006.
23. Independent Monitoring Commission, *12th Report*, October 2006; *The Times*, 5 October 2006.
24. Northern Ireland Office, *Proposals by the British and Irish Governments*, Belfast 2006.
25. *Daily Telegraph*, 14 October 2006.
26. *The Times*, 18 October 2006.
27. *Daily Telegraph*, 25 November 2006; *The Times*, 30 November 2006.
28. 'Suspended revolution' is the term used to describe the underlying lack of fundamental change in the structure of UK territorial politics in J. Bulpitt, *Territory and Power in the United Kingdom: An Interpretation* (Manchester: Manchester University Press, 1983).
29. Conservative Party press release, 7 February 2006; BBC News, 24 October 2006.
30. *Sunday Telegraph*, 26 November 2006.
31. Lord Falconer of Thoroton, speech to the ESRC Devolution and Constitutional Change programme final conference, London, 10 March 2006.

13
Local Government: Towards Strong and Prosperous Communities?

Steve Leach and Lawrence Pratchett

A trilogy of publications

The future of local government is supposed to have been the focus of three major reports in 2006. First, the interim report of the Lyons Inquiry into local government, *National Prosperity, Local Choice and Civic Engagement*,[1] was published in May 2006, setting out Lyons' arguments for a more devolved and responsible approach to place-shaping as a concept for both central and local government to tackle. It argues explicitly for a new central/local government settlement. Somewhat ironically, the impact of this heavily trailed report was lost in the sudden Cabinet reshuffle that took place the same week, creating an entirely new Department for Communities and Local Government (DCLG), with a new ministerial team headed by the former Education Secretary, Ruth Kelly.

Second, there was the publication, in October 2006, of the long-awaited local government White Paper, *Strong and Prosperous Communities*,[2] a document which paves the way for a number of significant changes, from structural reorganisation in some county areas to imposed changes on political leadership, and from a new streamlined performance and efficiency framework to an enhanced neighbourhood focus. Supposedly devolving more powers to localities, the White Paper met with only lukewarm support from much of the local government community, amid concerns that it was imposing a Whitehall vision of how local government should operate, far removed from the real world of local government.[3] Nevertheless, it is rapidly becoming a key vision for local government, with many of its proposals being enacted through a new Local Government and Public Involvement in Health Bill and many county areas responding to the restructuring opportunities that it offers.

The third and vital document in this trilogy, however, is notable primarily by its absence. The final recommendations of the Lyons Inquiry were expected to be published before the end of 2006, setting out not only a new financial settlement for local government but also a wider vision of the future role and function of local government. Such a vision would be the cornerstone of government policy towards localities. However, despite expectations in early December that it was expected 'to be submitted to the Treasury in two weeks time',[4] the final report appears to have been upstaged by three other reports that impact directly upon the Lyons recommendations: Sandy Leitch's report for the Treasury entitled *Prosperity for All in the Global Economy: World Class Skills*,[5] published 5 December 2006, poses a significant role for local government in delivering the new skills for a twenty-first-century economy; Kate Barker's report on *Land Use Planning*,[6] also for the Treasury, has a more obvious impact on local government, inviting a more streamlined planning process and more efficient use of land for economic purposes by making the planning process more responsive; and Sir Rod Eddington's study of *Transport's Role in Sustaining the UK's Productivity and Competitiveness*[7] suggests, among other proposals, new road-pricing mechanisms of potential value to local government. Lyons is responding to these reports but, in the meantime, the changes instigated by the White Paper and consequent Local Government Bill gather momentum, as do the proposals contained in all these other reports. The very real danger that Lyons now faces is that his extensive and detailed examination of local government's role, function and financing may arrive after the show has left town.

The timing of this succession of official publications could be seen as being, at best, poorly planned or, more critically, as being perverse and illogical. The sequencing of such key documents fails to deliver a coherent development of policy towards localities in general and local government in particular. At the very least, it seems reasonable to have expected the publication of the White Paper to have been delayed until after the final report of the Lyons Inquiry, so that the government could have responded to its recommendations and set out an integrated package of structural, functional and financial reforms. In previous analyses of local government, we have criticised central government for having a disjointed and incoherent approach to local government policy, with only the lead department for local government having the best interests of local government at heart and needing to defend those interests against the Treasury and other service-specific departments.[8] The sequencing fiasco lends a new twist to this criticism, however, with even the lead department, the newly formed DCLG, failing to show joined-up or coherent thinking. The most convincing explanation for this apparent lack of sequencing lies in the impending changes at prime ministerial level. Several of the key themes of the White Paper – elected mayors, community cohesion, choice in personal services – are long-term priorities of Tony Blair (who contributes a foreword to the White Paper). There is an assumption that he wishes to see these reforms embedded before he steps down, sometime in the summer of 2007.

There is, in fact, little connection between the arguments in the first Lyons Report and those set out in the White Paper, although the latter claims otherwise:

> The three priorities for reform that Sir Michael identified in this report in May – greater clarity about the respective roles of central and local government, greater recognition of local government's role as a place-shaper and co-ordinator of local services, and a recognition within local government of the need to improve its capability to do this job – are all key themes of this White Paper.[9]

In reality, although the White Paper does include a series of proposals for reducing the number of central controls and targets, and makes encouraging noises about providing more freedom and powers to local authorities and their partners, it does not address the relationship in the comprehensive way apparent in Sir Michael's report. Although the term 'place-shaping' is used regularly in the White Paper, it is interpreted in a much more limited way, with Local Area Agreements (the cornerstone of the place-shaping agenda, in the government's view) set to continue to be dominated by the straitjacket of central government priorities, which are focused around 'Children and Young People', 'Healthier Communities and Older People', 'Economic Development and the Environment' and 'Safer and Stronger Communities'. Although the White Paper claims to provide a vision of 'revitalised local authorities working with partners to reshape public services around the citizens and communities that use them',[10] it is a vision at a very high level of generality, which lacks the substance of Sir Michael's place-shaping agenda.

In this chapter, we explore a number of key themes that emerge in this putative trilogy. It is impossible to provide a detailed analysis of all the issues raised in the various documents, so instead we focus on four key particularly contentious issues. First, we explore the ongoing issue of political leadership, critically assessing the latest proposals in the White Paper to encourage 'strong' leadership. Second, we examine the return of local government restructuring onto the local government agenda and the tension between unitary and two-tier government in the shire counties. Third, we examine the continuing interest in creating semi-formal governance structures for city-regions in the form of 'Multi-Area Agreements'. Fourth, we analyse the emerging concept of place-shaping and the role of partnerships in both delivering and hindering such visions. Our argument throughout is twofold: first, in relation to each of the specific initiatives, there is an absence of detailed understanding of how local government works and, therefore, sensitivity to local needs and differences; second, overall, there is an absence of coherence to the proposals due, not least, to the sequencing problems of the various reports.

Political leadership

The well-established government belief in the value of strong leadership is illustrated by the following passage from the White Paper:

> Local democracy needs strong, visible leadership but the framework within which local authorities operate can be a barrier to the kind of leadership that prosperous communities require ... we are introducing stronger, more stable models of local authority leadership to build on the progress made so far.[11]

These beliefs are operationalised in a proposal for three models of 'strong leadership' which it is intended to introduce in legislative form in 2007, for implementation in 2008–09:

- a directly elected mayor with a four-year term
- a directly elected executive with a four-year term
- an indirectly elected leader with a four-year term.

In each model, all executive powers will be vested in the mayor or leader, who will have responsibility for deciding how they should be discharged. The key purpose is to give councils a stable leadership over a four-year term, regardless of how the wider political context of the council develops. As we will argue, there is little evidence to suggest that councils need or will benefit from such a change.

It should be noted that the requirement to submit a mayoral proposal to a referendum has now been removed, possibly because the majority of pre-2006 referendums produced the 'wrong' result (that is, a rejection of the mayoral option). A local authority can now simply choose to introduce an elected mayor model or, indeed, an elected executive. Authorities with a population of less than 85,000 can continue to operate with a streamlined committee system. It is widely anticipated that a large majority of all authorities will opt for the third model: the empowered council leader with security of tenure. The argument as to why security of tenure is so important is as follows:

> In most authorities leaders face election every year. This can make it hard to take and see through essential but difficult decisions that may in the short term be unpopular. It also brings uncertainties for senior management teams in pursuing and implementing longer term strategies.[12]

As we shall see, there is a sense in which security of tenure is a non-problem.

Although there is no explicit argument set out in the White Paper about the change in the balance of power from a more collective leadership focused on the party groups to a much more individualised model focused on the empowered leader, the lack of concern on the part of the government to clarify the position of the party group, or, indeed, party politics more generally, is illustrated by the lack of reference to both topics. Paul Wheeler made this point very well in relation to a 2005 government visioning document, *Vibrant Local Leadership*:

> All the agencies involved in local government improvement (Audit Commission, IDeA [Improvement and Development Agency] and ODPM [Office of the Deputy Prime Minister] amongst them) talk about community leadership, civic leadership, anything but political parties. It's as if there is a huge elephant in the room and everyone is trying to ignore it.[13]

There are two possible justifications for the government to prescribe the form and tenure of local political leadership, as they have done in the White Paper. The first would be if there were credible evidence that a particular approach to leadership resulted in *better performance*, assessed by indicators such as Comprehensive Performance Assessments (CPAs) or 'public satisfaction' measures. The second would be if there were credible evidence that a particular approach to leadership resulted in an *improved quality of democracy*, as assessed by measures such as public support, voter turnout, or accountability. If neither of these justifications is present then such prescription could reasonably be regarded as unwarranted interference in the right of local authorities to decide their own way of working.

At this point, it is useful to examine the evidence. In relation to performance, there is no real evidence linking leadership type with CPA results. Mayor-led authorities do not perform better than non-mayoral authorities. The previously much-quoted statistical relationship between 'authorities with strong leadership and strong scrutiny' and 'CPA performance' has wisely been omitted from the White Paper; it was not sustainable. An alternative measure might be public satisfaction with directly elected leaders. However, a New Local Government Network (NLGN) survey found no statistically significant difference between the public satisfaction ratings of mayoral and non-mayoral leaders.[14]

In relation to democratic justification, there are separate arguments around the relative visibility and accountability of 'strong' leaders. It is clear that elected mayors have greater visibility than other council leaders. The NLGN survey revealed recognition factors of 57 per cent and 25 per cent respectively. But this discrepancy is hardly surprising, given the fact of direct election and the high profile of mayors in the local media. There is no evidence that 'strong' council leaders, except where they are subject to the relatively unusual circumstances of direct election, are more or less recognisable than those not so categorised.

Beyond the higher visibility of elected mayors, there is little to support the democratic justification argument. It should be recalled that of 31 mayoral referendums carried out so far, only 12 (or 39 per cent) supported the idea of a mayor. Moreover, turnout at mayoral elections is no higher than at local elections where mayors are not involved. It is not possible to argue that elected mayors have caught the imagination of the public and led, in this sense, to democratic gains.

The argument about accountability is premised on the assumption that a single individual leader with overall executive responsibility will strengthen accountability because the public will be clearer as to whom they can hold responsible. As might be expected, however, all existing elected mayors delegate executive responsibility among selected Cabinet colleagues or identify a range of decisions that are to be taken collectively, or both. No doubt council leaders under the new proposals will do the same. As in Cabinet government at Westminster, it would be unjustifiable to hold the (mayoral) leader solely accountable for decisions outside his or her remit. If a Cabinet member for social services fails to identify and deal with an impending overspend, is it justifiable to hold the mayor responsible?

No one would be likely to dispute that the quality of local political leadership is important. The problem with the government's analysis lies in its use of the misleading term 'strong leadership'. First of all, it is something of a tautology – is anyone going to advocate 'weak leadership'? But what does strong leadership actually mean? The government's view emphasises qualities of individuality, visibility and executive power, with expectations (reading between the lines) that strong leaders are high profile, charismatic and entrepreneurial: the American examples typically cited always seem to have these qualities. A more helpful characterisation of leadership is that it should be *effective*: that is, it should succeed in articulating and delivering a clear vision for an area, leading to good performance and effective partnership working (or whatever outcomes are felt to be desirable). The reality is that such outcomes can be and are achieved by leadership styles which are not congruent with the government's ideal type. In a recent Rowntree Foundation research project on political leadership, examples were found of different leadership styles proving remarkably effective (in CPA terms) in different circumstances.[15]

There are a number of potential implementation problems in the government's related leadership proposals. The direct election of a 'slate' of executive members (including the leader) seems to be one that would have little real meaning for electors. The choice of an elected mayor has meaning, as does the choice of a local councillor. But would most electors have any basis for judging the suitability of a slate of up to ten people, the majority of whom they are unlikely ever to have heard of? It would, in addition, be problematic if an election produced a council with a composition that differed from the successful (presumably one-party) slate. It is also to be hoped that the 'vote of no confidence' principle could be extended to elected Cabinet members who proved ineffective in their roles.

The indirectly elected leader model, as set out in the White Paper, would be workable in an authority with elections every four years, although in a hung authority it is by no means unusual for coalitions between party groups to change over a period as long as this. But in authorities which elect by thirds, it is hard to see how a four-year term could be sustained if control changes during that period. There is, of course, the 'vote of no confidence' opportunity, but this seems a strange mechanism to use to reflect the fact that the existing leader's party no longer commands a council majority.

In any event, it is actually quite unusual for a council to change its leader during a four-year term or in authorities which elect by thirds, over a similar period, unless political control changes. Leaders have to face the possibility of an election every year, but in most cases their leadership is not contested. As a comparison of evidence in a sequence of Municipal Yearbooks demonstrates, there is more stability of political leadership than the government appears to think.

Our conclusion is that the decision to introduce legislation to prescribe the form and tenure of political executives in the way the government has done is not justified by the evidence, is based on a confusion between 'strong' and 'effective' leadership, shows little understanding of the way in which politics actually works in local councils, and constitutes an unnecessary intervention in the political management arrangements of local authorities.

Local government reorganisation

British local government is often held up as being unique because of the size of its principal authorities, which are significantly bigger than anywhere else in Europe.[16] Another, even more dubious distinction, however, is the frequency with which central government seeks to reorganise local government. No other country finds it either as attractive or as necessary to tinker with structural reform in the way British governments have done. Structural reorganisation appears to be a fall-back position for British governments, when their agenda for local government lacks substance or, indeed, when they perceive existing organisational structures to be a barrier to their wider objectives: Thatcher's abolition of the Greater London Council and the metropolitan counties is, arguably, the best example of this position. New Labour, when it was first elected in 1997, sensibly avoided revisiting the Banham reorganisations of the early 1990s, preferring to concentrate upon the substantive issues of local government performance and citizen engagement. However, over the last couple of years, it has been unable to resist the lure of reorganisation, being drawn inexorably towards another restructuring of the shire counties.

Having succumbed to the lure of restructuring, however, there is a strange and inconsistent recent history to the government's attitude to local government reorganisation. During David Miliband's time as Minister for Communities and Local Government, the official view, widely trailed in ministerial speeches, switched from what appeared to be a commitment to introduce 'unitary authorities' throughout those parts of England that do not already have them to a much more ambivalent and flexible attitude and then back again to a strong preference for unitaries. The proposals in the White Paper sit somewhat uneasily between prescription and flexibility. The government's preference in principle for unitary authorities is clear. It perceives unitary authorities (particularly large-scale ones) as more likely to deliver the Gershon-related efficiency savings that are required from local government. The concept is also more compatible with the government's vision of strong, visible accountable leadership, which it clearly regards as less feasible in a two-tier setting. There is also a suspicion in some quarters that the Department for Communities and Local Government would prefer a simplified system of some 180 unitary authorities, because it would be less complex to deal with than the current system, in which shire districts provide the largest grouping (238) within the overall total of 388 local authorities in England.

Scope for efficiency savings and administrative convenience, however, are arguably a totally inadequate basis for a local government reorganisation. As we pointed out in the 2005 Review, the strongest performers under the CPA system since its introduction have consistently been the shire counties, despite their apparent 'disadvantage' of having to work within a two-tier system.[17] A move to a uniform system of unitaries would reduce the number of elected councillors (parish and town councillors excepted) by up to 50 per cent, in a country where the average population served by a councillor is already much higher than in most European counties. Although it is technically feasible to operate services such as education over a wide range of population sizes (compare Rutland's 27,000 with Birmingham's more than 1 million), other types of decisions are clearly most appropriately made at different spatial levels. Land use and transportation planning cannot sensibly be done at shire district level, but it would make equally little sense for decisions on local planning and environmental issues to be made on a county-wide basis. 'Unitary authorities' are difficult to reconcile with the principle of subsidiarity.

In reality, the government's position on the two-tier versus unitary debate is more qualified than its position on shire government would suggest. It has introduced a two-tier system for Greater London, and can clearly see the benefits of a similar model for the metropolitan areas, even though its proposals fall short of the re-creation of the metropolitan counties.[18] In these circumstances it is, perhaps, not surprising that the White Paper proposals are somewhat equivocal. County areas can make bids to the DCLG for a 'unitary solution', but it has indicated that there is a limit to the number of bids it wishes to consider. At the same time, the government will consider bids from county areas to pioneer, as pathfinders, new two-tier models, with a similar implication that only a limited number of such bids will be accepted for implementation. However, by 1 February 2007, DCLG had received some 26 bids for unitary status and a further five proposals for pathfinder status in relation to enhanced two-tier working.

The unresolved issue regarding unitary bids is what the DCLG will do in the seven county areas where it has received competing bids for unitary status – Bedfordshire, Cheshire, Cornwall, Durham, Northumberland, Oxfordshire and Somerset. Will it disqualify the bids because they lack unanimity, or will it make its own choice from the menu provided, no doubt on a basis which places considerable emphasis on 'efficiency savings'? Whatever the outcome, what is proposed in the White Paper is messy and inconclusive, and liable to leave the local government map of England even less coherent than it was before.

City-regions

The government's position in the White Paper on local government structure (that is, a clear preference in principle for unitary authorities but a preparedness to tolerate the continuation of two-tier government in the shire areas, provided it can deliver equivalent Gershon-related efficiency savings) is further complicated by the reintroduction of city-regions as an important structural reference point. This renewed interest was signalled during David Miliband's brief period in charge of local government, and re-emerges in the White Paper, which devotes 25 pages to an analysis of their importance and of how, if our cities are to compete with continental equivalents such as Barcelona and Milan, they need to embrace a sphere of influence wider than the current boundaries of Manchester, Liverpool and Birmingham, all of which arbitrarily separate these city authorities from their wider catchment areas.

The logic of this argument would point to a re-creation of the metropolitan counties as 'strategic authorities', which could indeed link economic regeneration, transportation and planning policies for a viable journey-to-work catchment area. This was the purpose behind the creation by the first New Labour government of a new Greater London-wide authority (the Greater London Authority – GLA) in 2000. Two-tier local government is clearly perceived as viable in Greater London, and there is an equivalent argument for it in at least four of the former metropolitan county council areas.

Yet the White Paper chooses not to follow through this logic, possibly because of its incompatibility with the 'unitary is best' position elsewhere. Instead, what is offered is a good deal of encouragement for the groups of authorities in these areas to develop 'strong leadership' structures which provide a voice for the city-region, together with a proposal for a 'Multi-Area Agreement' instrument, which parallels the Local Area Agreements (LAAs) which are to be introduced elsewhere, but which brings with it dangers of a level of bureaucratic complexity approaching the unmanageable. There is already a de facto metropolitan county in Greater Manchester where the Association of Greater Manchester Authorities plays a key role in budget-setting for the Police, Fire and Passenger Transport Authorities, and acts as a clearing house for a range of other city region-wide issues. Elsewhere equivalent machinery is much more limited.

The government has suggested that elected mayors might be appropriate for city-regions, but there appears little local enthusiasm anywhere for this option. The alternative, a city-region leader selected (or elected) from the current range of city/district leaders, is fraught with problems. It would seem strange in national and international arenas if the city-region leaders of Greater Manchester, Merseyside and West Midlands were not from Manchester, Liverpool and Birmingham respectively. However, given the well-established suspicion of the 'big city' on the part of the adjacent authorities, this outcome is by no means guaranteed, and these three city-regions could end up being represented by politicians from Tameside, Knowsley and Sandwell respectively. Indeed, many of the French metropolitan agglomerations, such as Lyon and Lille, have had similar experiences, with representatives from small suburban municipalities coming to dominate these areas due, at least in part, to resistance among other suburban municipalities to the dominance of the main city.[19]

One reason for the failure of the White Paper to give real substance to its city-region agenda could be the known preference of the Chancellor for provincial regions as a more appropriate focus for sub-national government. Yet the option of elected regional assemblies is likely to remain dormant for some time, following its overwhelming rejection in the North-East referendum in 2005. In this respect, the city-region seems to be a poorly thought-through, stop-gap solution to the broader problem of metropolitan governance that is common to all developed countries.

Place-shaping and partnership

So far, the discussion has focused on aspects of the White Paper that have developed outside of the context of the Lyons Inquiry. One of the key themes of the first Lyons Report (May 2006), however, was that of 'place-shaping', which he characterises as follows:

> Place-shaping ... describes my view ... that the ultimate purpose of local government should not be solely to manage a collection of public services that take place within an area, but rather to take responsibility for the well-being of an area and the people who live there ... it should both reflect the distinctive identity and aspirations of the people and area, and function as a means of safeguarding their well-being and prosperity.[20]

Although there is a sense in which place-shaping is little more than a restatement of the importance of local authorities' community leadership (as opposed to service provision) role, with perhaps a greater emphasis on the case for changing the balance between central specification and local choice in favour of the latter, the term has quickly entered the vocabulary of ideas in good currency. The White Paper links its own agenda to the concept:

> In a rapidly-changing world, communities need strategic leadership to help bring together various local agencies and groups in order to build a vision of how to address a locality's problems and challenges in a co-ordinated way. This is what Sir Michael Lyons means when he talks about local authorities as 'place-shapers'.[21]

But the idea of 'place-shaping' requires an identification of what kind of places have most significance for governance: around what 'places' should decision-making structures and processes be built? On this issue, neither Sir Michael Lyons nor the government provides much in the way of guidance. In both cases, there is an assumption that place-shaping is relevant at all levels from large multi-county regions to small towns and to neighbourhoods within them. Yet elsewhere in the White Paper, emphasis is placed on the importance of city-regions and neighbourhoods as a focus for, in the first case, strategic planning and economic regeneration and, in the second, social cohesion.

Place-shaping is given particular emphasis in the section of the White Paper dealing with partnership working. There are a series of proposals for strengthening this function, and the role of local authorities as leaders within it. Thus, in various places the White Paper proposes that:

- a duty will be placed on local authorities to prepare the Local Area Agreement (LAA) in consultation with others
- there is an expectation that local authority leaders will play a leading role on Local Strategic Partnerships (LSPs) (and portfolio holders a key role on relevant thematic partnerships)
- a duty will be placed on the local authority and named partners to co-operate with each other to agree targets on the LAA
- a duty will be placed on relevant named partners to have regard to relevant targets agreed between them ... in LAAs.

Yet, although the commitment to enhanced partnership working is clear, and the spread of LAAs to all authorities is likely to enhance its significance for public and voluntary sector partners, one wonders how much difference the new provisions will actually make. For a start, requiring other agencies to participate in LSPs and LAAs and to 'have regard' to the content of the plans and targets which emerge is a response to a non-problem. With very few exceptions, such agencies already participate and 'have regard' to emergent plans and targets. The problem of securing involvement is much more significant in relation to the private sector and the White Paper does nothing to respond to this situation. What other agencies have not been required to do – and the White Paper does nothing to change this – is to support the priorities of local authorities themselves, which have generally assumed 'lead' responsibility for Community Strategies and LAAs. Thus the role of local authorities in relation to health and police authorities, for example, remains one of negotiation. They can seek to persuade health authorities to halt hospital closure programmes, or police authorities to focus resources on the authority's priority areas, but they lack effective levers or incentives in this negotiation process. The expectation must be that the other agencies whose participation in LAAs is now 'required' will continue to hold to their own organisational priorities (why should they do otherwise?), except for relatively uncontroversial LAA projects where additional resources are likely to result from co-operation.

The second major concern about the White Paper's partnership proposals is how much they remain dominated by central government. LAAs have become the key vehicle for local joined-up working. There is a requirement that LAAs are structured on the basis of four (central government) priorities: children and younger people, healthier communities and older people, safer and stronger communities, and economic development and the environment.[22] The diagram in the White Paper (the Outcomes, Targets, Indicators Framework) portrays what a straitjacket this categorisation embodies.[23] There are four levels of indicators based on these four priorities, only the last of which appears to provide scope for local choice (or more realistically, interpretation). Where is the scope for an authority to argue that crime and disorder, or economic regeneration is not a priority in its area? Where is the scope for other priorities, such as a lack of affordable housing, which do not fit easily into the framework? The much-heralded rebalancing of the central–local relationship is not demonstrated by the arrangements for LAAs, which remain centrally dominated and fail to provide the genuine local place-specific lead role proposed by the Lyons Report and others.[24]

Conclusion: awaiting episode one?

The development of local government policy in 2006 has suffered from sequencing problems of almost 'Star Wars' proportions. Just as George Lucas's defining 'episode 1' film of the Star Wars saga was not made until more than 20 years after the original (but later renamed the fourth) episode, so the various documents that constitute contemporary policy towards local governance are lacking the definitive steer that the Lyons Inquiry is supposed to have given it. In the absence of Sir Michael's definition of the role and function of local government and its accompanying financial settlement, the various proposals and developments contained in the White Paper and elsewhere lack the coherence that might otherwise be apparent. The extensive White Paper, comprising some 239 pages spread across two volumes, contains a wide range of ideas and proposals for both encouraging and directing local choice. We have touched on some of these proposals in this chapter, although many others around neighbourhood working, and so on, have not been addressed. However, at a detailed level, there is a significant lack of clarity and coherence about the proposals. As we have illustrated above, the White Paper shows a systematic lack of understanding or empathy for the way local government operates and, indeed, how it differs from place to place.

The problem is not simply one of sequencing. A year ago, the Lyons Report promised to be the most fundamental review of local government for at least a generation, possibly more: the inquiry itself still appears to want to achieve this ambition. However, as it responds, first to the White Paper and then to the agenda being set by the Leitch, Barker and Eddington Reports, it is difficult not to conclude that its fundamental review position has been undermined. The White Paper sets in train a whole range of restructuring and reform processes which will be under development, if not wholly in place, before the publication of the Lyons Report. Far from being the definitive statement on the future role and function of local government, therefore, the Lyons Report may simply be the 'post hoc prequel' to earlier decisions: Sir Michael's role has switched from one of defining the role and function of local government to one which must find some coherence and rationalisation of an increasingly complex and fragmented policy towards local governance.

In some respects, it is too soon to judge the impact of these documents on local government. The Lyons Report could still have a significant role to play in shaping its future role and function. The challenge that Sir Michael has always faced has been to develop a radical vision of change that empowers localities while, at the same time, bringing sceptical ministers and central government departments along with him. Moreover, the delays in publishing his report may enable the White Paper to be given a post hoc rationalisation of a radical shift in central–local relations that appears to be at the heart of what Lyons has set out to achieve. In the meantime, local government seeks its own coherence from a disparate and incoherent set of policy documents.

Notes

1. Lyons Inquiry, *National Prosperity, Local Choice and Civic Engagement: A New Partnership between Central and Local Government for the 21st Century*. Available at <www.lyons inquiry.org.uk>.
2. *Strong and Prosperous Communities*, Cm. 6939, October 2006.
3. *Local Government Chronicle*, 2 November 2006, p. 6.
4. Ibid., 7 December 2006, p. 1.
5. Available at <www.hm_treasury.gov.uk/independent_reviews/leitch_review/review_index.cfm>.

6. Available at <www.hm_treasury.gov.uk/independent_reviews/barker_review_land_ use_planning/ _index.cfm>.
7. Available at <www.hm_treasury.gov.uk/independent_reviews/eddington_trarnspor_ study/eddigton/_index.cfm>.
8. S. Leach and L. Pratchett, 'Local Government: A New Vision, Rhetoric or Reality?', *Parliamentary Affairs*, 58 (2005), 318–34.
9. Cm. 6939, p. 17.
10. Ibid., p. 7.
11. Ibid., p. 8.
12. Ibid., p. 55.
13. P. Wheeler, *Political Recruitment: How Local Parties Recruit Councillors* (York: Joseph Rowntree Foundation, 2006).
14. NLGN, *Mayors Mid-term: Lessons from the First 18 Months of Directly-elected Mayors* (London: NLGN, 2004).
15. S. Leach, J. Hartley, V. Lowndes, D. Wilson and S. Downe, *Local Political Leadership in England and Wales* (York: Joseph Rowntree Foundation, 2005).
16. See, for example, D. Wilson and C. Game, *Local Government in the United Kingdom*, 4th edition (Basingstoke: Palgrave Macmillan, 2006).
17. S. Leach and L. Pratchett, 'Local Government: A Second Wave of Modernisation?', in M. Rush and P. Giddings (eds), *Palgrave Review of British Politics 2005* (Basingstoke: Palgrave Macmillan, 2006), pp. 192–3.
18. See Cm. 6939, pp. 90–1.
19. Taoufik Ben Mabrouk, 'The Metropolitan Governance and the Democratic Issue: Democratic Deficit or Democratic Recognition Quest?', Paper presented to 'Local Governance: Developments and Democratic Challenges' Workshop, ECPR, Budapest, 8–11 September 2005.
20. Lyons Inquiry, *National Prosperity, Local Choice and Civic Engagement*, p. 39.
21. Cm. 6939, p. 94.
22. The last of these embraces transport, culture and sport as well as economic development and the environment – clearly an 'everything else' category!
23. Cm. 6939, p. 23.
24. Audit Commission/IDeA, *Fitness for Purpose in the 21st Century: Strategic Choice at Local Level in the New Millennium* (London: Audit Commission, 2005).

14
Foreign Policy: A Bleak Year

Christopher White

The ability to affect outcomes in international relations is limited by the power to shape events and by international society's governing norms: sovereignty and non-intervention. To punch above its weight, a middle-ranking power like the UK exploits its close relations with the US and membership of key international organisations, notably the United Nations Security Council (UNSC), the North Atlantic Treaty Organisation (NATO), the G8, the European Union (EU), and the Commonwealth. With the exception of the EU, all in one way or another are the result of Britain's once great power status. From the beginning, New Labour has seen this legacy as an opportunity to tackle the challenge of globalisation. To have any influence on the future, the argument goes, foreign policy must be geared towards shaping the direction that globalisation and change takes. On this view, the ability to affect outcomes in international relations affects the ability to shape what happens at home. Where possible, the UK has led on key issues: development and eradicating poverty, the promotion of human rights, democracy and good government, encouraging openness and liberalisation. Where necessary, working through multilateral and co-operative means, the UK has sought to exercise influence via the legitimacy of the arguments that it is able to wield.

In essence, New Labour's foreign policy is based on a liberal view of international relations and holds to a particular view of globalisation as a force for good that can benefit all, encouraging co-operation, the spread of democracy (a universal panacea) and human rights (the sine qua non of economic success). Security thus depends on deepening the process by establishing a more liberal international order. New Labour foreign policy has been consistent in these beliefs from the outset and, rather than calling for a rethink following 9/11, the call was merely to redouble one's efforts.

In a turnaround in fortunes, however, and in marked contrast to the previous year, key developments in 2006 have challenged many of the aspirations and assumptions associated with this view of international relations. An underlying theme of this chapter will be to detail these events and evaluate their significance for existing policy. New Labour's foreign policy may well be in need of renewal, confronted by a world still essentially realist in mindset and action, a world all the more threatening, in part, and perhaps paradoxically, as a result of UK policy.

Changing priorities?

Making sense of the future of British foreign policy proved a popular theme in 2006. In March, a revised version of the government's foreign policy priorities was published in a White Paper outlining nine strategic international priorities.[1] This was updated in June, with an additional goal added on the request of Margaret Beckett following her appointment as Foreign Secretary in the May Cabinet reshuffle.[2] The ten strategic priorities are:

1. making the world safer from global terrorism and weapons of mass destruction
2. reducing the harm to the UK from international crime
3. preventing and resolving conflict through a strong international system
4. building an effective and globally competitive EU in a secure neighbourhood
5. supporting the UK economy and business through an open and expanding global economy, science and innovation, and secure energy supplies
6. promoting sustainable development and poverty reduction, underpinned by human rights, democracy and good governance and protection of the environment
7. managing migration and combating illegal immigration
8. delivering high-quality support for British nationals abroad, in normal times and in crises
9. ensuring the security and good governance of the UK's Overseas Territories
10. achieving climate security by promoting a faster transition to a sustainable, low-carbon global economy (the added goal).

Energy security is now integrated with economic priorities, and the need to manage migration and combat illegal immigration is accorded the status of being a priority, as is the need to achieve climate security in a low-carbon economy. Reflecting the important connections between the domestic and the international, these objectives are for the government as a whole, not just the Foreign and Commonwealth Office (FCO), with lead roles for other departments in key areas; the Home Office, for example, in dealing with counter-terrorism.[3] The need for a reformed and more effective set of multilateral institutions, 'fit for purpose', is seen as one of a number of responses to the changing situation, alongside the need to renew key partnerships, particularly the transatlantic and European relationships. Nevertheless, the underlying evaluation remains unchanged: the UK can and should make a positive difference by applying abroad those values that guide action at home. Britain's security and continued prosperity continue to be premised on the pursuit of a progressive agenda geared towards the support of effective and accountable states.[4]

The White Paper recognised that 'the priorities cannot be pursued in isolation' but avoided ranking them, assuming that all could be pursued simultaneously. Judged against recent events, however, we can see that at times the objectives are either compromised by existing policy, for example the war in Iraq and counter-radicalisation policies, or stand in direct conflict with one another; for example, encouraging liberalisation and dealing with climate change.

International security

Terrorism

In an uncertain security environment, terrorism is identified as the primary threat to the UK. The government's counter-terrorism strategy, 'CONTEST', created in 2003, was made public in 2006. It involves four principal elements: preventing terrorism by tackling radicalisation, pursuing terrorists and those who sponsor them, protecting the public and key national services, and preparing for the consequences.[5] Progress towards achieving key targets (outlined in the Prime Minister's 'twelve point' plan for dealing with terrorism in August 2005) included the introduction of new grounds for deportation and exclusion by extending memoranda of understanding (now covering Algeria, Jordan, Libya and Lebanon), creating an offence of condoning or glorifying terrorism (one of a number of changes under the Terrorism Act 2006) and enabling the government automatically to refuse asylum to those involved in terrorism (one of a number of changes following the passage of the Immigration, Asylum and Nationality Act 2006).[6]

The FCO played an increasingly important role, particularly in dealing with radicalisation. In the financial year 2005–06, the Global Opportunities Fund spent £17.6 million on counter-radicalisation projects, sponsoring programmes such as a 'Scholars Roadshow' in the UK and funding a series of overseas visits allowing eminent British Muslims to discuss life in the UK.[7] The projects, part of a broader concern to alter adverse perceptions of the UK among Muslims, work in tandem with existing policies focused on political and economic reform.[8] The objective – countering negative perceptions in order to prevent radicalisation – nevertheless had to confront the argument that existing foreign policy, in Iraq and Afghanistan in particular, was working in the opposite direction and actually exacerbating the terrorist threat, a point recognised by the Foreign Affairs Committee in July with respect to Iraq.[9]

In many respects a key manifestation of globalisation, the terrorism issue links the multicultural, multi-faith context of the UK to foreign policy, suggesting the need for a redefinition of the national interest. That analysis is rejected by the government, which maintains it is possible to pursue a community-based solution to the terrorist threat while holding a consistent line on foreign policy.[10] The tension between the two objectives has been very evident in 2006, and will doubtless heighten should any terrorist attack occur in the future.

The position of the UN, long a key concern for the UK, advanced in 2006 with the General Assembly agreeing a comprehensive counter-terrorism strategy on 8 September.[11] Based on a report by the then Secretary-General, Kofi Annan, the strategy emphasises dissuasion, denial, deterrence, developing state capacity and defending human rights.[12] Given existing UNSC Resolutions 1373 and 1267 that renounce terrorism and oblige counter-terrorist policies, the UK was able to concentrate efforts on capacity-building measures, such as policing and forensics training.[13]

Counter-proliferation: Iran and North Korea

The second aspect of Strategic Priority 1 relates to counter-proliferation. Two countries in particular presented a fundamental challenge to UK interests in this respect: Iran and North Korea.

Following the breakdown of the EU3 (the UK, France and Germany) talks at the end of 2005, the dispute over Iranian nuclear ambitions was referred to the UNSC and the International Atomic Energy Agency (IAEA) in February. Reporting back to the UNSC in April, Mohamed El Baradei, Director General of the IAEA, indicated that Iran had increased, rather than suspended, its enrichment activities. When the permanent UNSC members and Germany met in London in May to discuss an appropriate response, the UK pushed for punitive sanctions that were 'incremental, proportional and reversible'. By the end of the month, in a significant move, US Secretary of State Condoleezza Rice had agreed to enter into talks with the EU3 and Iran with the proviso that enrichment activities were suspended. In an attempt to break the deadlock in early June, the EU's High Representative, Javier Solana, presented a comprehensive package of proposals in the hope of inducing compliance, but without success. With views hardening, the UK changed tack and argued for more robust sanctions. In July, a resolution (1696) was agreed, obliging Iran to suspend all enrichment-related activities or face possible sanctions. A deadline of 31 August was set, with the threat that failure to comply would lead to the adoption of appropriate measures under Article 41 of Chapter VII of the UN Charter. Although the resolution was seen at the time as a real breakthrough, the UNSC subsequently struggled to agree on the scope of sanctions with China and particularly Russia reluctant. Agreement on a package of punitive measures was eventually reached in December and adopted in UNSC Resolution 1737[14] which demanded the suspension of enrichment activities and heavy water-related projects and included a package of punitive economic – but no military – measures.

Relations with North Korea continued to deteriorate through the year. Following unfruitful talks, the UNSC passed Resolution 1625 in response to North Korea's conducting missile tests in July and then, after North Korea's successful detonation of a nuclear device in October, the more robust Resolution 1718 which demanded, inter alia, abandoning weapons of mass destruction and sanctioning selective embargoes on travel and luxury goods. Despite hopes that the resolution would be robustly enforced, implementation proved difficult, with the Chinese willing to 'inspect' but not 'intercept or interdict' imports.

From a UK perspective, the implications of either Iran or North Korea successfully developing a nuclear capacity are potentially dire: altering the regional balance, potentially precipitating a nuclear arms race, and fundamentally undermining the Non-Proliferation Treaty (NPT) regime, already weak in the eyes of many. The UK remains committed to the existing regime, but the events of 2006 suggest fundamental obstacles to its renewal. This in part explains the government's commitment to renew Trident, announced at the end of the year (itself a move that potentially undermines treaty commitments to disarm).

Conflict in the Middle East

The situation in the Middle East took a sharp turn for the worse in 2006: Iraq moved closer to civil war; Iran grew more belligerent and influential; and democratic advances, touted as an essential component of long-term peace in the region, failed to translate into greater stability and peace, in Iraq, in Palestine and Lebanon.

In Iraq, the situation deteriorated markedly in 2006, with increasing sectarian violence precipitating a situation approximating to civil war. In a leaked memo, the outgoing British Ambassador, William Patey, summed up this concern, predicting that 'the prospect of a low intensity civil war and a de facto division of Iraq is probably more likely at this stage than a successful and substantial transition to a stable democracy'.[15] Recognition of the seriousness of the situation altered expectations at home, adding to the view that a fundamental rethink was required, beginning with a change in expectations. Hope of achieving a prosperous, democratic, unified Islamic state gave way to a narrower, medium-term objective, focused on delivering stability, law and order. The tactics therefore turned to improving the Iraqi forces in the hope that responsibility could be transferred to the new Iraqi government, formed at the beginning of the year.

Relying on the new government, however, proved problematic, it being ostensibly a Shi'ite-dominated force, riddled with insurgent and criminal elements. In both the US and the UK, domestic political pressure heightened as casualties and civilian deaths rose. The US mid-term elections, seen by many as a vote on Bush's Iraq policy, returned a Democratic majority to both Houses. At the end of the year, despite the changing political environment, opinion remained divided over how best to achieve a basic stability, while retaining face and a sympathetic Western-orientated government, with little sign that Bush would significantly alter strategy in line with either the bipartisan Iraq Study Group recommendations or Democratic opinion.[16]

Throughout 2006, Blair faced criticism over his Iraq policy. His relationship with Bush led to charges that he was too closely allied to the US, that he had exercised little influence over the conduct of the war, and that his loyalty had achieved little in return with regard to the Middle East peace process. The former Defence Secretary, Geoff Hoon, one of a number of people to speak out about the 'special relationship', alleged that UK advice on dealing with the post-conflict situation, specifically on disbanding the Iraqi army and 'de-Ba'athification', was largely ignored.[17]

In the UK-administered south, the situation on the ground remained volatile through 2006, with UK forces operating in increasingly difficult circumstances, unable to make a positive difference as a result of the complexities of arbitrating between Shi'ite factions – all, in one way or another, suspicious, unco-operative and hostile. In a significant – and, for the government, embarrassing – public intervention in October, General Sir Richard Dannatt, Chief of the General Staff, suggested that the presence of British troops was in fact making the situation worse, adding that the hope of creating a liberal democracy had been 'naive' and the Iraq operation was 'exacerbating' the 'difficulties we are experiencing around the world'.[18]

With considerable pressure for withdrawal, steps were taken that focused on a timely exit. In February, Defence Secretary John Reid detailed criteria for a handover and suggested that significant reductions could be expected within 12 months.[19] In June, the Iraqi government assumed full responsibility for security in Muthanna, one of four provinces under British control in the south, and in the autumn the UK government announced its intention of making further reductions, subject to satisfactory progress, as part of a more complete stand-down of troops, leading up to a further withdrawal from Basra by the spring. In November, Saddam Hussein was sentenced to death, and, in December, in controversial circumstances, was hanged.

The situation in Iraq cannot be understood in isolation from the wider set of issues in the Middle East. Relations with Iran, a key actor in Iraq, remained fraught throughout the year. From a UK perspective, areas of concern are in essence threefold and relate to sponsoring insurgent elements in Iraq, developing nuclear weapons, and support of terrorism. Iran's growing influence in the region – suggesting a growing Shia arc of influence – was vividly demonstrated by the conflict that erupted between Israel and Lebanon in the summer.[20]

In July, Hezbollah seized two Israeli soldiers in a cross-border raid and targeted northern towns with Katyusha rockets provided by Iran. Describing the actions as an 'act of war', the Israeli Prime Minister, Ehud Olmert, responded with an aerial campaign that aimed at both military and civilian targets and a ground force incursion into Southern Lebanon. The UK reacted by stressing the importance of creating the necessary conditions for a lasting peace and resisted calls for an immediate ceasefire. The refusal to condemn the Israeli action as disproportionate drew considerable criticism from Muslim opinion in the region. It also angered members of Tony Blair's own party and highlighted the role Downing Street was taking in the matter, with suggestions that the FCO disagreed with the stance. During the G8 conference in St Petersburg that coincided with the beginning of the conflict, the UK took a lead in drafting UN Resolution 1701, adopted on 11 August.[21] The UK pledged £12.7 million in humanitarian assistance, but did not contribute to the peacekeeping force.

A cessation of the conflict followed, but the peace remained fragile, drawing attention to the fact that the underlying causes of the conflict remain; in particular, Hezbollah is unlikely to disarm (a requirement of the resolution). In the aftermath, a pro-Syrian Hezbollah campaign gathered momentum, with calls by the party for new elections after its support for the government had been withdrawn, effectively emasculating a democratically elected and pro-Western government. The domestic situation deteriorated further, following the assassination of the anti-Syrian Industry Minister, Pierre Gemayel, in November, suggesting a possible return to civil war in the region. Margaret Beckett showed her support for the Lebanese government by visiting in December, but the visit was controversial and demonstrated the dwindling influence of the UK in the region.

Elsewhere in the Middle East, the chances of a lasting peace settlement between Israel and the Palestinians seemed more distant, with the victory of Hamas in parliamentary elections in February. The UK refused to deal with Hamas on a bilateral basis, unless it renounced violence and accepted a two-state solution. In January, in a meeting in London, the EU, the UN, the US and Russia threatened to suspend aid to the Palestinian administration, but Hamas responded by appealing to Arab states to make up any shortfall, undermining the possibility of using aid to leverage influence.[22] The UK focused attention on President Abbas's 'National Dialogue' and his 18-point peace plan and, in December, Blair called for renewed talks, following meetings with the Israeli government and with President Abbas during a visit to the region. Meanwhile, fundamental obstacles to a solution grew as the struggle for power between Abbas's Fatah movement and Hamas continued.

Afghanistan

Five years after they were overthrown, the Taliban remain a powerful force in Afghanistan, controlling significant swaths of land along its southern periphery. Levels of fighting increased significantly in 2006, as NATO forces were deployed in the south as 'stage three' of its security operations in the country.[23] On 4 May, the UK-led Headquarters Group of NATO's Allied Rapid Reaction Corps assumed overall command of the International Security Assistance Force (ISAF) and, in the summer, a UK Provincial Reconstruction Team (PRT) took responsibility for Helmand province, a Taliban heartland and a major drug-producing area. UK troops faced fierce fighting, suffering high casualty rates as they sought to secure the area. Concerns over the ferocity of the fighting led to accusations that the deployment had been poorly planned, that troops were unnecessarily exposed, had poor backup and unsatisfactory equipment and supplies. This developed into a more comprehensive discussion regarding the role of the Ministry of Defence and with accusations that British forces were overstretched.[24]

Concerns over troop numbers and the composition of the ISAF forces in the south also led to acrimonious discussions between NATO members on their respective responsibilities in the region. Aware that its credibility is on the line, NATO met in Riga in November. Germany, France, Spain and Italy agreed to remove caveats that had hitherto limited their participation in combat operations and Poland agreed to an early deployment of 1,000 troops, but the organisation struggled to achieve the troop numbers deemed necessary.[25] Long-term concerns therefore remain, with worries that an unsuccessful campaign in Afghanistan could spell the beginning of the end for NATO. Part of the problem, as with Iraq, relates to the continued level of violence, which has prevented reconstruction and development work. In the case of Afghanistan, further complications flow from the difficulties of dealing with the narcotics trade, which accounts (according to some estimates) for some 80 per cent of Afghan trade. Eradication is seen as a vital component of any long-term success, but ISAF forces, mindful of the possibility of alienating locals and driving them into the hands of the Taliban, have hitherto refrained from destroying poppy cultivation.

A second difficulty relates to the role of Pakistan. Accusations that the Directorate of Inter-Services Intelligence (ISI), Pakistan's intelligence service, continues to support the Taliban worsened relations between the two countries. The resurgence of the Taliban was also attributed to Pakistan's policy of granting a tacit amnesty to pro-Taliban militants in Waziristan. President Musharraf is seen as a key UK ally in the 'war on terror', but Pakistan's ambiguous role called into question existing policy towards the country.

Protectionism on the rise: the failure of the Doha Round

Though Iraq and Afghanistan received the lion's share of attention in 2006, the failure to agree a deal at the World Trade Organisation (WTO) Doha 'development' Round of trade talks may well prove as important in the long term, signalling a new phase of globalisation. Early approaches to globalisation stressed the universal benefits of liberalisation and a need to humanise globalisation by managing the process in order to meet the interests of all – the purpose of Doha. More recently, however, responses have pointed in a decidedly protectionist direction, suggesting a return to bilateral trade deals based on a narrower, more mercantilist definition of the national interest. The UK worked hard to secure an agreement at Doha, but the five years of negotiations were fraught with difficulties, breaking down in Cancun as early as 2003. Essentially, the negotiations floundered because the US, the EU and the G20 could not agree on levels of farm tariff cuts, trade-distorting subsidies and industrial tariff cuts.

United Nations

Strategic Priority 3 places an emphasis on the need for a stronger international system, better able to prevent and resolve conflict. A key aspect of this objective relates to the UN: improving the institution to make it more 'fit for purpose'. Two important new institutions, the Peacebuilding Commission (PBC) and the Human Rights Council, began work in 2006. Both were welcomed by the UK, though they are rather weaker institutions than originally envisaged in the 2004 High Level Panel report. Originally proposed to address the problem of 'failed states' and to improve the capacity of the UN to provide better post-conflict transition management, disagreement over whether the PBC should be an organ of the Security Council or of the UN Economic and Social Council (ECOSOC), its mandate and membership, meant that the new PBC will in effect operate in an advisory capacity rather than the monitoring and preventative role originally envisaged. It is supported by a new Peacebuilding Support Office and a Peacebuilding Fund. It is intended that the Human Rights Council will offer a more robust forum to discuss and implement human rights standards across the UN and replace the largely discredited Human Rights Commission.[26]

Energy security and the environment

Issues related to climate change and energy security now figure high on the foreign policy agenda and are explicitly included in Strategic Priorities 5, 6 and 10.[27] They also relate to Strategic Priorities 3, 4 and 7, as energy security and climate change are increasingly recognised as potential sources of conflict and, in the long term, precipitate mass migration.

UK policy on climate change is to arrive at an agreed international framework to deal with carbon emissions that balances the needs of developing countries to grow, the right of wealthier countries to maintain existing standards of living, and the necessity to prevent environmental disaster. The outline of a new approach developed after the Gleneagles summit of 2005, with the UK increasingly recognising the possibilities that the G8 affords, alongside the UN (through the United Nations Framework Convention on Climate Change process) and the EU, a key forum to agree environmental targets; in effect, tacitly recognising the limitations of Kyoto.[28]

In October the government published the Stern Report which reviewed the economic costs of rising temperatures.[29] It advised early spending to offset the consequences of a 4–5°C rise in temperatures, suggesting a carbon target of no more than 450–550 ppm (parts per million) CO_2, seen as a balance between overly high adjustment costs and doing nothing. Three policy measures were recommended: carbon pricing, technology policy, and energy efficiency.

In addition to climate change, energy security rose up the agenda in 2006. In the next decade the UK will become a net importer of gas and oil, importing 90 per cent of its gas needs compared with 10 per cent today, at a time when global energy demand is set to rise. The results of the government's review of energy strategy were announced in a statement to the House of Commons on 11 July.[30] Chief among its concerns were the need to secure supplies, avoid dependence and diversify energy sources. It was with this in mind that the UK pushed for an accord on energy security at the G8 in St Petersburg in July. A plan to enhance energy security was agreed, with action promised in the following areas:

- increasing the transparency, predictability and stability of global energy markets
- improving the investment climate in the energy sector
- enhancing energy efficiency and energy saving
- diversifying the energy mix
- ensuring the physical security of critical energy infrastructure
- reducing energy poverty
- addressing climate change and sustainable development.[31]

The strategic implications of energy supplies were brought home in 2006, as Europe became aware of the leverage that Russia, its principal gas exporter, could exert. In January, gas supplies to the Ukraine were cut off, signalling Russia's willingness to use energy supply as a political tool. The strategy appeared to involve negotiating bilaterally within the EU, and, in its near vicinity, exerting political pressure for a less pro-Western position on the part of the Ukraine, Georgia, Belarus and Azerbaijan. The European Energy Charter, signed in 1994 (though not ratified) and designed to provide freer access to energy resources and the energy transit infrastructure in Russia, was tacitly rejected by the Putin government, as Gazprom took a more aggressive stance in ensuring key controlling stakes over new oil and gas fields. In a confidential study leaked to the *Financial Times*, NATO experts suggested that Russia was trying to form a gas cartel with key gas suppliers, such as Algeria, Qatar, Libya and Iran, at a time when the EU is seeking greater diversification in its gas supply.[32] In spite of the warm words of mutual dependence during talks in

Finland between the EU and Russia in October, the fundamentals point to a medium-term dependence on Russia for supplies, with all that that entails.

More broadly, energy matters fed into a number of key security matters, including in Africa, where, notably, China has been playing an increasingly influential role as it expanded its efforts to secure energy and raw materials. This played out most tangibly in the Sudan, where the UK and the US pushed for a strengthened role for UN peacekeeping forces in Darfur, but experienced difficulties in the Security Council, as China initially refused to endorse a robust position.

Conclusion: time for a reappraisal

It is a curiosity of UK foreign policy that the UK tends to see its interests and those of the international society as one and the same. This deeply ingrained *Weltanschauung* accounts for the underlying confidence in globalisation and explains why universal values and interests are a recurring theme, orientating UK policy and underpinning its essentially utopian confidence that the challenges associated with the contemporary environment can be solved by an act of collective will.[33] Much has been spoken of New Labour's ethical approach to foreign policy. But underlying it is the perception that globalisation brings with it a new set of conditions, pregnant with utopian possibilities. Globalisation doubtless does bring with it novel conditions, but perhaps less utopian than Blair initially hoped.

The decision to invade Iraq and the immense problems of the post-conflict situation have proved to be disastrous, contributing to the Prime Minister's decision that he would leave office earlier than anticipated. Confidence that democracies can be created from the outside now seems misplaced and, given the situation in Lebanon and the Palestinian territories, the assumption that democratic states necessarily create a more benign and stable environment is open to question. In time, this may be so, but in the case of Iraq, time is a luxury that intervening states can ill afford. Iran and North Korea, part of Bush's 'axis of evil' and Blair's 'reactionary' states, edged closer to joining the nuclear club, suggesting a failure of existing policy. How to deal with these states is now a paramount concern, as is the possibility that their action may well precipitate a new nuclear arms race. As Iraq has floundered, so Iran has grown in influence and power, crucially altering the Middle East 'balance'. The uncomfortable fact is that the US and the UK now need Iran if they are to exit from an orderly Iraq. The quid pro quo may well be acquiescing in the presence of another nuclear power in the region.

2006 called into question the character of the 'special relationship' between the US and the UK, with evidence suggesting that the influence the latter is able to bring to bear on the US in return for its alliance is rather limited. Questions were asked as to whether it was damaging to the UK's interests to be so closely allied to the US. The American refusal to enter into discussions with Iran and its apparent lack of commitment to a broader Middle East peace process suggest a significant divergence. Add to this the reasons underlying the failures of the WTO talks, along with the current impediments to dealing with climate change, and we see major factors that may strain Anglo-American relations in the future.

The utopian elements of UK policy have economic roots. The suspension of the WTO Doha (development) Round represented a setback for the UK, a step backwards with respect to its commitment to encouraging development in Africa through trade, and a setback with respect to its concern to advocate globalisation qua liberalisation as a force for good. Instead, protectionist impulses are now on the rise, and may be felt in the form of regionalism. It may well be this that proves to be the most significant of changes in the long run. In short, 2006 was a bleak year, suggesting the need for a fundamental reappraisal of UK foreign policy.

Notes

1. *Active Diplomacy for a Changing World: the UK's International Priorities*, Cm. 6762, March 2006.
2. Margaret Beckett is the first female Secretary of State for Foreign and Commonwealth Affairs. The Cabinet reshuffle also saw the appointment of Geoff Hoon, the former Secretary of State for Defence, as Minister of State for Europe, and Ian McCartney, former Chair of the Labour Party and Minister without Portfolio, as Minister of State for Trade, as ministers outside the Cabinet but with the right of attendance. In July Sir Peter Ricketts succeeded as Permanent Under-Secretary following the retirement of Sir Michael Jay.
3. See Michael Jay, 'Foreign Policy and the Diplomat: The End of an Affair?', speech delivered at the London School of Economics, 27 July 2006; Foreign Affairs Committee, *Minutes of Evidence, 8 November 2006*, evidence of Lord Hannay of Chiswick, Sir Jeremy Greenstock and Mathew Kirk, Qs 1–19, HC 167, 2006–07.
4. Jack Straw, 'Active Diplomacy for a Changing World', launch of the White Paper, 28 March 2006.
5. *Countering International Terrorism: the United Kingdom's Strategy*, Cm. 6888, July 2006.
6. See ibid., Annex A.
7. For a detailed list of the projects see *Global Opportunities Fund Annual Report 2005–2006*, <www.fco.gov.uk>.
8. See Peter Gooderman, Director Middle East and North Africa, 'Economic Reform in the Middle East and North Africa', speech delivered in London, 29 March 2006; Dr Kim Howells, 'Relations between Islam and the West: Perceptions and Realities', speech delivered at Wilton Park, 2 May 2006; Frances Guy, 'Democracy in the Muslim World as Seen from the Seat of a Great Power', speech delivered at the Royal Society of Edinburgh, 6 May 2006; Lord Triesman, 'The Government's Relations with Islam at Home and Abroad', speech delivered at the Centre for Islamic Studies, 7 June 2006; the British Council, *British Muslims: Media Guide*, 2006.
9. 'The situation in Iraq has provided both a powerful source of propaganda for Islamist extremists and also a crucial training ground for international terrorists', Foreign Affairs Committee, *Fourth Report, Foreign Policy Aspects of the War Against*

Terrorism, HC 573, 2005–06. This view added to the chorus of criticism with respect to the government's counter-terrorist strategy. See also Rachel Briggs, Catherine Fieschi and Hannah Lownsbrough, *Bringing it Home: Community-based Approaches to Counter-terrorism* (London: Demos, 2006) p. 48.

10. The problem accordingly is diagnosed in terms of poor communication and understanding of existing policy. See *Government Response to the Fourth Report from the Foreign Affairs Committee*, Cm. 6905, September 2006.

11. *The United Nations Global Counter-Terrorism Strategy*, A/RES/60/288.

12. Kofi Annan, *Uniting Against Terrorism: Recommendations for a Global Counter-terrorism Strategy*, A/60/825. S/RES/1373 (2001); S/RES/1267 (1999).

13. *Global Opportunities Fund Annual Report, 2005–06.*

14. S/RES/1734 (2006).

15. 'Iraq Civil War Warning for Blair', 3 August 2006, <http://news.bbc.co.uk/1/hi/uk/5240808.stm>

16. Chaired by James Baker and Lee Hamilton, the bipartisan group recommended: opening dialogue with Iran and Syria; phased withdrawal of all combat troops (leaving only embedded forces by 2008); calls for a renewed US commitment to the Arab-Israeli peace process. 'Staying the course', it suggested, was no longer a viable option. Bush welcomed the report but distanced himself from the recommendations.

17. According to Mr Hoon, 'we would not have disbanded the Iraqi army … We were very concerned in the final stages of the conflict that the Iraqi army was a force for stability in Iraq and I think we would have preferred for that army to remain intact. I don't think we would have pursued the de-Ba'athification policy in quite the same way', <www.telegraph.co.uk/news/main.jhtml?xml=/news/2006/12/09/wirq109.xml>.

18. *Daily Mail*, 13 October 2006.

19. Speech given to the Foreign Press Association, 7 February 2006.

20. See Jack Straw, 'Iran: The Path Ahead', speech delivered at the International Institute for Strategic Affairs, 13 March 2006.

21. Resolution 1701 works alongside existing Resolutions 1559 and 1680. S/RES/1701 (2006); S/RES/1680(2006); S/RES/1559 (2004).

22. A 'Temporary International Mechanism' currently provides a means to filter aid. Set up in the EU, it currently filters over €100 million in aid. See Quartet Statement (US, UN, EU, Russia), S163/06, <www.consilium.europa.eu/ueDocs/cms_Data/docs/pressData/en/declarations/90137.pdf>.

23. The first two stages involved taking responsibility, first in the north, then, in the spring of 2005, in the west.

24. General Sir Michael Jackson, Dimbleby Lecture 2006. See also Defence Committee, *Ministry of Defence Annual Report and Accounts 2005–06*, HC 57, 2006–07.

25. Riga Summit Declaration, NATO Press Release, <www.nato.int/docu/pr/2006/p06-150e.htm>.

26. General Assembly Resolution A/RES/60/251.

27. See 'Our Energy Future – Creating a Low Carbon Economy', Department of Trade and Industry White Paper, February 2003, Cm. 5761.

28. See G8's 'Plan of Action for Climate Change, Clean Energy and Sustainable Development'.

29. Stern Review on the Economics of Climate Change, HM Treasury, <www.treasury.gov.uk/independent_reviews/sternreview_economics_climate_change/stern review_index.cfm>.

30. Department of Trade and Industry, FCO & DEFRA, *UK International Priorities: The Energy Strategy*, Cm. 6887, July 2006.
31. G8 press communiqué, <http://en.g8russia.ru/docs/11.html>.
32. *Financial Times*, 14 November 2006.
33. See the Prime Minister's speech on the Middle East to the Los Angeles World Affairs Council, 1 August 2006, <www.number-10.gov.uk/output/Page9948.asp>.

15
Britain and Europe: A Pause for Reflection?

Tim Bale

After the no votes in France and the Netherlands stopped ratification of the Constitutional Treaty in its tracks in mid-2005, a 'pause for reflection' was called for on all sides. In 2006 it became a standing joke that this process entailed rather more pause than it did reflection – a situation that arguably suited a less enthusiastic member state like the UK than it did those which hoped somehow to put the pieces back together and carry on regardless. The conclusions of the European Council that took place in June 2006 were a clear signal that little progress had been or would be made in the near future: notwithstanding the fact that parliamentary ratification of the treaty has proceeded in some countries, discussion on what to do next was booted into the long grass of 2008. And reports that the council meeting in December would see Germany seek to accelerate progress under its forthcoming presidency came to nothing.

This decision eased any residual international or indeed domestic pressure that the issue might have exerted on the British government – a government more than happy to take a breather after its fairly fraught stint as EU President during the second half of 2005.[1] In any case, when it came to matters European, Her Majesty's Loyal Opposition was otherwise occupied: the Conservative Party's new leader, David Cameron, was busy trying to tidy up the fallout from his campaign promise to end the link between Conservative Members of the European Parliament (MEPs) and the European People's Party group in Strasbourg and Brussels. The Liberal Democrats, meanwhile, were too busy with their own leadership contest to worry much about Europe, even if the latter is an issue which some in the party are beginning to feel deserves a bit of a rethink now that they face stiffer competition from a voter-friendly Conservative Party for the support of a largely Eurosceptical electorate.[2]

Yet the fact that direct, full-frontal domestic debate on the issue was comparatively muted in 2006 did not mean that little of importance went on in and around Europe. The EU, after all, is still seeking to adjust to the enlargement of 2004. And, as it faces the prospect of incorporating not just Bulgaria and Romania but also Turkey and the western Balkans, some of its members are clearly beginning to wonder whether bigger really is better – a debate which, along with that over the organisation's role in global trade, conflict and security, the UK can hardly avoid entering. In any case, British membership of the EU, and the blurring of the national and the international it inevitably entails, means that there is a European dimension to many supposedly domestic issues, most notably in 2006 immigration policy.

Selling (and getting) 'a Europe of results'

It would be wrong to write off the government's response to the stalling – or maybe strangling – of the Constitutional Treaty simply as one of relief. Inasmuch as there was reflection and debate on the future, ministers outlined a clear preference for concentrating on policies that will produce the tangible benefits that (rightly or wrongly) they believe stand some chance of reconnecting ordinary people with Europe or at least convincing them that it does them more good than harm. The good governance of the expanded EU may require institutional fixes and patches in the long term – even some of those which were mooted in the Constitutional Treaty itself, although only the UK Commissioner (and former Labour minister) Peter Mandelson was brave (or foolhardy) enough to admit this out loud.[3] But what was needed more urgently, as the government's new Minister for Europe, Geoff Hoon, stressed in a number of keynote speeches, was seeing the EU deliver 'real value' for its citizens. Whether he was as unhappy as some suggested with the demotion to a post formally outside the Cabinet from which he had been promoted some years previously, he showed little sign of it in public.[4] Instead, he made it his business to carry on where his predecessor, Douglas Alexander, had left off, by continuing to push for the economic liberalisation that the UK – and other member states in Scandinavia and Eastern and Central Europe – insist must now be the EU's central thrust.[5] Noting that only three or four out of every ten Britons thought they had benefited from EU membership, Hoon called for a renewed effort to show how Brussels makes a positive difference not just to people's daily lives but also to the big issues – security, climate change and development – that they also profess to care about.[6]

This is not necessarily a pipedream. As the spring 2006 Eurobarometer showed once again, the British public is much more persuaded of the case for joint European action in fields where a single country acting alone is clearly powerless, especially tackling terrorism, organised crime and environmental protection.[7] The UK's willingness to support the extension of the EU's already rather ambitious emissions trading scheme (ETS) to air travel (now a major source of CO_2) may in part be explained by this, as well as by the support expressed by British Airways and the UK's budget airlines for what they see as an alternative to a flat-rate tax. Whether this public support for European action extends to development issues, however, is arguable: there, the common perception that the EU wastes money makes people suspicious of the idea that co-ordination would help. And, as Hoon himself noted, the situation was not exactly helped in 2006 by the fact that EU (as well as US) intransigence was widely blamed for lack of progress on a world trade agreement that might conceivably assist poorer countries.[8] Beyond supporting Peter Mandelson in his role as Trade Commissioner, and working behind the scenes to persuade other countries to give him even more room for manoeuvre on tariff reform, there is little that the UK by itself could do about the situation.

On international trade, the EU at least has the competence to act. When it comes to both foreign policy and the domestic economic reforms that UK politicians routinely urge on countries like Germany, Italy and France (whose serious social unrest in the early part of the year seemed to attract as much British gloating as sympathy), the EU has less traction. With regard to the former, world events once again revealed both the strength and weakness of the UK's attachment to the so-called Common Foreign and Security Policy (CFSP). On the one hand, the UK stood shoulder-to-shoulder with France and Germany (the so-called EU3) in deciding to refer Iran's nuclear programme to the UN Security Council. Likewise, it was fully on board with the EU's decision to suspend direct aid payments to the Hamas government in Palestine and with the tough line taken with Serbia, to whom it was made clear that closer relations would have to wait on its getting serious about catching war criminals. The British government is also at the forefront not just of moves toward a common energy policy but to incorporate energy questions into rethinking the EU's relations with its near neighbours in Eurasia, including Russia, whose hard line on gas supplies to Ukraine caused considerable concern during the winter. But when it came to the summer conflict in Lebanon, the UK eschewed calls for Europe to speak with one voice, showing considerably more sympathy with Israel than most other member states. One reason, perhaps, why in mid-November the government apparently only learned of a new Middle East peace initiative put together by Spain, France and Italy via a BBC news item![9] Then again, while the British government can hardly be said to have made the running in the establishment of what will be the EU's biggest ever military mission – the 7,000 strong peacekeeping force for Lebanon – it did nothing to block the mission and made at least a token contribution.

In the field of domestic economic reform in Europe, where again the EU's writ doesn't run very deep, one should not write off the nitty-gritty work done by the UK to help along EU legislation designed to make the Lisbon agenda (the creation of a dynamic and competitive European economy) a reality rather than a pathetic joke. The most obvious of these was the so-called Services Directive, which aimed to make the single market a reality for the sector which, in modern economies, is as (if not more) important than tradable goods – a sector in which the UK has a considerable comparative advantage. While it is true that the directive probably does not go far enough for some business interests, and perhaps not as far as the UK government would have liked, the fact that the Council of Ministers was able to adopt a common position that satisfied both the Commission and Parliament – and calmed public opinion in less-than-liberal member states – was a major achievement.[10] Whether the freeing-up of the logjam that bogged down the measure in 2005 had much to do with the UK government, as opposed to, say, Labour and Conservative MEPs' work in their respective European party groups, is, however, a moot point: some would even suggest that progress could only resume once the British had finished their stint as President.

Showdown averted: the Conservatives

The positive role played by Conservative MEPs was, as usual, obscured by the party's internal arguments over Europe. And, as usual, any wounds that resulted were largely self-inflicted. During the 2005 Conservative leadership contest, David Cameron, momentarily concerned about the progress the even more sceptical Liam Fox seemed to be making, had thrown a bone to right-wing MPs by promising to take Conservative MEPs out of the European People's Party and European Democrats (EPP-ED) party group to which they belonged in Strasbourg and Brussels. However, after Cameron had attained the prize he sought, it quickly became apparent that this was a promise he was going to have trouble keeping. For one thing, a considerable number of the MEPs themselves were unhappy about being used as pawns in a wider game and a small but vocal Europhile minority made it clear that they would refuse to go along with the plan. Predictably, an equally vocal minority – both at Westminster and in Strasbourg and Brussels – insisted, at least initially, that anything less than immediate fulfilment of the pledge would cast doubt on Cameron's credibility more generally. More awkward still was the rapidly growing awareness that the Conservatives were going to struggle to find sister parties in Europe who were sufficiently like-minded, and sufficiently mainstream, to help them form a new party group in the EP. Meanwhile, leaders of the continent's largest centre-right parties made clear their continuing displeasure with Cameron (who once again chose not to attend their pre-European Council gathering), with the German leader Angela Merkel going as far as to break with protocol and meet Gordon Brown as if he were already her British counterpart.[11]

Despite the promises and the best efforts of the former leader and now Shadow Foreign Secretary, William Hague, weeks turned into months. By the summer, Cameron had to make the best of a bad job by declaring, alongside the leader of the Czech Civic Democrats but not – as had been hoped – a Polish counterpart, that a new group would indeed be formed, but only after the next European elections in 2009. Some activists were undoubtedly unhappy.[12] The compromise was enough, however, for most Conservatives and their supporters in the media: few sceptics wanted to make trouble for a leader who appeared to be well on the way to giving them a fighting chance (and, in one or two individual cases, a safe seat) at the next general election; pro-Europeans were also prepared to accept the compromise, either because they believed that even a new group would eventually be obliged to engineer some kind of arrangement with the EPP or, as some suspicious sceptics alleged, they had secured a quid pro quo whereby sceptical grassroots members would have less say in the adoption and ranking of candidates at the next European Parliament elections.[13] Meanwhile, Labour was too preoccupied with its own problems – its poor polling, its cash-for-peerages scandal, and of course the continuing question of the Blair–Brown succession – to make that much of what was clearly a climb-down. Given the fact that Europe is not an issue ever likely to win it many votes – unless of course the Conservatives are arguing furiously over it – this was entirely rational. The same went for the Liberal Democrats.

For the Conservatives, however, the EPP climb-down and the relatively mild controversy it created usefully obscured some rather interesting and perhaps significant steps along the road to a more pragmatic European policy.[14] No one should understate the extent of scepticism on the Conservative benches, front and back, and in the constituency associations the length and breadth of England, and in Scotland and Wales too. And some would argue that if the party can manage to maintain that stance while avoiding internal arguments, it may yet pay electoral dividends.[15] Nevertheless, there are signs that the Conservatives have not only made up their minds that 'less is more' on Europe, but also that they are beginning to adjust their own position in the light of Labour's tilt towards what Tony Blair, in rather a reflective speech in February, labelled 'practical scepticism', namely:

a genuine, intellectual and political concern about Europe as practised; not about Europe as an ideal or a vision or even a set of values. This is not about xenophobia, nor devotion to undiluted national sovereignty, but a worry about Europe's economy being uncompetitive, its institutions too remote, its decision-making being too influenced by the lowest common denominator.[16]

However, any move on the part of the Conservatives to accommodate Labour's increasing emphasis on what Blair called 'a Europe that is open, free, Atlanticist and ready, willing and able to compete' was not so much shouted from the rooftops as signalled by smoke – and sometimes a few mirrors as well. At the beginning of September, for instance, the American-owned supermarket chain, Asda, took it upon itself to call for UK withdrawal from the Common Fisheries Policy – something that the Conservatives have themselves hoped to negotiate.[17] Called onto the BBC's flagship *Today* programme, however, the party's representative, Scottish MEP Struan Stevenson, sounded extremely reluctant about such a course of action, confirming to many the rumours that the idea had been buried at sea somewhere in the preceding months. By the middle of the month, the party announced the overwhelming endorsement (at least among the quarter of party members who voted) of its new statement of aims and values, *Built to Last*.[18] However, sceptics would have had to look at the small print for any mention of Europe, and even then it was no more than an assurance that the party would be 'Opposing any proposed European Constitution that would create a single European superstate' – an assurance, note, that would leave the party more than enough room in the future to support a document whose aims, it could argue, stopped short of such a cunning plan.

In fact, even the man whose emphasis on Europe when he was Conservative leader had encouraged hardline sceptics to think that things were slowly but surely moving their way was beginning to sound less strident. No one hearing William Hague's thoughtful speech to the Open Europe think-tank in June would have labelled him a Europhile.[19] Yet his scepticism was measured, his calls for reassertion of national control limited to particular dossiers, and his criticisms of the EU's apparent desire to do too much were qualified by a recognition of the practical achievements and potential of the single market and an enlarged Union. True, he wanted no more talk of constitutions, and no attempt to slip some of the rejected treaty's provisions in through the back door. He also revived the idea of a multi-speed Europe. But he acknowledged the need for institutional change to cope with an EU of 27-plus members, called for a 'realistic assessment' not just of what the EU 'should stop doing' but also what it 'needs to do more of', and declared himself 'a firm believer that Britain's place is in the European Union, a strong player in Europe, not at the margins'. His criticism of the government – 'no sign of a strategic vision, let alone the effort to persuade others of its merits, nor of any bottom line and sticking to it. We mean to do better' – smacked strongly of valence rather than position politics, of differences over delivery, not an ideological divide.[20]

Europe and immigration: invasion?

If, on Europe, the Conservatives were continuing to turn down the volume and even quietly changing the channel, then the same could be said of immigration. Although the issue is seen (not altogether wrongly) as a potential vote-winner by some, 'Team Cameron' is widely thought to share the opinion – most cogently stated by wealthy supporter Lord Ashcroft – that concentrating on it ends up alienating the voters the Conservatives need, firstly, because it contributes to their image as 'the nasty party', out of touch with twenty-first-century Britain and, secondly, because it crowds out their arguments on more bread-and-butter issues. This decision to soften the focus, however, coincided with the country's right-wing newspapers striking gold once again with seemingly endless revelations concerning, firstly, dodgy-dealing, as well as plain old incompetence, in the UK's immigration regime and, secondly, the hundreds of thousands of migrant workers 'flooding' into the country from some of the EU's newest member states, thereby making a mockery of government estimates in the run-up to enlargement in 2004.

Such headlines placed the Labour government in an awkward position, as any coverage of migration tends to do. As a self-styled progressive centre-left party, its natural inclination was still towards tolerance, inclusivity and multiculturalism. And this tendency was reinforced in Labour's case by its commitment to a business-friendly, flexible and pan-European labour market that keeps employment high but inflation down – precisely the model it insisted on crowing about to other EU member states whenever it got the chance. On the other hand, the party's strategists, as well as some of its more outspoken and/or nervous MPs, were acutely aware of the evidence that voters – and not just those who are racially prejudiced or in direct competition for jobs, housing and services with the new arrivals – were rather less positive about the influx.[21] Despite the fact, then, that immigration from the new Europe was by and large a success – a view supported by the liberal media and by the EU's own widely reported research[22] – the government declared in late October that it would, as widely predicted, limit the right of Bulgarian and Romanian citizens to work in the UK when their countries joined the EU in January 2007. No less predictably, the scheme announced by the supposedly hardline Home Secretary, John Reid, was condemned both by advocates and, even more strongly, by opponents of migration.[23]

Thus far, the Conservatives have been as sanguine as Labour about enlargement, not least because they share the analysis that 'widening' makes 'deepening' more difficult. They are also aware of a good deal of support from businesses for a strategy, which, by expanding the market for labour as well as goods and services, should help to combat wage growth.[24] Yet the Conservatives could hardly ignore public anxiety about Poles and other Eastern European workers coming into the country. Given the fact that it was already apparent that the government and even the employers' organisation, the Confederation of British Industry (CBI), were beginning to consider a more restrictive stance on migration from Bulgaria and Romania, it was probably, therefore, smart politics for the Conservative immigration spokesman, well-known moderate Damian Green, to hammer home his call for just such a policy, making the now traditional argument that 'Controlled immigration also helps to promote much better cohesion between existing and new people in this country.'[25]

Turkey: still a cheerleader, but for how long?

Notwithstanding this switch toward a harder line on migrant labour from the EU's newest members, there were no signs that either Labour or the Conservatives have cooled on their support for the accession – albeit in a decade or so's time – of Turkey, where, in January, the former Foreign Secretary, Jack Straw, accepted the Bosphorus Award for European Understanding in recognition of his role in helping Ankara begin entry negotiations last year. This consensus is interesting: an influx of visibly different, mainly Muslim people from that country would likely provoke media hysteria in the UK; yet all the mainstream parties apparently contemplate it with equanimity. This is presumably because any concerns are trumped by foreign policy priorities: Turkey is a loyal member of the North Atlantic Treaty Organisation (NATO), a long-standing US ally and a potential bridge into 'the Islamic world'. Economic interests also play a part: over 400 British companies operate in Turkey, including BP, which is a major shareholder in its oil and gas pipelines; the UK is the second largest market for Turkish exports; and bilateral trade is worth over £5 billion per annum. Accordingly, the UK worked as hard as any other member state to avoid a 'train crash' (to use Enlargement Commissioner Olli Rehn's words) over Ankara's intransigence over the opening of its ports and airports to Cyprus: the government may not have been able to prevent the EU suspending discussions with Turkey on eight out of the 35 'chapters' that have to be signed off before accession, but it helped ensure that the other 27 remained open and that no specific deadline for the opening of ports was insisted upon.

For some time, this pro-Turkey policy has looked a reasonable bet in terms of domestic public opinion: polls in recent years suggested that the British (over 1.5 million of whom go to Turkey on holiday each year) were notably less worried about Turkish accession than many of their fellow EU citizens.[26] How long this will last, however, is surely a moot point. In June, the Austrian presidency, backed by France, made an attempt to bounce the European Council into declaring that the EU's 'absorption capacity' would henceforth be considered a criterion for future enlargements. It was forced into dropping the demand – as well as a demand that a reference to public opinion also be inserted – by a coalition co-led by the UK and without a word of protest from the Conservative Opposition. Should British public opinion turn negative in the coming years – and Eurobarometer results published in mid-December hinted that it was already doing so – it will be interesting to see whether this 'enlightened' consensus holds.[27]

Going behind our backs?

The same European Council meeting in Vienna did, however, see something of a U-turn by the British government. During its own term in the presidency last year, the UK had apparently called for the EU's decision-making processes to be thrown open to the cameras. Yet, when, after more work on the issue by Austria, a concrete proposal for doing exactly that was ready, it looked as if the new Foreign Secretary, Margaret Beckett, wanted to reject it, her argument being that broadcasting council meetings would merely drive the real discussion into the corridors rather than the committee rooms of power. When it became clear, however, that this would have seen the UK portrayed as an enemy of transparency, the Prime Minister agreed to opening things up. The first internet broadcast of proceedings – featuring a meeting of ECOFIN (Economics and Finance Council) – went ahead on 11 July, although the cameras were switched off as soon as the more sensitive matters on the agenda (notably the Stability and Growth Pact) were reached!

Otherwise, despite the best endeavours of Eurosceptic pressure groups and papers, there was little the government did during 2006 to worry anyone but the most suspicious observer of the relationship with Brussels. A case in point is the Tampere meeting of justice and home affairs ministers that took place towards the end of September. As the meeting approached, the devoutly Eurosceptical *Daily Mail* – possibly primed by background research done by campaigning think-tanks like Open Europe[28] – blew the gaff on an apparent attempt by the government to accede to federalist demands to allow qualified majority voting (QMV) on criminal justice matters.[29] In fact, the government – at that stage anyway[30] – had not come to a decision on a matter which, given concerns about international terrorism and organised crime, at least deserved consideration. Such moves, it could have argued, are consistent with plans for greater co-operation on security matters announced by EU ministers after a meeting in London in August.[31] As such, they could even garner public support, assuming the pooling of sovereignty could somehow be confined to those subjects rather than entailing (as the Commission wanted) a wholesale transfer of 'pillar three' matters into 'pillar one' (where QMV is the norm). In any case, such demands were turned down at Tampere even by supposedly Europhile governments like Germany and Italy. Predictably enough, of course, this apparently bathetic ending to the story, such as it was, barely made it into the media in the following day or so. No doubt, though, it had done its duty, serving in its own small way to reinforce – in drip-drip fashion – the overall message that Labour cannot wait to sell out on Europe while we are all looking the other way.

Conclusion

The Labour government did not give up trying to sell Europe to Britain in 2006. The new 'Britain in Europe' website of the Foreign and Commonwealth Office (FCO) contained an animated guide to the EU, while the Prime Minister enlisted the help of the comedian and actor, Eddie Izzard, who came up with a predictably offbeat podcast on the European Council.[32] But in his speech to an audience in Oxford in February, during which he reflected not just on the bruising experience of negotiating a budget deal the previous December but on decades of ambivalence and awkwardness, Tony Blair ruefully observed that

> The British problem with our membership of the EU may derive from the curious and tortured circumstances of its birth. But, long since, it has taken on a unique life of its own. The dilemma of a British Prime Minister is acute to the point of ridiculous. Basically you have a choice: co-operate in Europe and you betray Britain; be unreasonable in Europe, be praised back home, and be utterly without influence in Europe. It's sort of: isolation or treason.[33]

This dilemma is unlikely to disappear anytime soon. The BBC, stung by criticism of its European coverage by an independent report in 2005, may have upped its game on the issue, but a Damascene conversion among the editors of most of Britain's national newspapers is a long way off.[34] However, the Prime Minister, faced with that dilemma, will change, and so, too, might the willingness of his successor to risk the kind of headlines that Blair routinely put up with as a price for securing continental compromise. If that successor turns out to be Gordon Brown, many predict that the UK would have a leader less worried about alienating foreign opinion than alienating domestic opinion. According to the *Spectator*, when the budget deal negotiated by Blair at the end of 2005 comes up for review in two or three years' time, Labour insiders are forecasting a showdown with the French: Brown, they argue, 'has more appetite for a fight than Blair. Blair wants to be liked and have other leaders on the phone. Gordon would be much more comfortable being isolated in Brussels, lapping up the praise from the press back home.'[35] No one, then, should expect a post-Blair Labour government to be any more enthusiastic – at least on the outside – about Europe. Indeed, even before the handover of power, the media were reporting (in November) that the Foreign Secretary, Margaret Beckett, was seeking to assert control over her Europe Minister. Apparently, Geoff Hoon was more relaxed than more senior members of the government about suggestions that some of the streamlining of decision-making called for by the failed Constitutional Treaty could be pushed through in some sort of 'mini-treaty', thereby bypassing the need for a referendum.

Labour's ambivalence will not of course prevent it from trying to use Europe to undermine the Conservative Party and its leader. An early sign of this was a jointly authored press piece in June by two ministers arguing that 'David Cameron's hostility to Europe makes a mockery of his claimed green credentials' – an argument bolstered later on in the year when the Commission got admirably tough with member state governments, which (unlike good-boy Britain) attempted to introduce ridiculously generous carbon allowances into the second phase of the ETS, the EU's trading scheme.[36] Cameron might, however, prove more of a moving target than they hope: he ended the year seeming to play it both ways on Europe – and, interestingly, being allowed to do so by the media. Business-friendly broadsheet the *Financial Times*, reported Cameron had sought to 'shrug off his party's reputation for hostility towards Europe' and 'lavished praise' on the Commission when he visited it for talks in early December – a message so well spun by 'Team Cameron' that by the time it reached the notoriously sceptic *Sun*, the tabloid was happy to report that the Tory leader 'gave them a rocket' and 'slammed the EU's "culture of hopelessness"'.[37] But for all the subtle signs that the Conservatives may be tacking towards a more pragmatic (or Janus-faced) stance on the EU, their leader – who knows his move to the centre risks alienating key media players, core voters and many members – is unlikely to renounce the Euroscepticism that they regard as an article of faith, particularly when an end-of-year survey of the latter group suggested that nearly half of them thought the UK Independence Party (UKIP) was the other party closest to their views (and not just on Europe).[38] Whether, though, a stridently sceptical stance would prove as useful to him in government as it might in opposition is (as John Major could no doubt tell him) another matter entirely. Pause for reflection?

Notes

1. See Tim Bale, 'Britain and Europe: Less of the Poison?', in Michael Rush and Philip Giddings (eds), *The Palgrave Review of British Politics 2005* (Basingstoke: Palgrave Macmillan, 2006), pp. 213–27.
2. In December 2006, Eurobarometer (the EU's public opinion survey) noted that the proportion of people thinking membership of the EU was 'a good thing' was, at 34 per cent, the lowest in all the member states. Some 31 per cent of British respondents thought membership a bad thing, with 28 per cent seeing it as neither good nor bad, <http://ec.europa.eu/public_opinion/archives/eb/eb66/ eb66_highlights_en.pdf>.
3. See 'Mandelson's EU constitution call', 6 April 2006, at <http://news.bbc.co.uk/1/ hi/uk_politics/4882332.stm>.
4. Geoff Hoon is one of two ministers outside the Cabinet who attend its meetings, having previously been members, the others being Ian McCartney, former party chairman, now Minister of State in the DTI. The government Chief Whip in the Lords also attends Cabinet and the Attorney General does so when necessary. Hoon's predecessor as Minister for Europe also attended the Cabinet, although not then a member.
5. Geoff Hoon, 'How Patriotic is Economic Patriotism', speech to City of London, 9 May 2006, available at <www.britainusa.com/sections/articles_show_nt1.asp?a =41806&i=41066&L1=41012&L2=41066&d=-1>.
6. Geoff Hoon, 'Making the Case for Europe: A New Agenda', speech to the Centre for European Reform, 14 June 2006, <www.britischebotschaft.de/en/news/ items/060614a.htm>.
7. See Eurobarometer 65, July 2006, <http://ec.europa.eu/public_opinion/archives/ eb/eb65/eb65_en.htm>.

8. For a bracing Eurosceptic critique, see Neil O'Brien, 'How Europe Betrays the Poor', *Spectator*, 8 December 2005, <www.openeurope.org.uk/analysis/betrayingpoor. pdf>. For a careful consideration of the vexed question of who stands to benefit from a trade and agriculture deal, see Ken Ash and Stefan Tangermann, *Agricultural Policy and Trade Reform: Potential Effects at Global, National and Household Levels* (Paris: OECD, 2006).

9. 'European Middle East peace plan ignores UK', *Guardian*, 17 November 2006.

10. See Council of the European Union, *Services in the Internal Market*, 24 July 2006, <www.consilium.europa.eu/uedocs/cms_Data/docs/pressdata/en/misc/90635. pdf>.

11. *Guardian*, 3 June 2006.

12. Witness some of the comments on influential Conservative blog, ConservativeHome, <http://conservativehome.blogs.com/Conservativediary/2006/07/interview_with_ .html>.

13. See <http://conservativehome.blogs.com/Conservativediary/2006/09/conservative_ me.html>.

14. See Tim Bale, 'Between a Soft and a Hard Place? The Conservative Party, Valence Politics, and the Need for a New "Eurorealism"', *Parliamentary Affairs*, 59 (2006), 385–400.

15. See Jane Green, 'When Voters and Parties Agree: Valence Issues and Party Competition', *Political Studies*, forthcoming.

16. Tony Blair, 'Europe Emerging from "Darkened Room"', speech made in Oxford, 2 February 2006, <www.number-10.gov.uk/output/Page9003.asp>.

17. See 'Asda Joins Calls for Common Fisheries Policy to be Scrapped', 5 September 2006, <www.asda-press.co.uk/pressrelease/49>.

18. <www.conservatives.com/pdf/BuiltToLast-AimsandValues.pdf>.

19. William Hague, 'The Future of Europe: Freedom and Flexibility', speech to Open Europe, 7 June 2006, <www.conservatives.com/tile.do?def=news.sConservative. page&obj_id=130249&speeches=1>.

20. Ibid. On the distinction between valence and position politics, see Bale, 'Between a Soft and a Hard Place', and Green, 'When Voters and Parties Agree.'

21. Lauren M. McLaren and Mark Johnson, 'Resources, Group Conflict, and Symbols: Explaining Anti-Immigration Hostility in Britain', *Political Studies*, forthcoming.

22. See, for example, 'So far, migrant workers have been just the job', *Observer*, 27 August 2006, and <http://ec.europa.eu/employment_social/emplweb/news/ news_en.cfm?id=119>.

23. See <http://news.bbc.co.uk/1/hi/uk_politics/6076410.stm>. Most opponents had already made up their minds anyway: when the government first hinted at its plans to restrict entry, the *Daily Express* (27 September) ran the screamer 'Thousands of Romanians and Bulgarians get green light to invade Britain'.

24. Polls conducted by YouGov for the admittedly pro-European Business for a New Europe, February and March 2006, showed at least two-thirds support among business people for the single market, enlargement and EU membership in general. See <www.bnegroup.org/info/ugovfull2a.pdf>.

25. *Observer*, 20 August 2006.

26. The difference between the pro and con camps in the UK, even now, is not that great, however. See *Special Eurobarometer on Attitudes towards European Union Enlargement*, July 2006, available, online at <http://ec.europa.eu/public_opinion/ archives/ebs/ebs_255_en.pdf>, p. 71.

27. See <http://ec.europa.eu/public_opinion/archives/eb/eb66/eb66_highlights_ en.pdf>, pp. 29–31.
28. See Open Europe, 'New Poll: 72% Oppose Giving Up the Veto on Crime and Justice', 21 September 2006, available online at <www.openeurope.org.uk/ media%2Dcentre/pressrelease.aspx?pressreleaseid=24>.
29. See 'Labour ready to surrender more powers to Brussels', *Daily Mail*, 22 September 2006.
30. Later, in early December, Home Secretary John Reid called publicly for the scrapping of the supposed plan to end the veto. See <http://news.bbc.co.uk/1/hi/ uk_politics/6208042.stm>.
31. See 'Europe-wide security net to counter terrorism', *Guardian*, 17 August 2006.
32. See <www.fco.gov.uk/servlet/Front?pagename=OpenMarket/Xcelerate/ShowPage &c=Page&cid=1007029391674> and <www.pm.gov.uk/output/Page9684.asp>.
33. See note 16 above.
34. For the report, the research that went into it and the BBC's response, see <www. bbcgovernors.co.uk/docs/rev_eu_coverage.html>. In 2005, the BBC appointed its heavyweight political correspondent to a new position as Europe editor. See Mark Mardell, 'Why I'm Taking on Europe', *British Journalism Review*, 16 (2005), 31–35, also available online at <www.bjr.org.uk/data/2005/no3_mardell.htm>. Mardell's brief seems, sensibly enough, to provide context for EU stories, not least by improving coverage of the domestic politics of other member states. Anyone interested in high-level (but intelligible) analytical coverage of the EU on the BBC should also go to its website and search under 'The Record Europe', which brings up the weekly edition of a TV programme devoted to goings-on in Brussels presented by Shirin Wheeler. The 18 December edition, for instance, contained a fascinating discussion by MEPs about the REACH legislation on chemicals that was controversially watered down at the last minute as it was passed right at the end of the year.
35. Mark Leonard, *Spectator*, 26 August 2006, available online at <http://cer.org.uk/ articles/leonard_spectator_26aug06.html>.
36. *Guardian*, 22 June 2006. On the ETS, see <http://news.bbc.co.uk/1/hi/business/ 6194092.stm>.
37. *Financial Times* and the *Sun*, 8 December 2006.
38. See <http://conservativehome.blogs.com/torydiary/2006/12/tory_members_ ar.html>.

16
Politics and the Media: The Stormy Year Before the Calm?

Dominic Wring

During 2006, sections of the media continued to enjoy their role as a source of opposition to a now somewhat diminished government. Whereas the two main parliamentary opposition parties seemed preoccupied with re-establishing themselves under new leaders, journalists of various persuasions were involved in a series of critical investigations into ministerial affairs, both of a political and a personal nature. The compromising stories that emerged hardly enhanced the already much derided reputation of Tony Blair and showed how media reporting reflected and influenced events. His tense relationship with Gordon Brown was widely reflected in news coverage, as were David Cameron's attempts to rebrand the Conservative Party. Aside from the Liberal Democrats' difficulties, a variety of minor party figures won legal cases against the media, notably the UK's bestselling *News of the World* title, which endured an especially expensive year. These incidents highlighted the degree to which it is often those politicians belonging to smaller, less well-known parties who are willing to fight journalists in court to defend their reputations. More mainstream figures appear less willing or able to take the risk, despite their protestations about the treatment they receive from the media.

Labour

A year to forget

The government has faced an avalanche of criticism, much of it from journalists, since its re-election in May 2005. During 2006 several Cabinet members were subjected to attacks on their competence, including the minister responsible for media, Culture Secretary Tessa Jowell. The *Sunday Times* led an investigation into a 'gift' to Jowell's husband David Mills, estimated by

La Republica newspaper (although this figure varied in other reports) to be £350,000, from the then Italian Prime Minister, Silvio Berlusconi. The story over this particular relationship had featured in satirical magazine *Private Eye* some years ago but it was only now, after considerable national press speculation, that the couple separated and Mills was indicted by Rome's legal authorities. Jowell's Parliamentary Private Secretary (PPS), Huw Irranca-Davies, attacked journalists for their 'cynical spin' on the marriage breakdown as a career-saving move while others detected the influence of Alastair Campbell in helping the minister survive.

The Education Secretary, Ruth Kelly, found herself at the centre of a controversy over government monitoring of sex offenders teaching in schools. The *Sun* pointed out lax procedures surrounding the operation of the so-called List 99 of banned individuals when men convicted of sexual offences were offered work in schools. Kelly survived a torrent of media criticism, only to be moved in a subsequent reshuffle. Similarly, several journalists had been critical of Patricia Hewitt's performance as Health Secretary and, when she was prevented from finishing her speech to the Royal College of Nursing by hecklers, it was portrayed as a symbol of the wider malaise within the NHS.

Perhaps most embarrassing was the *Daily Mirror*'s revelation of John Prescott's affair with his diary secretary, Tracey Temple. The *Sunday Times* followed up with claims by a former party press officer that Prescott had tried to grope her. Temple then hired the services of PR consultant Max Clifford and sold her story to the *Mail on Sunday* for a reported £250,000. The subsequent publicity laid Prescott open to the charge that he, like Blair, was a 'lame duck' leader. The *Mail* later published photographs of the Deputy Prime Minister playing croquet on the lawn of his official Dorneywood residence, implying that he was indulging himself at public expense. The paper and its fellow Associated Press title, the *Evening Standard*, also investigated Prescott's involvement with a wealthy US financier hoping to purchase the Millennium Dome to turn it into a casino. If this was not enough, the Deputy Prime Minister was also singled out for special criticism by his former Cabinet colleague, David Blunkett, in memoirs that were abridged for the *Mail*, the *Guardian*, radio and television.[1] Furthermore, several candidates declared themselves candidates for Prescott's role as deputy leader of the party, in anticipation of his retirement.

In the main, Cabinet ministers who faced a torrid press proceeded with care in response to media criticism. Home Secretary Charles Clarke and his replacement, John Reid, took a different approach in the belief that what they were doing would best protect the public. Although their more draconian policies garnered sympathy from the right-wing press, they alienated liberal commentators such as the *Independent*'s Simon Carr and Henry Porter of the *Observer*. Clarke dismissed these critics as 'pernicious' for their opposition to ID cards and measures, although his own credibility was questioned when it was revealed that the Home Office did not know the whereabouts of 1,000 foreign ex-prisoners, many of whom were supposed to have been deported on release. The media rounded on him and, in the wake of poor local election results, he was sacked in the ensuing reshuffle.

On succeeding Clarke, John Reid maintained a similarly high profile, notably when he and Transport Minister Douglas Alexander appeared in a televised address to warn air travellers of a potential terrorist attack during the summer. Reid was so confrontational in various exchanges with journalists that even his brooding predecessor suggested he was overly 'media-led' in his approach. Prison reformer Juliet Lyon went further by denouncing the new Home Secretary for surrendering policy to the *Sun*, following his announcement of further 'crackdowns' on assorted offenders. Even one Chief Constable, Terry Grange, suggested that ministers were overly sensitive to the views of the *News of the World*. As Alastair Campbell's former deputy Lance Price put it: 'the influence of the Murdoch press on immigration and asylum policy would make a fascinating PhD thesis'.[2]

If Charles Clarke's sacking was predictable, less so was the removal of Jack Straw as Foreign Secretary. Straw had apparently alienated the Bush administration by suggesting that any plan to attack Iran would be 'inconceivable'. The American neo-conservative, Irwin Stelzer, in the *Spectator*, and the more traditional right-wing columnist, William Rees-Mogg, of *The Times*, agreed that the White House had orchestrated the Foreign Secretary's departure. Straw's successor, Margaret Beckett, was an experienced domestic minister, but Israel's invasion of Lebanon left her little time to settle into her new post, and this crisis, together with Iraq, precipitated considerable media criticism. Beckett had particularly fraught encounters with Radio 4 *Today* presenters James Naughtie and John Humphrys. Far from fading from view, Straw became Leader of the House of Commons and expressed the contentious view that the veil worn by some of his Muslim constituents was 'a visible statement of separation and of difference'. His comments in the *Lancashire Evening Telegraph* initiated an intense debate and the lurid *Express* headline, 'Veil should be banned say 98 per cent'.

Trouble at the top: the leadership

Tony Blair's announcement in October 2004 of his intention to retire after what he hoped would be a third victory in 2005 may have had some electoral benefit, but in the longer term it left him open to endless media speculation as to when he would depart and who would take his place. Chancellor Gordon Brown's prominent intervention to shore up Labour's 2005 campaign ensured that he remained the obvious successor. Inevitably, press coverage turned to the Blair–Brown relationship and every utterance by them or their associates was forensically analysed. As *The Times* columnist Peter Riddell's book, *The Unfulfilled Prime Minister*, suggested, Blair was a politician in a hurry to make an impact during his final years in office.[3] Yet it soon became clear how much his fate depended on the (in)actions of his party colleagues, the White House, the Conservatives and the media.

The representation of Blair as George Bush's 'poodle' was reinforced by opinion formers from the highly conservative *Mail* to the liberal *Independent*. This image was compounded when the President's 'Yo Blair' greeting of the Prime Minister and what they had assumed was a private conversation during a G8 meeting in July was broadcast. Journalists interpreted Bush as having dismissed Blair's offer to visit the Middle East as a broker for peace in favour of sending Secretary of State Condoleezza Rice. The Prime Minister's authority was further challenged in a *Mail* interview with General Sir Richard Dannatt, Chief of the General Staff, in which he questioned government commitment to troops in Afghanistan and Iraq. This was followed in December by the publication of photographs showing poor accommodation provided for troops in the UK and their families, a matter then taken up by Major-General Richard Shirreff, commander of the British forces in Iraq.

Closer to home, Blair was reliant on Conservative support to ensure the passage of a schools reform bill designed to weaken the role of local authorities. Endorsed by the *Sun*, the plans were denounced by ex-leader Neil Kinnock and former Education Secretary Estelle Morris in an energetic campaign by party pressure group Compass, criticising Blair for trying to 'appease Murdoch and the *Mail*'. A greater threat to his remaining Prime Minister came with the loans for peerages' scandal, a story initially driven by web-blogger Guido Fawkes. Electoral Commission returns indicated Labour's 2005 campaign had been reliant on money borrowed from wealthy supporters, some of whom were subsequently nominated for peerages. Party Treasurer Jack Dromey's surprise statement that he had no knowledge of the estimated £13.9 million involved raised further questions about the legality of these transactions. Various newspapers, among them the *Sunday Times* and the *Sunday Telegraph*, implicated Downing Street aides, as well as Blair's long-time fundraiser, Lord Levy. His subsequent arrest featured prominently on *BBC News 24*. The admission by Nick Bowes, Labour's former head of corporate fundraising, that Blair 'was up to his neck' in the loans affair was publicised by the Conservative web-blogger, Iain Dale. Labour enjoyed some relief when the media spotlight turned on the Conservatives' own long list of donors and the funding the Liberal Democrats had received from fraudster Michael Brown. But the focus soon returned to Labour: more people were questioned about Labour's loans, including former head teacher Des Smith, who had solicited financial backers for specialist schools. He bitterly resented his treatment by the police and denounced the Prime Minister in a *Mail on Sunday* interview, suggesting he should be interrogated. Blair duly became the first occupant of 10 Downing Street to be interviewed by detectives, although this occurred on what several journalists, using Jo Moore's notorious 9/11 phrase, called 'a good day to bury bad news', with the publication of Lord Stevens's report into the death of Princess Diana and Lord Goldsmith's extraordinary decision to curtail a Serious Fraud Office investigation into British arms deals with Saudi Arabia.

The 2006 local elections demonstrated the Blair-led Labour Party's vulnerability to defeat by the rejuvenated Conservatives and MP Lynne Jones, speaking on the BBC *Politics Show*, led calls for her leader to resign. The Prime Minister responded by launching a public dialogue entitled 'Let's Talk', which critics likened to the earlier 'Big Conversation', and dismissed it as offering the illusion of consultation.[4] Blair was arguably most vulnerable when, on returning from summer holiday, he gave an interview to *The Times* in which he refused to indicate a date for his departure. Within days there was intensive press speculation over the existence of a private letter drafted by formerly loyalist MPs Siôn Simon and Chris Bryant, urging their leader to retire. Publication of their names led signatories junior Defence Minister Tom Watson and seven PPSs to resign. Watson denied a recent visit to the constituency home of Gordon Brown was related to his support for the letter, but this did little to stem speculation that allies of the Chancellor had, in the reported words of one Cabinet member, been attempting to mount a 'coup'. The statement by the Environment Secretary, David Miliband, on Radio 4's *Today* programme that Blair would resign within a year was reinforced by the *Sun*'s categorical 'Blair will go on 31 May 2007'. The claim was overshadowed by the *Mirror*'s ridicule of a schedule devised by his aides for the Prime Minister's departure that included appearances on *Blue Peter* (he later did), *Songs of Praise* and Chris Evans's Radio 2 programme, before concluding that the public should be left 'wanting more' of their leader.[5]

The tension between Blair and Brown provided a story at least as old as the government, but the sense that the in-fighting between their supporters was reaching its dramatic climax encouraged further speculation, following criticism of the Chancellor's tax credit system by Stephen Byers and Alan Milburn. The latter, the *Sunday Mirror* suggested, was the Prime Minister's choice to succeed him. Brown's tax policy was also attacked by a former Downing Street economics adviser, Derek Scott, in *The Times* and ex-minister Gisela Stuart in a *Telegraph* piece that was sympathetically reported by the *Sun*. Byers returned to the fray during the summer, with a provocative *Sunday Telegraph* article denouncing inheritance tax as a blight on the aspirational middle class.

More extraordinary were the personalised criticisms by the former Home Secretary, Charles Clarke, who attacked Brown because of a photograph published at the height of the alleged 'coup' showing him 'grinning' while leaving Downing Street. Clarke intensified his attack by telling the *Telegraph* that the Chancellor was a 'control freak' with 'psychological issues'. Journalists duly leapt on the comment 'that's a lie' allegedly made by Cherie Blair in earshot of a reporter, when Brown talked about his affection for her husband during his Labour Party Conference speech. Similarly, a dubious BBC *Newsnight* focus group exercise, suggesting voters favoured John Reid as leader, received greater attention than it deserved, and certainly more than John McDonnell, the only declared leadership candidate.

Blair–Brown tensions were also evident when the former refused to answer press questions during their joint appearance to launch the party's local election campaign. The Chancellor's spin-doctors' briefings were subsequently revealed on ITV News by political editor Tom Bradby. Brown remained above the fray, at least in public, and concentrated on promoting what correspondents began to term 'Project Gordon'. This involved him discussing non-economic matters such as British identity, his musical tastes and family life. An appearance on Sky saw an emotional man talking about the death of his infant daughter Jennifer. Intriguingly, although the *Mail* responded critically to Brown over his budget, the staunchly Conservative title also labelled him a 'man of the future' and its editor, Paul Dacre, told the *Leeds Student* (which he once edited) that Brown was a 'remarkable politician'. *The Times* and the *Sun* were more ambiguous, signalling that they were waiting for proprietor Rupert Murdoch to endorse Brown or David Cameron.

Brand Cameron: the Conservatives

David Cameron's energetic publicity strategy was aimed at a variety of audiences his party had neglected in recent years. Here Cameron applied his own experience as former head of corporate communications for Carlton media and, for £276,000 a year, recruited consultant Steve Hilton to oversee the Conservatives' rebranding. Other recruits were Ali Gunn as public relations adviser, George Eustice as press officer, the agency Karmarama, and Chris Roycroft-Davis, an influential *Sun* executive, as speechwriter. Few policy proposals emerged, but plenty of photo-opportunities were set up to promote Cameron as a politician of vision. His first year as leader contrasted with those of his immediate predecessors and, like Margaret Thatcher three decades before, he seized the opportunity to remake the party in his own image. Cameron's media-conscious approach was reminiscent of William Hague's attempts to relaunch the party prior to 1999 but, by contrast, was accompanied by considerably better ratings against a now diminished Blair premiership. The Conservative message has been relayed in a series of carefully orchestrated public relations initiatives that, contrary to past leaders' experiences, have sought to set rather than merely respond to the media or government agenda while simultaneously promoting the relatively new, youthful Cameron to the public at large.

Cameron's interest in environmentalism was promoted through a trip to Svalbard in Norway, where he was photographed driving a dog sleigh in an attempt to draw attention to the melting polar ice cap. Critics questioned the value of the initiative, but it secured considerable coverage, much of which was free of the ridicule attached to Hague's early appearances as leader. As Nicholas Boles of the think-tank Policy Exchange put it: 'The picture is all that counts. It's complete gold dust. The idea that he'd have been better off spending the day trooping around a shopping centre is nonsense.'[6] The photo-opportunity anticipated an agenda promoted by the Stern Report later in the year confirming the precarious state of the environment and the need to remedy the situation. The leader further boasted his green concerns by biking to work, although his sincerity was queried by *Today* presenter John Humphrys, who challenged Cameron over his reliance on an accompanying car to ferry his baggage.

Cameron's rebranding strategy featured a new party logo in the form of a tree, progressive sounding newspaper adverts, a so-called 'A-list' of prospective candidates, and the document *Built to Last*, overwhelmingly endorsed in a membership ballot. It led Blair to respond with a charge routinely levelled against himself: 'The Tories have got themselves a slick PR strategy. But give them a real-life policy decision and they flunk it. They think "strategy" is all. It isn't ...'[7] Cameron's approach also involved disassociating himself from his predecessors' most contentious policies. Thus he repudiated the party's stance over apartheid South Africa and was photographed alongside Nelson Mandela. He also made a break with traditional Conservative law and order rhetoric by speaking about the importance of tackling the causes of youth crime in a speech that was derided by media critics as urging people to 'hug a hoodie'.

Consciously following on from Blair's lead, Cameron made appearances on less formal political programmes including *GMTV*; chose pop music as a guest on Radio 4's *Desert Island Discs*; gave an interview to the men's magazine, *GQ*; and appeared with mothers from the mumsnet web forum. During the buildup to the World Cup, the Conservative leader was a guest of *Sun* editor Rebekah Wade at David Beckham's celebrity charity dinner. More daringly he appeared on *Friday Night with Jonathan Ross*, hosted by an irreverent Labour supporter. Cameron avoided a potentially embarrassing question about his youthful devotion to Margaret Thatcher, that outraged the *Daily Mail* but which he dismissed in a calm, unflappable way. The launch of the WebCameron site also enabled the leader to communicate directly with voters with his first appearance featuring him talking in his kitchen while washing dishes.[8]

Where party criticism of Cameron was muted, it was more forceful in the press, given that dissidents on the right have, unlike their equivalents on the Labour left, ready access to many column inches. The *Mail*'s Melanie Philips and *Telegraph* commentator Simon Heffer have respectively denounced 'Blue Labour' and the 'overpaid teenagers' advising the 'stupid, shallow', 'PR spiv' leader. And, although the *Express* did endorse the Conservatives in the local elections, it urged readers to 'hold your nose' when voting. Cameron can, however, rely on sympathetic coverage from those like *Mail* and *Spectator* columnist Peter Oborne, a scourge of the Blair government. Furthermore, Will Lewis becoming *Daily Telegraph* editor may help renew the party's once close relationship with the paper, despite the likely protestations from contributors like Heffer. Cameron has already been cultivating the Barclay brothers, owners of the *Telegraph*, although the revelation that frontbencher Greg Clark has lauded *Guardian* commentator Polly Toynbee's writings on relative poverty may not help this particular cause. Nor will this endear the party to former ally Rupert Murdoch, whose admission that he has not been impressed by Cameron has been reflected in *Sun* stories about 'Dave the Dope', 'Cam a Cropper' and 'green with a little g'. The paper has not, however, ruled out supporting the Conservatives in the future.

After Kennedy: the Liberal Democrats

The Liberal Democrats' unusually high media profile at the beginning of 2006 was partly a consequence of the destabilising impact of David Cameron's victory. Charles Kennedy's ability to continue as leader subsequently dominated the media agenda. The willingness of his parliamentary colleagues to use journalists to raise doubts about Kennedy weakened his position, especially when Lembit Opik was the only frontbencher willing to defend him. When the Liberal Democrat MEP, Chris Davies, said his leader was a 'dead man walking', it marked the beginning of the end. Other prominent Liberal Democrats offered sympathy but expressed concern about Kennedy continuing after his candid admission of alcoholism.[9] There was speculation whether what had been a secret between senior party figures had come into the public domain via former Liberal Democrat press officer turned ITV political correspondent Daisy McAndrew, although her editor later denied this was the case.

Kennedy resigned, having contemplated seeking a mandate to continue from the party membership. However, he would have been aware this risked alienating his colleagues, given that BBC2's *Newsnight* claimed that only 13 of his 63 MPs wanted him to stay. The episode once again demonstrated how even the most internally democratic of the major parties could be influenced by an elite axis of journalists with determined political contacts. There was more drama during the nomination stage of the leadership race. Remarkably, an initial challenger for the post, Shadow Home Affairs spokesperson Mark Oaten, made his former leader's problems appear comparatively mundane after he withdrew from the contest through lack of parliamentary support. However, his higher profile led the *News of the World* to run a lurid front-page story detailing the MP's relationship with male prostitutes. In a *Sunday Times* account, for which he was allegedly paid £20,000, Oaten was frank about what he called his 'midlife crisis'. Meanwhile, his wife, Belinda, who stood by him, contributed a *Mail* article on her experiences, following revelations in the paper about Conservative MP Gregory Barker ending his marriage for a male lover.[10] Oaten eventually announced that he would be standing down at the next general election.

Sexuality dominated the coverage of another potential Liberal Democrat leader: Simon Hughes denied he was gay in an *Independent* interview but retracted when the *News of the World* reported his use of male chatlines. The paper made homophobic jokes about 'LimpDems' but other journalists questioned Hughes's credibility, given that he entered Parliament after a notoriously fractious 1982 by-election in which the orientation of his gay Labour opponent, Peter Tatchell, had been highlighted by the popular press and in a Liberal leaflet. However, it was a magnanimous Tatchell who calmed the debate, declaring that he supported his former rival's candidature because of his promotion of homosexual equality. A beneficiary of Hughes's discomfort was the low-profile Chris Huhne, the only other candidate to stand against the frontrunner and Liberal Democrat deputy leader, Sir Menzies Campbell. A former journalist, Huhne secured the *Independent on Sunday*'s endorsement and shared the platform in a special leadership hustings edition of BBC1's *Question Time*, but the resulting debate was uneventful and strengthened the position of the dull but safe Campbell, who had already gained most MPs' support. He duly won the membership ballot, having secured favourable coverage from the key opinion-forming *Guardian* and *Independent* newspapers.

Campbell subsequently struggled for media attention against the renewed Conservatives and the constant stream of speculation over the Blair succession. A *Telegraph* poll in June suggested that he had made little impact, and even the revelations over funding that plagued the major parties provided little opportunity when it was revealed the Liberal Democrats' wealthiest election donor, Michael Brown, who had given £2.4 million, had pleaded guilty to fraud charges during the summer. There was some media attention to the party's decision to propose raising environmental rather than income taxes, but this was overshadowed by the revival of Charles Kennedy's political career with a Channel 4 documentary on the decline of democratic participation, and *News of the World* speculation that he was contemplating an attempt to regain the leadership. The ephemeral nature of media attention to the Liberal Democrats was further highlighted by the coverage of frontbench MP Lembit Opik's relationship breakdown and his new partner, one of the sisters in a Romanian pop duo, the Cheeky Girls. Aside from the gossip, journalists claimed Opik had acted inappropriately by asking the relevant minister about the migration status of his consort.

The media and the courts

Legal proceedings ensured several politicians attracted media coverage during the year, the most senior being London Mayor Ken Livingstone, who won an appeal against being suspended from office following an altercation with *Evening Standard* reporter Oliver Finegold. Aside from Livingstone, it was mainly minor party leaders who found themselves embroiled in cases that involved them challenging journalists. Thus the trial of the British National Party chairman, Nick Griffin, following earlier revelations made in a BBC undercover investigation into his conduct ended in his acquittal amid more publicity than he would otherwise have attracted. At the other end of the political spectrum, there was also a victory for Tommy Sheridan, the former Scottish Socialist leader, who had left the party when several of his fellow MSPs had supported allegations in the *News of the World* detailing his extramarital affairs and visits to private clubs to pursue them. Following his triumph and the awarding of £200,000 damages, Sheridan denounced Britain's bestselling newspaper and News International as 'pedlars of falsehood', claiming they were part of a conspiracy to destroy him. The *News of the World* faced further embarrassment in court when one of its most experienced journalists, Clive Goodman, admitted to having hacked into the private telephone messages of, among others, aides to Prince William, and Simon Hughes, the Liberal Democrat leadership contender.

Respect MP George Galloway, arguably the highest-profile minor party leader, also scored a notable victory against the *News of the World* when he won the right to publicise the photograph of its elusive reporter, Mazher Mahmood, whom he had denounced as an 'agent provocateur'. Mahmood was better known as the 'fake sheikh' who tricked various celebrities into revealing compromising details about themselves. Consequently, when he approached the Respect leader in the guise of a potential donor to the party, Galloway dismissed him for making anti-Semitic comments in an attempt to compromise the MP. More importantly for Galloway, his success in a libel case against the *Daily Telegraph* over allegations that he had profited from his charitable work in the Middle East was upheld by the Court of Appeal. He was not, however, in court to celebrate because of his participation in Channel 4's celebrity version of *Big Brother*.

Galloway's stint on *Celebrity Big Brother* generated much media attention, but did little for his reputation. Channel 4's recruitment of a serving MP was denounced in news bulletins by the then government Chief Whip, Hilary Armstrong, who claimed he had abandoned his constituents. Galloway had thought the programme would enable him to promote his anti-war views, but he seemed unaware of its highly editorialised format which focused more on domestic rather than formal politics. Galloway did, however, become embroiled in a series of unseemly rows with housemates.

Media manoeuvring

Channel 4 provided ITV with a rare boost during a bad year, when it agreed a deal that ensured that the latter continued to produce its news programming. One ITV executive talked of the troubled channel needing a 'Clause IV moment', and the shock announcement that the BBC Chairman, Michael Grade, would be returning to the network as its chief executive may provide it. In contrast, the purchase by Sky of 17.9 per cent of ITV for £940 million, to become the largest shareholder, was attacked as a retrograde step that could weaken the beleaguered broadcaster. The intervention prevented others from acquiring the shares and led Sir Richard Branson, the leading backer of rival bidder NTL, to mount a passionate, overtly political attack: 'The government are scared stiff of Murdoch. Perhaps his empire should be looked at. If you add ITV to his papers and Sky, you may as well as let Murdoch decide who becomes PM.' Branson was perhaps mindful of former Downing Street spin-doctor Lance Price's earlier observation that 'Rupert Murdoch doesn't leave a paper trail that could ever prove his influence over policy, but the trail of politicians beating their way to him and his papers tells a different story ... like the 24th member of Cabinet ... his presence is always felt.'[11]

Sky's chief, James Murdoch (son of Rupert), made clear who he felt threatened media pluralism by attacking the 'broadcasting establishment' as 'authoritarian' and 'elitist', and saying that Lord Reith, the BBC's first Director General, had had 'a pretty firm view of the need to keep the lower classes in their place'. He spoke in the hope of changing policy, not least because, as Des Freedman suggests, governance of this arena is heavily influenced by a determined elite of relatively few actors.[12] A recent focus of this network has been Ofcom, which, under the new management of former Downing Street aide Ed Richards, has been given greater regulatory powers over broadcasters. The Corporation was faced with further changes courtesy of the government's White Paper, *A Public Service for All*,[13] which proposed replacing the Board of Governors with a new oversight Trust. The renewal of the BBC Charter was followed by Director General Mark Thompson's bid to increase the licence fee above the rate of inflation in order to fund various initiatives including the proposed relocation of major facilities from London to Manchester. Although seen as sympathetic to the BBC, Culture Secretary Tessa Jowell nevertheless criticised the considerable sums paid to leading presenters such as Jonathan Ross when his and other celebrities' salary details were leaked to the *Daily Mirror* and the *Sun*. As the year ended, it was reported that the Chancellor would, at best, offer a below-inflation increase in the licence fee.

Conclusion

2006 witnessed the resolution of much of the doubt as to who would guide each of the three main parties into the next general election. While Menzies Campbell became Liberal Democrat leader, David Cameron carefully consolidated his position, and Gordon Brown ended the year looking virtually unstoppable in his as yet undeclared bid to succeed Tony Blair as Prime Minister. The attendant discussions within each of the parties over their respective futures created quite distinctive, introspective debates between supposed colleagues rather than with their electoral opponents. This situation arguably gave journalists more influence to shape agendas, particularly where they related to intra- rather than inter-party disputes. Consequently, the various media-driven crises that confronted a succession of Cabinet ministers were often represented through the prism of how they related to the unresolved leadership question. But dissenters such as John Pilger castigated fellow journalists for becoming sidetracked from what he argued were the real, more substantive issues:

> the insidious censorship of 'current affairs', a loose masonry uniting politicians and famous journalists who define 'politics' as the machinations of Westminster, thereby fixing the limits of 'political debate'. No more striking example currently presents itself than the relentless media scrapping of the political twins, Blair and Gordon Brown, and their tedious acolytes, drowning out the cries of the people of Iraq, Gaza and Lebanon.[14]

Significantly, Pilger's essential point, that the mediation of contemporary politics was overwhelmingly dominated by evaluation of personality rather than policy, was shared by non-leftists such as the former Conservative minister George Walden when he lamented: 'who would have predicted that an Etonian of three years' parliamentary standing (whose experience of life had been predominantly as a PR executive for a TV company notorious for its low standards) would be elected leader of the Conservative party?'[15] However, Cameron, unlike his predecessors, was not so easily ridiculed nor ignored by journalists during the year. Rather it was the Liberal Democrats whose own largely self-inflicted leadership crisis at the beginning of 2006 generated much unwelcome publicity. Menzies Campbell has struggled to gain the kind of media attention the party enjoyed in the two previous Parliaments, when the Conservatives were distracted by their own problems. Ironically, the rise of David Cameron also boosts the Liberal Democrats' hopes of participating in a coalition government should the next election result in a hung Parliament. That possibility will inevitably foster journalistic interest in the leaders and will exercise the party spin-doctors. Furthermore, it remains to be seen whether and when the major opinion-forming media, the popular newspapers, will embrace any of the alternatives with much enthusiasm or sincerity. On the very last day of the year, Gordon Brown's acolytes let it be known that he 'is serious about doing something fundamental to change the culture of spin'.[16] That does not mean, however, that a Brown premiership would presage the end of this contentious practice.

Notes

1. David Blunkett, *The Blunkett Tapes: My Life in the Bear Pit* (London: Bloomsbury, 2006).
2. *Guardian*, 1 July 2006. It should also be noted that, following the murders of five prostitutes in Ipswich, a former special adviser at the Home Office complained that ministers had failed to protect the women by decriminalising prostitution because they feared a 'hostile media response' (*Observer*, 17 December 2006).
3. Peter Riddell, *The Unfulfilled Prime Minister: Tony Blair's Quest for a Legacy* (London: Methuen, 2006).

4. *Guardian*, 18 November 2006.
5. 2006 coincided with the 30th anniversary of another Labour Prime Minister's demise and was marked by two drama documentaries, BBC1's *The Plot Against Harold Wilson* and BBC4's *The Lavender List*, as well as ITV's more conventional offering, *Wilson*. The BBC also aired a wholly fictional series, *The Amazing Mrs Pritchard*, featuring a shop manager, with limited previous political experience, replacing Blair as Prime Minister sometime in the near future.
6. *Guardian*, 22 April 2006.
7. *Guardian*, 27 June 2006.
8. The site received an unexpected publicity boost when Labour MP Siôn Simon posted a spoof mocking Cameron's performance on the popular YouTube online video forum.
9. Greg Hurst, *Charles Kennedy: A Tragic Flaw* (London: Politico's, 2006).
10. The Barker story came and went, as did *News of the World* allegations about Boris Johnson's extramarital affair with a journalist. Perhaps a reflection of the changing Conservative Party, neither story resulted in a swift deselection and/or resignation.
11. *Guardian*, 1 July 2006.
12. Des Freedman, 'Dynamics of Power in Contemporary Media Policy-making', *Media, Culture and Society*, forthcoming.
13. Cm. 6763, March 2006.
14. *Guardian*, 15 September 2006.
15. *Guardian*, 22 September 2006.
16. *Sunday Telegraph*, 31 December 2006.

17
Waiting for Gordon?

Philip Giddings

> *Estragon:* Charming spot. Inspiring prospects. Let's go.
> *Vladimir:* We can't.
> *Estragon:* Why not?
> *Vladimir:* *We're waiting for Godot.*
> (Samuel Beckett: *Waiting for Godot*, 1955, Act 1)

At the end of 2006, the sense of waiting in Whitehall and Westminster is palpable. It is probably 'Waiting for Gordon', but there are still those who want to hedge their bets. Prime Minister Blair's political authority has been waning for months, because of both Iraq and the advanced, but undated, announcement of his retirement. With the outer limit of the desired 'smooth transition' known to be the next Labour Party Conference, the balance of power within the government is swinging ever more strongly away from Blair. This 'waiting' background has been the context of so much that happened in British politics in 2006. Notwithstanding the third successive Labour victory the previous year, with what was in historical terms a very comfortable majority, the sense has grown that this is an interim administration, marking time for the new incumbent in Number 10.

Deferred hope

'Waiting' has two perspectives: looking forward – the object of our waiting, the event we are expecting to happen; and looking back – the ground of our waiting, the reason for our expectation that the event will happen. 'Hope deferred maketh the heart sick' says the proverb. What ails many former and current supporters of the current government is the deferred hope – the delivery problem. When the Blair government was first elected in 1997 there were high hopes on education, health, crime, human rights, an ethical foreign policy, constitutional reform, economic growth and stability, and improved standards of conduct in public life. For many people, it seems, those hopes have either been disappointed or have yet to be fulfilled. This is not simply the perspective of Labour's political opponents who could be expected to take that line. It has been, and is, the view of many who voted Labour in 1997 but have not done so in subsequent elections or are no longer intending to do so. More seriously, it is also the view of many members of the Labour Party, including those who joined in the 1990s, who have 'had enough'.

There seem to be three strands to this climate of disappointment and disaffection. The first strand is frustration that, notwithstanding much passing of legislation and spending of money, public and private, the hoped-for improvements in public services, particularly the education and health services, have not occurred. The second is the character and political style of the government – the perennial Blairite/Brownite sniping in the media, and the sleazy media controversies highlighted by Dominic Wring in Chapter 16. The third is the Prime Minister's identification with the Iraq war, and the perception of Blair as 'Bush's poodle'.

None of those strands is unique to 2006. In response to each, Blair apologists can say, and have said, in effect. 'Please be patient – what you desire is coming: public appreciation of the real improvements in public services which this government's investment is producing; the blowing away of the negative media froth; pacification, democracy and stability in Iraq (and Afghanistan), with a Middle East peace settlement.' The government's problem is that fewer and fewer of its supporters, never mind its opponents, are convinced, presenting David Cameron and Menzies Campbell with a significant opportunity.

Policy frustration: constitutional reform

The judgements of voters, and even party members, are very broad-brush, often the product of impressions and images. The analyst and the commentator probe more deeply and usually reveal a more complex picture. That is certainly the case with the performance of this government: notwithstanding the reports of disappointment and disaffection, it has substantial achievements which have to be weighed in the balance of judgement as well. Indeed, in some areas it is the fact that expectations have been further fuelled by those achievements that has contributed to some of the perceptions of disappointment. Constitutional reform illustrates the point. Devolved assemblies established in Scotland and Wales and in prospect in Northern Ireland; a Human Rights Act and a Freedom of Information Act on the statute book and brought into operation; hereditary peers mostly excluded from the House of Lords; significant procedural changes in the Commons. It is a substantial catalogue of achievement.

But, as 2006 has demonstrated, those 'constitutional reform' achievements are being overshadowed by some of the problems coming in their wake.

The West Lothian question, and an apparent surge of nationalist support in Scotland, suggest that the devolution legislation may not be the complete answer in that country, and the Wales package has already been substantially amended. In Northern Ireland we are once again at one of those crux moments: will Sinn Fein complete the reversal of their long-held positions and accept *all* the political institutions of Northern Ireland, *including* the police force – or will the peace process once again stall or even collapse? Similarly, the Human Rights Act is proving a mixed blessing in the minds of politicians anxious to pursue the strong counter-terrorist and law-and-order agendas, causing embarrassing clashes between the executive and the judiciary and with Parliament, or at least the majority in the Commons, as well. Excluding most of the hereditary peers seems to have had the paradoxical effect for a Labour government of producing a more confident and assertive second chamber willing to challenge, and therefore delay, some of the government's key legislative proposals, at least in detail if not in principle. Completing the reforms seems no nearer, even after the deliberations of the Joint Committee on Conventions. Jack Straw's appointment as Leader of the House in May resulted in a further attempt to move the issue forward, but at the end of 2006 the reality was that reform of the Lords had begun, but had not been completed: the third Parliament with a safe Labour majority – 'charming spot'; manifesto commitment in 2005 to complete the reform so that it is a modern and effective revising chamber – 'inspiring prospects'; but still 'Waiting for Godot'?

A similar point could be made about modernisation of the Commons: yes, a Modernisation Committee has been established and produced several reports, but there is little evidence that the resulting changes have convinced even the majority of Labour's own backbenchers that the inspiring prospects of democratic renewal and a more accountable politics of the 1997 manifesto are being realised. In 2006, there were certainly some developments, particularly the change to public bill committees, following the Modernisation Committee's report on *The Legislative Process* (see Chapter 8), but it remains to be seen whether the changes introduced will improve the effectiveness of Parliament's contribution to the legislative process. Much will depend – as it always has – on the willingness of ministers and government business managers to respond constructively at committee stage. As it seems politically easier for ministers to engage with criticisms and suggested amendments to their proposed legislation at the *pre*-legislative stage, evidence sessions at committee stage may be little more than window-dressing. We must wait and see.

The key issue here is the willingness of ministers and government business managers to engage constructively with the backbenchers and the opposition parties. It is tempting for governments with secure majorities to fall back automatically on steamroller tactics, perhaps tossing the occasional bone to their own backbenchers as a reward for loyalty. Philip Cowley's work has shown that government backbenchers are becoming more willing to stand out against this approach, as the rebellions in 2005–06 have confirmed (see Chapter 8). Towards the end of the year the Modernisation Committee launched its inquiry into strengthening the role of the backbencher, which may provide more constructive ways of engagement. There are echoes here of the 1960s and the Crossman experiment with select committees which some saw as a means of finding interesting things for backbenchers to do, in contrast to the desire of others to rebalance the relationship between executive and legislature.[1] One suspects that while some MPs are grateful for even the small procedural advances that have been achieved, many Labour supporters inside and outside the Commons are still waiting for the more decisive change in that executive–legislature balance, which the inspiring prospects of 'democratic renewal and more accountable politics' were taken to apply. As they still wait at the end of 2006, they are likely to be asking. 'Will a Brown-led government make the change?'

Public service reform: 'still ploughing on'

Turning from Westminster to Whitehall, we come to expectations of public service reform. Here there are real tensions within the Labour movement over the Blair government's direction of travel. Many have become increasingly anxious that, far from reversing the 'enabling state' and approaches of the Thatcher–Major era, Blair and Brown have taken them further, particularly in regard to outsourcing the provision of services and cutting civil service numbers in response to the Gershon review. Those taking that view are not encouraged by the realisation that Gordon Brown has been in the vanguard of that approach and they cannot therefore expect a change of direction, if and when he does succeed Tony Blair as Prime Minister.

But there is another, and perhaps more general reason for the sense of disappointment with the Blair government's performance with the public services. Expectations were high that the return of a Labour government would bring major improvements to the quantity and the quality of provision, particularly in health, social services and education. Very substantial increases of public spending in those areas have been made, and seem likely to continue. But the stories of cuts, closures and poor quality have not gone away, and the year ended with Cabinet member and Labour Party chairman Hazel Blears herself joining a demonstration protesting about the closure of the maternity unit in a hospital in her Salford constituency. She was in good company: Chief Whip Jacqui Smith had similarly protested about a closure in Redditch and, earlier in the year, Home Secretary John Reid had campaigned against the closure of an A&E unit in his Monklands constituency.[2]

Clearly, the delivery problem, identified by the Prime Minister towards the end of the 1997 Parliament, remains unresolved. A plethora of initiatives, programmes and targets have come and gone, but even Labour ministers, not to mention the public, are unconvinced that the expected improvements have been achieved. As Andrew Gray and Bill Jenkins put it in Chapter 6, the delivery machine has been creaking under pressure: to the long-standing problems of the Child Support Agency have been added those of the Rural Payments Agency and the succession of spectacular failures by the Home Office and its agencies. Famously, even the Home Secretary himself declared publicly that his department was not fit for purpose. Delivery remains a serious problem.

In his summer series of lectures Blair had set out his vision of an enabling state – a notion associated with the Conservative Environment Secretary Nicholas Ridley in the late 1980s, which would empower the individual and involve 'public service risk takers and open up provision to the independent and voluntary sectors'. This, the Prime Minister argued, would meet the public's desire for services that were responsive, effective and of high quality. Setting aside the controversial question of what purpose public services *should* serve, the Prime Minister's speeches were effectively an admission that after ten years of New Labour, several volumes of legislation and many millions of pounds in public expenditure, responsiveness, effectiveness and quality were still lacking. As Andrew Hindmoor put it in Chapter 11, it is a case of 'ploughing on': in health, education, social services, and pensions, New Labour's full harvest is still awaited. Fulfilment of the Blair vision will be in the hands of his successor.

Style of government

In spite of their joint authorship and ownership of the New Labour project, there has been continued conflict between Blair and Brown at the heart of the government. This is more than the impatience of Brown and his entourage to get their hands on the levers of power. The repeated reports of feuding and sleaze at the highest level have contributed significantly to the growth of disaffection among Labour members and voters.

The difficult relationship between Blair and Brown has been an ongoing motif since the beginning of the life of this government, and it was on show again when Blair declined to answer questions at the somewhat counter-productive press conference in the run-up to the local elections. Cherie Blair's 'that's a lie' stage whisper at the party conference kept the pot boiling. But potentially the most dramatic turn came in early September, when a junior minister and seven Parliamentary Private Secretaries resigned in what looked like an attempted anti-Blair coup. By then, Blair had already been forced to be more specific about the date of his resignation, but talk of a 'smooth transition' remained unconvincing.

The image of disarray at the top of the government was reinforced by the continuing saga of 'misfortunes' of the Deputy Prime Minister, who was stripped of his department in the May reshuffle. That he insisted on keeping the use of the grace-and-favour country residence Dorneywood and was then forced to give it up 'to save his flagging political career' added to the damage. As Dominic Wring has shown in Chapter 16, the media misfortunes of Tessa Jowell and Ruth Kelly and, above all, the phenomenon of the 'cash for peerages' affair extending ever nearer to the Prime Minister himself further reduced the diminished reputation of the whole government. The contrast with Blair's 'whiter than whiter' declaration soon after taking office in 1997 is stark. The echoes of the final periods of the Macmillan, Wilson and Major administrations resound down the years.

Opposition opportunity

Disappointment and disaffection with a government should be a golden opportunity for the opposition parties. The election of David Cameron as Conservative Party leader raised expectations that that party would at last present a credible, electable alternative to Labour. Cameron's personality and style, and his commitment to 'rebranding' his party suggested that, under his leadership, the Conservatives might at last break through. Although they performed well in the local government elections, and in several months were ahead of Labour in the opinion polls, as Michael Cole and Tim Jones showed in Chapter 3, 2006 produced only a modest Conservative resurgence. The party's improved polling performance was more a function of declining support for Labour than a positive surge for the Conservatives. It is, of course, early days: after its third successive defeat in 1959, Labour continued to lose ground in 1960 before the recovery began which brought it to office (with a modernising agenda) with a tiny majority in 1964 and a substantial one in 1966. Cameron has to encourage his supporters to be patient as he seeks to lay the ground for victory at the next general election. His current strategy of focusing upon values and principles but shying away from detailed policy commitments may be prudent, but the pressure for more specifics, particularly as the philosophical divide between the parties narrows, is bound to grow. He too has to wait to see if it really will be Gordon Brown who succeeds Blair, and then he has to stake out in more detail a distinctive programme for a Conservative government. The Conservatives are in a better spot than they were, but it is hardly 'charming'; the prospect of power is certainly 'inspiring'; but before they can go, they must wait for Gordon – and for a fuller programme from David Cameron.

With Labour losing ground and the Conservative recovery still awaited, the situation should be ideal for the Liberal Democrats. However, the leadership trauma, which saw Menzies Campbell substituted for Charles Kennedy, has not resulted in a strengthening of their position, and in Scotland and Wales it seems to be the nationalists who are gaining most from disillusion with Labour. So it remains the case that none of the three main British political parties is strongly connecting with the electorate, and especially not with young voters. The challenge to make connections remains a formidable one, which may well prove a serious problem when the Phillips Report on party funding appears in the wake of the 'cash for peerages' affair. As Andrew Russell suggested in Chapter 4, the party system may be edging towards bankruptcy in more senses than one.

Disengagement from the established political parties does not mean that the public in general, or younger people in particular, are therefore disengaged from politics itself. This is evident from the growth in interest group activity, particularly cause groups. The Countryside Alliance, Make Poverty History, Fathers 4 Justice, a whole host of 'green' groups at local level, animal rights groups, the various groups campaigning about the Iraq war, all show the vibrancy of the desire to participate and influence public policy and service delivery at international, national, regional and local levels. The use of the media and the internet demonstrate that these groups have not been slow to adapt to and exploit the information age, with its great potential for empowering the mass population. Much as the government might desire to systematise (and control?) the processes of consultation and policy formulation, there was plenty of evidence in 2006 that groups were willing to take advantage of those processes but not to be overly constrained by them. The phenomenon of business leaders joining a protest march (see Chapter 5) in support of their cause well illustrates the point – and their failure reminds us that government still holds most of the cards in the end.

The experience of war

The 'NatWest Three' affair and protests about the Iraq war underline the growing internationalisation of politics and government. There is no doubt that Tony Blair's power and reputation within the United Kingdom have been deeply affected by his commitment to the American-led invasions of Afghanistan and Iraq in pursuit of George Bush's 'war on terror'. But these international developments affect more than the power and reputation of individual leaders, important as those are. They can also have a major impact upon policy and administration. Students of post-war British politics will be well aware of the significance of international economic and political events for the well-being of the British economy, particularly when sterling was a reserve currency. Students of previous Labour governments will know of the significance for Attlee of the Cold War and Korea, and for Wilson of Vietnam. The latter in particular contributed significantly to the disaffection of many ordinary Labour Party members from its leadership. And, in the year of the fiftieth anniversary of Anthony Eden's disastrous Suez expedition, we need no reminder that the ramifications of international affairs, especially of wars, are not respecters of parties.

Nevertheless, for the Blair government the experience of war has been especially damaging: not only is the Iraq war widely judged to have been immoral if not illegal, it is also increasingly seen by many to have failed in its purpose. Its critics argue that peace and stability have been brought neither to Iraq nor to the Middle East. On the contrary, they say, it appears that the condition of the Iraqi people is no better, and in many cases actually worse, than it was under Saddam Hussein. The 'war on terror', far from being contained or eradicated, has actually spread, poisoning community relations in many states and local communities across the world. The critics' case does not go unanswered, but apologists for the war have a difficult case to make while television screens across the world are showing pictures of what looks very much like civil war in Iraq and increased Taliban activity in Afghanistan. President Bush has suffered the consequences in the mid-term congressional elections. Blair will, we assume, leave office before the next British general election, but there is no doubt that confidence in his government and in his leadership has been seriously dented. As Christopher White has shown in Chapter 14, 2006 was not a good year for the United Kingdom's government in the field of foreign affairs.

The fortunes and misfortunes of war should remind us that political prophecy is exceedingly risky. In his memoirs, the former Conservative Chancellor, Norman Lamont, headed the chapter about the long-delayed recovery from recession in the earlier 1990s with a quotation from Dostoyevsky which is a warning to all politicians and political analysts: 'Of all human follies prophecy is the most gratuitous.'[3] Who, at the end of 1981, would have predicted an Argentinian invasion of the Falkland Islands, a British taskforce succeeding in retaking them, and the consequent transformation of Margaret Thatcher's political fortunes? At the end of 2006, many are 'Waiting for Gordon', and he is without doubt the clear favourite to succeed Tony Blair. Although even the hottest favourite has been known to lose, most of the significant players in national politics are preparing for a Brown government. They are also aware that 2007 brings the Comprehensive Spending Review, in which he has played the key role, and which will decisively shape medium-term policy-making for this government – whether or not he becomes Prime Minister.

Waiting or shaping?

As even that is not at this point certain, we can be sure that 2007 will bring unpredictable events at home and abroad which will shape the political year. The outcome of the Scottish parliamentary elections could have a decisive effect on the future of the United Kingdom as a political entity, as could German Chancellor Merkel's endeavour to revive the proposed constitution for the European Union. Sinn Fein's agreement to recognise and co-operate with the Police Service of Northern Ireland could finally launch fully devolved, power-sharing government in Northern Ireland – or its refusal to do so could bring the Belfast Agreement peace process to an end. Much effort will need to be expended upon reviving the trade negotiations after the collapse of the WTO Doha Round, and similar effort will be needed if anything of substance is to be put in place of the Kyoto protocols. It is more than a truism to say that we live in a global world. And in a global world it is often necessary to wait upon events, while at the same time seeking to shape them. That is the art of diplomacy. It is a first requirement for national politics also. 'Waiting for Gordon' could be a recipe for caution and immobilism. It is also an opportunity to shape the game.

Notes

1. See Victor Wiseman, 'The New Specialised Committees', in A. Hanson and B. Crick (eds), *The Commons in Transition* (London: Fontana, 1970); R. Butt, *The Power of Parliament* (London: Constable, 1969), pp. 363–83.
2. The *Guardian* reported on 13 January 2007 that 11 government ministers had been involved in campaigns against closure of services at NHS hospitals.
3. Norman Lamont, *In Office* (New York: Little Brown, 1999), p. 137: when describing his preparation for the 1992 budget, he referred to the expectations of recovery as 'a case of waiting for the dawn that never came' (p. 160).

Statistical Appendix

Ross Young

A. Parties and elections

Note: The Statistical Appendix in the 2005 edition of the Review included data on general election results since 1945, European Parliament, Scottish Parliament, National Assembly for Wales, Northern Ireland Assembly, London mayoral, and Greater London Assembly election results. These have been omitted from the current appendix, but will be included in future editions, as appropriate.

Table A.1 Local elections

	Con. %	Lab. %	Lib. Dem. %	Green %	SNP/PC %	Ind. %	Other %
Year							
2001[a]							
Votes	39.4	30.9	25.1	1.0	n.a.	2.8	0.8
Seats	44.0	33.6	18.5	0.1	n.a.	3.0	0.7
2002[a]							
Votes	32.2	35.2	23.7	2.7	n.a.	3.0	3.2
Seats	34.0	40.6	21.4	0.2	n.a.	2.2	1.6
2003[b]							
Votes	31.5	27.9	24.2	1.6	3.8	7.4	3.6
Seats	37.9	25.7	22.8	0.3	1.6	9.8	2.0
2004[c]							
Votes	29.6	28.7	23.9	3.0	1.9	6.3	6.5
Seats	28.2	37.0	21.1	0.4	2.9	7.9	2.6
2005[a]							
Votes	39.8	25.0	27.6	2.3	n.a.	2.9	2.3
Seats	49.9	25.6	20.7	0.4	n.a.	2.3	1.1
2006[a]							
Votes	34.6	28.0	23.5	4.6	–	2.4	6.9
Seats	41.2	28.0	20.7	0.7	–	1.5	3.3

Note: Although local elections normally take place in May, not all take place simultaneously in the constituent parts of the UK or in all authorities.

[a] England.

[b] England and Scotland.

[c] England and Wales.

Sources: 2000: C. Rallings and M. Thrasher, 'Elections and Public Opinion', *Parliamentary Affairs*, 54 (2001), p. 328; 2001: Rallings and Thrasher, 'Elections and Public Opinion', *Parliamentary Affairs*, 55 (2002), p. 355; 2002: Rallings and Thrasher, 'Elections and Public Opinion', *Parliamentary Affairs*, 56 (2003), p. 273; 2003: Rallings and Thrasher, 'Elections and Public Opinion', *Parliamentary Affairs*, 57 (2004), p. 390; 2004: M. Lambe, C. Rallings and M. Thrasher, 'Elections and Public Opinion', *Parliamentary Affairs*, 58 (2005), p. 342; 2005: M. Cole, T. Jones, C. Rallings and M. Thrasher, 'Elections and Public Opinion', *Palgrave Review of British Politics 2005* (Basingstoke: Palgrave Macmillan, 2006), Table 3.6; M. Cole and T. Jones, 'Elections and Public opinion', *Palgrave Review of British Politics 2005*, Table 3.5.

Table A.2 Estimated national equivalent vote at local elections, 1997–2006 (%)

Year	Con.	Lab.	Lib. Dem.
1997	31	44	17
1998	33	37	25
1999	34	36	25
2000	38	30	26
2001	32	41	18
2002	34	33	25
2003	35	30	27
2004	37	26	27
2005	33	36	23
2006	39	26	25

Source: House of Commons Library, *Research Paper 05/93: Local and Mayoral Elections, 2005* (2005), Table C. C. Rallings and M. Thrasher, *Local Elections Handbook* (Local Government Chronicle Elections Centre, 2006).

B. Government and administration

Table B.1 Composition of the government

Year	1992		1997		2001		2006	
Prime Minister	Major		Blair		Blair		Blair	
Party	Con.		Lab.		Lab.		Lab.	
Rank	No.	%	No.	%	No.	%	No.	%
Cabinet	22	20	22	20	23	20	23	19
Law Officers	4	4	4	4	3	3	2	2
Ministers of State	30	28	30	27	30	26	30	25
Junior ministers	32	29	33	29	35	31	41	35
Whips	21	19	22	20	23	20	23	19
Totals	109	100	112	100	114	100	119	100
MPs	85	78	88	79	91	80	97	82
Peers	22	20	22	20	23	20	22	18
Non-parliamentary	2	2	2	2	0	0	0	0

Source: Cabinet Office.

Table B.2 Cabinet committees

	Major 1994	Blair 2000	Blair 2006
Committees			
Ministerial committees	4	14	32
Ministerial sub-committees	16	12	17
Other committees	2	5	5
Ministerial groups	3	0	0
Total Membership	25	31	54
Mean size	11	12	13
Range	4–20	5–22	4–23[a]
Chairs			
Prime Minister	7	6	20
Deputy Prime Minister	1	4	9
Departmental ministers	12	7	18
Non-departmental ministers	6	14	7

[a] Excluding the Civil Contingencies Committee, of which only the Home Secretary is a full member.

Source: Cabinet Office.

Table B.3   Number of civil servants, 1975–2005[a]

| | Permanent staff | | | Casual staff | Total FTE[b] |
	Non-industrial	Industrial	Total		
1975	526,050	178,480	704,530	16,540	721,070
1976	570,510	180,390	750,900	11,100	762,000
1977	573,220	175,650	748,870	7,120	755,980
1978	569,240	169,570	738,800	6,320	745,130
1979	567,770	167,660	735,430	7,560	742,990
1980	549,410	158,520	707,930	6,000	713,930
1981	541,790	150,940	692,730	6,160	698,880
1982	529,790	139,190	668,980	6,920	675,900
1983	520,220	131,010	651,230	9,090	660,320
1984	505,940	120,250	626,190	7,450	633,640
1985	499,790	101,520	601,320	10,670	611,990
1986	500,430	95,950	596,370	10,790	607,160
1987	510,090	90,730	600,820	11,850	612,670
1988	509,530	73,390	582,920	10,310	593,230
1989	503,190	69,710	572,900	11,100	584,000
1990	499,100	67,480	566,580	13,120	579,700
1991	494,660	64,150	558,810	13,610	572,420
1992	509,450	61,390	570,840	16,860	587,700
1993	508,760	51,680	560,440	18,260	578,700
1994	494,140	46,150	540,290	21,110	561,410
1995	474,880	42,020	516,890	18,240	535,140
1996	458,660	35,920	494,570	20,010	514,580
1997	439,630	36,030	475,660	19,610	494,660
1998	430,460	32,800	463,270	17,670	480,930
1999	428,850	30,750	459,600	16,770	476,370
2000	445,980	29,440	475,420	11,300	486,720
2001	453,770	28,930	482,690	12,260	494,950
2002	462,940	27,280	490,220	12,550	502,780
2003	490,190	21,110	511,300	9,630	520,930
2004	503,550	20,030	523,580	10,820	534,400
2005	498,200	20,230	518,430	7,890	526,320

[a] Figures rounded to the nearest ten.
[b] Full-time equivalent.

Source: Cabinet Office, *Civil Service Statistics, 2005*.

Table B.4   Civil servants by function, 2000 and 2005

	Percentage of FTE staff	
	2000	2005
Work and Pensions[a]	27	23
Revenue	19	14
Law and Order	17	14
Defence	20	18
Health	1	1
Other	16	30

[a] Social Security and Employment (2000).

Source: Cabinet Office, *Civil Service Statistics, 2005*.

Table B.5   Civil servants by department and agency, 2005[a]

Dept./agency/org.	Departmental	Executive agencies[b]	Other[b]	Total
Cabinet Office	1,770	290 (1)	–	2,060
Central Office of Information	–	550 (1)	–	550
Security & Intelligence Services	4,720	–	–	4,720
Dept. for Media, Culture & Sport	520	100 (1)	–	620
Ministry of Defence[c]	46,980	41,730 (23)	2,350 (1)	91,060
Office of the Deputy Prime Minister	3,340	960 (3)	–	4,300
Ordnance Survey	–	1,470 (1)	–	1,470
Dept. for Education & Skills	4,550	–	2,320 (1)	6,870
Dept. for Environment, Food & Rural Affairs	5,680	3,860 (6)	–	9,540
Office of Water Services (Ofwat)	–	–	240 (1)	240
Rural Payments Agency	–	2,810 (1)	–	2,810
Foreign & Commonwealth Office	5,870	60 (1)	–	5,930
Dept. of Health	2,300	1,160 (3)	–	3,460
Food Standards Agency	–	700 (1)	–	700
Meat Hygiene Service	–	1,460 (1)	–	1,460
Home Office	21,480	5,600 (3)	–	27,080
Assets Recovery Agency	–	–	110 (1)	110
Charity Commission	–	–	530 (1)	530
HM Prison Service	–	45,960 (1)	–	45,960
Dept. for International Development	1,880	–	–	1,880
Law Officers	40	8,750 (3)[d]	–	8,790
Dept. for Constitutional Affairs	2,010	10,610 (4)	–	12,620
HM Land Registry	–	7,820 (1)	–	7,820
National Archives	–	520 (1)	–	520
Dept. of Trade & Industry	4,410	4,740 (6)	–	9,150
Advisory, Conciliation & Arbitration Service (ACAS)	–	–	890 (1)	890
Export Credit Guarantee Dept.	–	–	310 (1)	310
Office of Fair Trading	–	–	630 (1)	630

Table B.5   continued

Dept./agency/org.	Departmental	Executive agencies[b]	Other[b]	Total
Office of Gas & Electricity Markets (OFgem)	–	–	260 (1)	260
Postal Services Commission (POSTCOMM)	–	–	40 (1)	40
Dept. for Transport	1,940	14,690 (6)	–	16,630
Treasury	1,060	–	–	1,060
Debt Management Office	–	80 (1)	–	80
Office of Govt. Commerce	–	260 (1)	380 (1)	640
HM Customs & Excise	–	23,420 (1)[d]	–	22,590
Govt. Actuary's Dept.	–	–	100 (1)	100
Inland Revenue	–	78,660 (1)[d]	–	78,660
National Savings & Investment	–	12 (1)	–	12
Office for National Statistics	–	3,720 (1)	–	3,720
Royal Mint	–	730 (1)	–	730
Dept. for Work & Pensions	12,950	104,150 (5)	–	117,100
Health & Safety Executive	–	–	3,790 (1)	3,790
Northern Ireland Office	160	–	–	160
Privy Council Office	50	–	–	50
Scottish Executive	4,460	7,880 (15)	–	12,340
Crown Office & Procurator Fiscal	–	–	1,390 (1)	1,390
General Register Office for Scotland	–	–	220 (1)	220
National Archive for Scotland	–	160 (1)	–	160
Registers of Scotland	–	1,380 (1)	–	1,380
Scotland Office	80	–	–	80
National Assembly for Wales	3,630	450 (2)	–	4,080
Estyn (Office of Ch. Inspector of Schools in Wales)	–	–	90 (1)	90
Totals	129,880	374,960 (100)	13,540 (15)	518,380

[a] Figures rounded to the nearest ten.
[b] Figures in parentheses indicate no. of agencies.
[c] Excluding service personnel.
[d] Operating on 'Next Steps' lines (i.e. as executive agencies).

Source: Cabinet Office, *Civil Service Statistics, 2005*.

Table B.6   Number of permanent civil servants by location, 2005

Location	FTE
London	89,550
South East	57,630
Total London and South East	147,180
East	30,600
East Midlands	22,878
North East	34,460
North West	59,720
South West	52,360
West Midlands	34,550
Yorkshire and the Humber	38,670
Total England	420,410
Scotland	48,130
Wales	32,680
Northern Ireland	6,250
Unreported and elsewhere	10,960
Grand total	518,430

Source: Cabinet Office, *Civil Service Statistics, 2005*.

Table B.7   Number of permanent civil servants by level of responsibility and gender, 2005[a]

	Male	Female	Total
Non-industrial staff	234,590	198,990	433,580
Senior civil service (SCS)	3,270	1,110	4,380
Grades 6/7	18,030	8,020	26,050
SEO/HEO[b]	53,690	31,770	85,460
EO[c]	58,980	52,900	111,880
AO/AA[d]	90,430	102,940	193,370
Unknown	10,200	2,250	12,450
Industrial staff	16,900	2,250	19,750
Total	251,490	201,840	453,330

[a]   Figures rounded to nearest ten.
[b]   Senior officer/higher executive officer.
[c]   Executive Officer.
[d]   Administrative officer/administrative assistant.

Source: Cabinet Office, *Civil Service Statistics, 2005*.

Table B.8 Number of permanent civil servants by level of responsibility, ethnicity, and disability, 2005[a]

	White	Asian	Black	Chinese	Mixed	Other	Non-response	Total	% ethnic minority[b]	Disabled	% disabled
Non-industrial staff	371,140	15,750	10,370	840	3,770	2,780	124,810	529,460	8.3	23,730	4.5
Senior Civil Service (SCS)	3,480	60	20	10	30	20	1,030	4,640	2.5	110	2.3
Grades 6/7	20,460	490	240	40	210	150	6,940	28,540	5.3	870	3.1
SEO/HEO	68,370	1,880	1,350	140	650	490	21,240	94,110	6.2	3,730	4.0
EO	97,820	4,510	3,270	220	980	760	29,330	136,880	9.0	6,610	4.8
AO/AA	171,730	8,740	5,450	420	1,870	1,330	62,850	252,390	9.4	12,050	4.8
Unknown	9,270	80	50	10	30	50	3,420	12,290	2.3	370	2.9
Industrial staff	12,940	60	100	10	70	80	7,280	20,550	2.4	850	4.1
Total	384,080	15,810	10,480	850	3,840	2,860	132,090	550,010	8.1	24,580	4.5

[a] Figures rounded to nearest ten.
[b] As a proportion of known ethnic origin.

Source: Cabinet Office, Civil Service Statistics, 2005.

C. Legislation

Table C.1   Public general acts and statutory instruments since 1975[a]

Year	Non-consolidation Acts	Consolidation Acts	Total	Statutory instruments
1975	67	16	83	2,251
1976	75	11	86	2,248
1977	48	5	53	2,202
1978	50	9	59	1,977
1979	44	16	60	1,770
1980	55	13	68	2,051
1981	60	12	72	1,892
1982	50	7	57	1,900
1983	52	8	60	1,965
1984	51	11	62	2,072
1985	65	11	76	2,080
1986	64	4	68	2,344
1987	56	1	57	2,278
1988	49	6	55	2,311
1989	43	3	46	2,503
1990	42	4	46	2,667
1991	63	6	69	2,953
1992	51	10	61	3,359
1993	43	9	52	3,276
1994	38	3	41	3,334
1995	48	6	54	3,345
1996	57	6	63	3,291
1997	62	7	69	3,114
1998	47	2	49	3,319
1999	35	–	35	3,488
2000	45	–	45	3,424
2001	25	–	25	4,147
2002	43	1	44	3,271
2003	44	1[b]	45	3,354
2004	38	–	38	3,452
2005	24	–	24	3,599

[a] Excluding Northern Ireland Acts and statutory rules.
[b] Including one Act under the Tax Law rewrite provisions.

Sources: House of Commons Library and Office of Public Sector Information.

Table C.2 Public bills since 1997–98

(a) Introduced in the Commons or introduced in the Lords and sent to the Commons

Session	Government bills			Private Members' Bills		
	Commons	Lords	Total	Commons	Lords	Total
1997–98	35	18	53	135	14	149
1998–99	22	9	31	93	11	104
1999–2000	28	12	40	97	7	104
2000–01	19	7	26	61	2	63
2001–02	26	13	39	118	5	123
2002–03	26	10	36	93	9	102
2003–04	25	11	36	89	0	89
2004–05	25	7	32	69	2	71
2005–06	42	16	58	112	9	121

Source: House of Commons, *Sessional Returns*.

(b) Received royal assent

Session	Government bills			Private Members' Bills		
	Commons	Lords	Total	Commons	Lords	Total
1997–98	34	18	52	8	2	10
1998–99	18	9	27	7	1	8
1999–2000	27	12	39	5	1	6
2000–01	14	7	21	0	0	0
2001–02	26	13	39	7	1	8
2002–03	23	10	33	13	0	13
2003–04	22	11	33	5	0	5
2004–05	14	7	21	0	0	0
2005–06	37	16	53	3	0	3

Source: House of Commons, *Sessional Returns*.

(c) By House of introduction

Session	Government bills			Private Members' Bills		
	Commons	Lords	Total	Commons	Lords	Total
1997–98	66	34	100	91	9	100
1998–99	71	29	100	89	11	100
1999–2000	70	30	100	93	7	100
2000–01	73	27	100	97	3	100
2001–02	67	33	100	96	4	100
2002–03	72	28	100	91	9	100
2003–04	69	31	100	100	0	100
2004–05	78	22	100	97	3	100
2005–06	72	28	100	93	7	100

Source: House of Commons, *Sessional Returns*.

Table C.2   continued

(d)   Received royal assent

Session	Government Bills		Private Members' Bills	
	Commons	Lords	Commons	Lords
1997–98	97	100	6	14
1998–99	82	100	8	9
1999–2000	96	100	5	14
2000–01	74	100	0	0
2001–02	100	100	6	20
2002–03	88	100	14	0
2003–04	88	100	6	0
2004–05	56	100	0	0
2005–06	88	100	3	0

Source: House of Commons, *Sessional Returns*.

Table C.3   Consideration of bills by standing committees in the House of Commons since 1997–98

Session	Bills considered	Committee sittings
1997–98	40	246
1998–99	31	219
1999–2000	39	353
2000–01	21	126
2001–02	39	269
2002–03	43	315
2003–04	36	243
2004–05	14	81
2005–06	46	274

Source: House of Commons, *Sessional Returns*.

Table C.4 Draft Bills published since 1997–98 and committee consideration

Session	Draft Bills published	Consideration		
		Departmental committee	Joint committee	Ad hoc committee
1997–98	3	2	0	0
1998–99	6	1	2	2
1999–2000	6	3	0	0
2000–01	2	1	0	0
2001–02	7	3	3	0
2002–03	10[a]	5	5	0
2003–04	12	6	4	0
2004–05	5[b]	2	1	0
2005–06	3	2	1	0

Note: All data refer to the session in which the draft bill was published. However, draft bills may be considered in committee in a subsequent session to that in which they were introduced.
[a] Includes draft clauses of the Police (Northern Ireland) Bill and the Gambling Bill.
[b] Includes draft clauses of the Company Law Bill.

Source: House of Commons Library, *Pre-Legislative Scrutiny* (Standard Note Series).

Table C.5 Delegated legislation laid before the House of Commons since 1997–98

Statutory instruments laid before the House	1997–98	1998–99	1999–2000	2000–01	2001–02	2002–03	2003–04	2004–05	2005–06
Instruments subject to affirmative procedure	225	178	180	123	262	233	207	126	271
Instruments subject to negative procedure	1,591	1,266	1,241	717	1,468	1,216	1,038	660	1,583
Other instruments[a]	40	35	35	28	58	25	36	7	31
Total	1,856	1,479	1,456	868	1,788	1,474	1,281	793	1,885

Number of statutory instrument pages[c]	1997	1998	1999	2000	2001	2002	2003	2004	2005[b]
	8,660	7,480	10,760	8,770	10,830	9,070	9,330	10,236	8,868

Regulatory Reform Orders (RROs):	1997–98	1998–99	1999–2000	2000–01	2001–02	2002–03	2003–04	2004–05	2005–06
RRO draft Orders laid before the House	5	4	0	2	12	10[d]	5	6	3

Remedial Orders made under the Human Rights Act 1998:	1997–98	1998–99	1999–2000	2000–01	2001–02	2002–03	2003–04	2004–05	2005–06
Remedial Orders[e]	0	0	0	0	0	1	1	0	0

a Instruments subject in part to affirmative and negative procedure; instruments not subject to parliamentary proceedings but laid before Parliament; Special procedure Orders; Bills of Acts of the Northern Ireland Assembly.
b To 31 August 2005.
c Number of pages in the Office of Public Sector Information bound set, excluding some local and unpublished instruments and, most recently, those of the Welsh Assembly.
d Including one draft order laid in 2001–02.
e Laid under the urgent procedure, considered and approved by the House.

Source: House of Commons, *Sessional Returns*.

D. The House of Commons

Table D.1 Party composition of the House of Commons, 1 January 2007

	Total no. MPs	No. women MPs	% women
Labour[a]	353	96	27
Conservative[a]	198	17	9
Liberal Democrat	63	9	14
Democratic Unionist	9	1	11
Scottish Nationalist	6	0	0
Sinn Fein	5[b]	1	20
Plaid Cymru	3	0	0
Social Democratic and Labour Party	3	0	0
Respect	1	0	0
Ulster Unionist	1	1	100
Independent	2	0	0
Independent Labour	1	1	100
Speaker	1	0	0
Total	646	126	20

[a] Including deputy speakers (1 Lab., 2 Con.).
[b] Have not taken their seats.
Source: House of Commons, *Weekly Information Bulletin*.

Table D.2 MPs' salaries and allowances, summary of rates (November 2006) and year of introduction

Introduced	Salaries/allowances	Rate	
1912	Parliamentary salary	£60,277	p.a.[a]
1964	Pension	[b]	
1974	Resettlement grant	[c]	
1969	Staffing allowance	£87,276	p.a. (max.)
2001	Incidental expenses provision (IEP)	£20,000	p.a.
2001	IT equipment (centrally funded)	£3,000	p.a. (circa)
2003	Pension provision for members' staff	[d]	
1972	Additional Costs Allowance	£22,110	p.a. (max.)
1972	London Supplement	£2,712	p.a.
1981	Winding-up Allowance	£35,095	max.
1924	Car mileage:		
	– first 10,000 miles	£0.40	p.a. (per mile)
	– in excess of 10,000 miles	£0.25	p.a. (per mile)
1998	Motorcycle allowance	£0.24	p.a. (per mile)
1998	Bicycle allowance	£0.20	p.a. (per mile)

[a] With effect from November 2006.
[b] Pension payable at 65 (or 60 with reduced benefit) according to length of service (minimum of 4 years' service).
[c] Resettlement grant – lump sum equivalent to 50–100% of salary, depending on age and service.
[d] Staff pension – group stakeholder arrangement.
Sources: House of Commons, *Library Research Paper 06/47*, 2005; House of Commons Department of Finance and Administration.

Table D.3   Parliamentary Questions since 1997–98

	Oral[a]	Written[b]	Urgent	Private Notice	Sitting days	No. answered Oral	No. answered Written
1997–98	3,382	52,652	–	28	241	14	218
1998–99	1,943	32,149	–	12	149	13	216
1999–2000	2,106	36,781	–	9	170	12	216
2000–01	906	16,716	–	7	83	11	201
2001–02	2,203	72,905	–	10	203	11	359
2002–03	2,206	55,436	10	–	162	14	342
2003–04	2,060	54,875	12	–	132	16	416
2004–05	848	22,962	4	–	65	13	353
2005–06	2,712	95,041	14	–	208	13	457

[a] Total number reached for answer.
[b] Total for written answer on a named day and for ordinary written answer.

Source: House of Commons, *Sessional Returns*.

Table D.4   Early Day Motions (EDMs) since 1997–98

Session	Total	Of which statutory instruments[a]	Sitting days	EDMs per day
1997–98	1,757	300	241	7
1998–99	1,009	51	149	7
1999–2000	1,198	25	170	7
2000–01	659	24	83	8
2001–02	1,864	54	203	9
2002–03	1,939	42	162	12
2003–04	1,941	18	132	15
2004–05	1,033	13	65	16
2005–06	2,924	48	208	14

[a] Prayers for the annulment of statutory instruments.

Source: House of Commons, *Sessional Returns*.

Table D.5 Select committees – party affiliation of chairs

Committee	January 2007	2001–05 Parliament (April 2005)
Departmental committees:		
Communities & Local Government	Lab.	Lab.[a]
Constitutional Affairs	Lib. Dem.	Lib. Dem.
Culture, Media & Sport	Con.	Lab.
Defence	Con.	Lab.
Education & Skills	Lab.	Lab.
Environment, Food & Rural Affairs	Con.	Con.
Foreign Affairs	Lab.	Lab.
Health	Lab.	Lab.
Home Affairs	Lab.	Lab.
International Development	Lib. Dem.	Con.
Northern Ireland Affairs	Con.	Con.
Science & Technology	Lib. Dem.	Lab.
Scottish Affairs	Lab.	Lab.
Trade & Industry	Con.	Lab.
Transport	Lab.	Lab.
Treasury	Lab.	Lab.
Welsh Affairs	Lab.	Lab.
Work & Pensions	Lab.	Lib. Dem.
Other committees:		
Environmental Audit	Con.	Con.
European Scrutiny	Lab.	Lab.
Public Accounts	Con.	Con.
Public Administration	Lab.	Lab.
Regulatory Reform	Lab.	Lab.
Human Rights (Joint)	Lab.	Lab.
Statutory Instruments (Joint)	Con.	Lab.
Administration[b]	Lab.	[b]
Finance & Services[c]	Lab.	Lab.
Liaison[c]	Lab.	Lab.
Procedure[c]	Con.	Con.
Selection[c]	Lab.	Lab.
Standards & Privileges[c]	Con.	Con.

	Con.	Lab.	Lib. Dem.	Total
Departmental committees:				
New Parliament	5	10	3	18
Old Parliament	3	13	2	18
All committees:				
New Parliament	10	18	3	31
Old Parliament	10	23	2	35

[a] Formerly the responsibility of the Office of the Deputy Prime Minister.
[b] Formerly 5 committees (3 Con. and 2 Lab. chairs).
[c] Salaries for chairs from July 2005, for other chairs from 2003–04.

E. The House of Lords

Table E.1 Composition of the House of Lords (8 January 2007)

	Total	Life peers	Bishops	Elected by party	Elected office-holders[a]	Royal office-holders[a]	Total hereditary peers	Women peers[b] No.	%
					Hereditary peers				
Conservative	206	159	0	38	9	0	47	33	16
Labour	211	207	0	2	2	0	4	54	26
Liberal Democrat	78	73	0	3	2	0	5	20	26
Crossbench	202	169	29	2	2	2	33	30	15
Bishops	26	0	26	0	0	0	0	0	0
Other	13	11	0	2	0	0	2	3	23
Total	736[c]	619	26	74	15	2	91	140	19

[a] (1) Earl Marshall (the Duke of Norfolk) (Crossbench); (2) Lord Great Chamberlain (the Marques of Cholmondley (Crossbench).
[b] Including 3 hereditary woman peers (Baroness Darcy de Knayth, Countess of Mar, Lady Saltoun of Abernethy).
[c] Excluding 12 peers on leave of absence – total House membership: 730.

Source: House of Lords Information Office (based on writs of summons issued).

Table E.2 House of Lords statistics, 1997–2006

	1997–98	1998–99	1999–2000	2000–01	2001–02	2002–03	2003–04	2004–05	2005–06
Sitting days	228	154	177	76	200	174	157	63	206
Average daily attendance	417	446	352	347	370	362	368	388	403
Starred Questions[a]	832	539	630	270	713	687	634	228	743
Unstarred Questions[b]	129	83	87	28	81	59	50	14	89
Written Questions	5,729	4,322	4,511	1,993	5,798	5,084	4,524	1,877	7,374
Govt. defeats in divisions[c]	39	31	36	2	56	88	64	37	62
as proportion of all divisions (%)	22	31	19	5	33	39	36	55	32

[a] Short oral Questions not leading to a debate.
[b] Oral Questions leading to a full debate.
[c] Government defeat is defined as a division in which at least one of the tellers on the losing side is a government whip.

Source: House of Lords, Sessional Statistics.

Index

Note: 'n' after page reference indicates an endnote on that page.

elections
  by-elections, local, 35–6
  by-elections, devolved, 29, 49, 50
  by-elections, parliamentary, 29, 36–7,
    50, 101–2
  dual candidacies, ban on in Wales, 17,
    168, 169
  local, 29, 32–6, 42, 71, 222, 240–1
  mayoral, 29, 34–5, 181–2
  statistics, 240–1
  see also electoral fraud *and*
    referendums, mayoral
Electoral Administration Act 2006, 113
Electoral Commission, 9, 40, 58, 113,
    114, 120, 221
electoral fraud, 43, 48, 229
electoral reform, 34
Electoral Reform Act 2006, 23
Eli Lilly, 56
energy policy, 59, 153–5, 161, 200
English Parliament, proposed, 174–5
Enron Corporation, 63, 143
Environmental Audit Committee, 154–5
environmental policy, 59, 60, 206–7
Environmental Pollution, Royal
    Commission on, 59
Environment, Food and Rural Affairs
    Committee, 75
Environment, Food and Rural Affairs,
    Department for (DEFRA), 62, 75
Equitable Life, 84
EU3, 194, 207
Europe, Council of, 138
Europe, Eastern and Central, 155–6, 206
European Commission, 156, 214
European Constitution, proposed, 205,
    206–8, 210, 212–13, 238
European Convention on Human Rights
    (ECHR), 13–14, 15, 16, 90, 134–5,
    136, 137, 138, 140, 143
European Council, 212–13, 213
European Court of Human Rights,
    135–6, 137
European Democrats, 208
European Energy Charter, 200
European Parliament, 205
European People's Party, 205, 208, 209
European Union (EU)
  and climate change, 206–7, 214
  Common Fisheries Policy, 210

Constitutional Treaty, 205, 206 *see
    also* European Constitution,
    proposed
  Council of Ministers, 208
  and crime, 206
  Economic and Finance Council
    (ECOFIN), 213
  economic reform of, 207–8
  enlargement of, 156, 160–1, 206, 211,
    212
  and energy policy, 201
  and environmental policy, 200–1,
    206–7, 210
  and farm payments, 75
  and foreign policy, 191, 201
  and immigration, 7–8, 155–6, 206,
    210–12
  and policy consultation, 61
  qualified majority voting, 213
  Services Directive, 208
  Stability and Growth Pact, 213
  and world trade, 199, 206
  Turkish entry, 206, 212
Eustice, George, 223
Evening Standard, 219, 226
Ewing, Margaret, 36, 163
Exmoor Foxhounds, 62
executive agencies, 75–6, 244–5
extradition, 63, 143, 237
Extradition Act 2003, 143

*Fair, Effective, Transparent and Trusted:
    Rebuilding Confidence in Our
    Immigration System*, 156
Falconer, Lord, 15–16, 20, 97, 98, 123,
    138, 175
Farage, Nigel, 37, 50
Farmers for Action (FFA), 64
farm payments, 69, 75
Fathers 4 Justice, 63, 63–4, 237
Field, Frank, 155–6
Financial Times, 59, 200, 215
Finegold, Oliver, 226
Finland, 201
First Minister
  Northern Ireland, 171, 172
  Scotland, 163
  Wales, 167
Fisheries and Angling Conservation
    Trust, 63